Agent-Based Social Systems

Volume 13

This series is intended to further the creation of the science of agent-based social systems, a field that is establishing itself as a transdisciplinary and cross-cultural science. The series will cover a broad spectrum of sciences, such as social systems theory, sociology, business administration, management information science, organization science, computational mathematical organization theory, economics, evolutionary economics, international political science, jurisprudence, policy science, socioinformation studies, cognitive science, artificial intelligence, complex adaptive systems theory, philosophy of science, and other related disciplines.

The series will provide a systematic study of the various new cross-cultural arenas of the human sciences. Such an approach has been successfully tried several times in the history of the modern science of humanities and systems and has helped to create such important conceptual frameworks and theories as cybernetics, synergetics, general systems theory, cognitive science, and complex adaptive systems.

We want to create a conceptual framework and design theory for socioeconomic systems of the twenty-first century in a cross-cultural and transdisciplinary context. For this purpose we plan to take an agent-based approach. Developed over the last decade, agent-based modeling is a new trend within the social sciences and is a child of the modern sciences of humanities and systems. In this series the term "agent-based" is used across a broad spectrum that includes not only the classical usage of the normative and rational agent but also an interpretive and subjective agent. We seek the antinomy of the macro and micro, subjective and rational, functional and structural, bottom-up and top-down, global and local, and structure and agency within the social sciences. Agent-based modeling includes both sides of these opposites. "Agent" is our grounding for modeling; simulation, theory, and realworld grounding are also required.

As an approach, agent-based simulation is an important tool for the new experimental fields of the social sciences; it can be used to provide explanations and decision support for real-world problems, and its theories include both conceptual and mathematical ones. A conceptual approach is vital for creating new frameworks of the worldview, and the mathematical approach is essential to clarify the logical structure of any new framework or model. Exploration of several different ways of real-world grounding is required for this approach. Other issues to be considered in the series include the systems design of this century's global and local socioeconomic systems.

More information about this series at http://www.springer.com/series/7188

Yutaka Nakai • Yuhsuke Koyama • Takao Terano
Editors

Agent-Based Approaches in Economic and Social Complex Systems VIII

Post-Proceedings of The AESCS International Workshop 2013

Springer

Editors
Yutaka Nakai
Faculty of Systems Engineering
and Sciences
Shibaura Institute of Technology
Saitama, Japan

Takao Terano
Department of Computational
Intelligence and Systems Science
Tokyo Institute of Technology
Yokohama, Japan

Yuhsuke Koyama
Shibaura Institute of Technology
Saitama, Japan

ISSN 1861-0803
Agent-Based Social Systems
ISBN 978-4-431-55235-2 ISBN 978-4-431-55236-9 (eBook)
DOI 10.1007/978-4-431-55236-9

Library of Congress Control Number: 2015940090

Springer Tokyo Heidelberg New York Dordrecht London

Printed on acid-free paper

Springer Japan KK is part of Springer Science+Business Media (www.springer.com)

Preface

Recently the world of social sciences has been changing rapidly. Many researchers collaboratively confront critical issues in social and economic problems. These researchers come not only from standard disciplines in the social sciences such as economics, political science, sociology, and others, but also from natural science fields such as physics, mathematics, and computer science. This interdisciplinary research now attracts an increasing number of researchers and leads them to initiate new series of conferences and to establish new academic organizations. One of them is the International Workshop on Agent-Based Approaches in Economic and Social Complex Systems (AESCS) organized by the Pan-Asian Association for Agent-Based Approach in Social Systems Sciences (PAAA). The seven AESCS workshops were held in Shimane (2001), Tokyo (2002), Kyoto (2004), Tokyo (2005, 2007), Taipei (2009), and Osaka (2012). Since 2006, PAAA has sponsored the biennial World Congress on Social Simulation (WCSS) with the European Social Simulation Association (ESSA) and the Computational Social Science Society of America (CSSSA). They held their conferences in Kyoto (2006), Fairfax (2008), and Kassel (2010). Following these assemblies, PAAA had its biennial workshop from AESCS2012 in the beginning of 2012. PAAA organized the succeeding workshop AESCS2013 at the Shibaura Institute of Technology, Tokyo, Japan. At AESCS2013, we had 22 presentations on September 11 and 13, 2013. In addition to these regular presentations, three keynote speeches were delivered by David L. Sallach (Argonne National Laboratory, University of Chicago, USA) on the topic "Topos Modeling of Social Conflict: Theory and Methods," Hiroshi Deguchi (Tokyo Institute of Technology, Japan) on the topic "Research Program for Social Architecture Design via Agent-Based Modeling," and Misako Takayasu (Tokyo Institute of Technology, Japan) on the topic "Modeling of Japanese Business Transactions; Evaluation of Systemic Risks, and Stress Tests." As in the previous events hosted by PAAA, we also prepared a post-conference publication to archive selected papers from the conference proceedings. Fourteen papers were selected to be included in this volume after the reviewing process with at least three referees. These fourteen papers are grouped into three parts: "Conflicts, Humans, and Culture," "Public Issues and Economy," and "Management and Business."

Saitama, Japan Yutaka Nakai

Committee Members of AESCS2013

Workshop Chair
Takao Terano, Tokyo Institute of Technology, Japan

Organizing Committee Chair
Yutaka Nakai, Shibaura Institute of Technology, Japan

Organizing Committee Members
Manabu Ichikawa, Tokyo Institute of Technology, Japan
Yusuke Goto, Iwate Prefectural University, Japan
Yusuke Koyama, Shibaura Institute of Technology, Japan
Takashi Yamada, Tokyo Institute of Technology, Japan

Program Committee Chair
Yusuke Koyama, Shibaura Institute of Technology, Japan

Program Committee Members
Akihiro Sato, Kyoto University, Japan
Akira Sasaki, Hosei University, Japan
Albert Bakhtizin, Central Economics and Mathematics Institute of Russian Academy of Sciences, Russia
Chung-Ching Tai, Tunghai University, Taiwan
Galina Besstremyannaya, Central Economics and Mathematics Institute of Russian Academy of Sciences, Russia
Hajime Kita, Kyoto University, Japan
Hideki Tanuma, Tokyo Institute of Technology, Japan
Hiroshi Deguchi, Tokyo Institute of Technology, Japan
Hiroyuki Matsui, Kyoto University, Japan
Isamu Okada, Soka University, Japan
Keiki Takadama, University of Electro-Communications, Japan
Kotaro Ohori, Fujitsu Laboratory, Japan

Makoto Mizuno, Meiji University, Japan
Manabu Ichikawa, Tokyo Institute of Technology, Japan
Masayuki Ishinishi, Ministry of Defense, Japan
Reiko Hishiyama, Waseda University, Japan
Ryuichi Yamamoto, National Chengchi University, Taiwan
Setsuya Kurahashi, Tsukuba University, Japan
Shingo Takahashi, Waseda University, Japan
Shu-Heng Chen, National Chengchi University, Taiwan
Takashi Yamada, Tokyo Institute of Technology, Japan
Toshiyuki Kaneda, Nagoya Institute of Technology, Japan
Utomo Sarjono Putro, Institut Teknologi Bandung, Indonesia
Yusuke Goto, Iwate Prefectural University, Japan
Yutaka Nakai, Shibaura Institute of Technology, Japan

Sponsors

Pan-Asian Association for Agent-Based Approach in Social Systems Sciences (PAAA)
Shibaura Institute of Technology
The Society for Instrument and Control Engineers

Contents

Contributors

Mark Abdollahian School of Politics and Economics, Claremont Graduate University, Claremont, CA, USA

Shuang Chang Department of Computational Intelligence and Systems Science, Tokyo Institute of Technology, Yokohama, Kanagawa, Japan

Shu-Heng Chen AI-ECON Research Center, Department of Economics, National Chengchi University, Taipei, Taiwan

Bin-Tzong Chie Department of Industrial Economics, Tamkang University, New Taipei City, Taiwan

Hiroshi Deguchi Department of Computational Intelligence and Systems Science, Tokyo Institute of Technology, Yokohama, Kanagawa, Japan

Shiro Horiuchi COC Promotion Office, Yamagata University, Yamagata, Japan

Manabu Ichikawa Department of Computational Intelligence and Systems Science, Tokyo Institute of Technology, Yokohama, Kanagawa, Japan

Tae-Seok Jang Department of Economics, BK21Plus, Seoul National University, Seoul, Republic of Korea

James Kaplan Department of Computer Science, Harvey Mudd College, Claremont, CA, USA

Fumiaki Kawachi Faculty of Systems Engineering and Sciences, Shibaura Institute of Technology, Saitama, Japan

Kumiko Kiso Graduate School of Engineering, Fukui University, Fukui, Japan

Setsuya Kurahashi Graduate School of Business Sciences, University of Tsukuba, Tokyo, Japan

Hao Lee Department of Informatics, Graduate School of Integrated Science and Technology, Shizuoka University, Hamamatsu, Japan

Teruyuki Monnai Department of Architecture, Graduate School of Engineering, Kyoto University, Kyoto, Japan

Masayoshi Muto Faculty of Systems Engineering and Sciences, Shibaura Institute of Technology, Saitama, Japan

Yutaka Nakai Faculty of Systems Engineering and Sciences, Shibaura Institute of Technology, Saitama, Japan

Patrick deWerk Neal School of Politics and Economics, Claremont Graduate University, Claremont, CA, USA

Isamu Okada Department of Business Administration, Soka University, Hachioji, Tokyo, Japan

Chathura Rajapakse Department of Computational Intelligence and Systems Science, Tokyo Institute of Technology, Yokohama, Japan

David L. Sallach Argonne National Laboratory, University of Chicago, Chicago, IL, USA

Ichiro Takahashi Department of Business Administration, Soka University, Hachioji, Tokyo, Japan

Takao Terano Department of Computational Intelligence and Systems Science, Tokyo Institute of Technology, Yokohama, Japan

Dirk Van Rooy Research School of Psychology, Faculty College of Medicine, Biology and Environment, The Australian National University, Australian Capital Territory, Australia

Jiao Xue Department of Computational Intelligence and Systems Science, Tokyo Institute of Technology, Tokyo, Japan

Zining Yang School of Politics and Economics, Claremont Graduate University, Claremont, CA, USA

Takashi Yoshida Graduate School of Business Sciences, University of Tsukuba, Tokyo, Japan

Part I
Conflicts, Humans, and Culture

Chapter 1
Human Development Dynamics: Network Emergence in an Agent Based Simulation of Adaptive Heterogeneous Games and Social Systems

Mark Abdollahian, Zining Yang, Patrick deWerk Neal, and James Kaplan

Abstract In the context of political modernization and economic development, the complex adaptive systems framework can help address the coupling of macro social constraint and opportunity with individual agency. Using a simple evolutionary game approach, we fuse endogenously derived socio-economic system dynamics from Human Development (HD) Theory with Prisoner's Dilemma spatial intra-societal economic transactions. We then explore a new human development dynamics (HDD) model behavior via quasi-global simulation methods to explore technological progression on economic development, cultural plasticity, social and political change. Using network analysis, we then investigate the impact of technology proliferation on communications ease and the resulting compression of social space on individual wealth and political preference formation. As economic and social capital is created, past transaction histories tend to reinforce future success, and networks emerge and solidify at different rates depending on technology. Increasing social connectivity in small populations has an immediate and positive impact on wealth creation, yet those effects become negative as technology proliferates and population size increases. This suggests not only diminishing marginal returns to increasing communications' payoffs to individuals but moreover crowding out effects. We believe complex adaptive or evolutionary systems approaches are necessary to understand both near and potentially catastrophic, far-from-equilibrium behavior and societal outcomes across all human scales of modernization.

M. Abdollahian • Z. Yang (✉) • P. deWerk Neal
School of Politics and Economics, Claremont Graduate University, Claremont, CA, USA
e-mail: mark.abdollahian@cgu.edu; zining.yang@cgu.edu; patrick.neal@cgu.edu

J. Kaplan
Department of Computer Science, Harvey Mudd College, Claremont, CA, USA
e-mail: jek@purelyfunctionalcapital.com

Y. Nakai et al. (eds.), *Agent-Based Approaches in Economic and Social Complex Systems VIII*, Agent-Based Social Systems 13, DOI 10.1007/978-4-431-55236-9_1

Keywords Economic development • Modernization • Democratization • Co-evolution • Game theory • Agent based model • Network analysis • Techno-social simulation • Complex adaptive systems

1 Introduction

Rooted in comparative political economy, the HD perspective is a qualitative, trans-disciplinary approach to understanding modernization and development through the lens of interdependent economic, cultural, social and political forces across individual, institutional and societal scales. Here we extend Abdollahian et al.'s (2012, 2013, 2014) novel, quantitative systems dynamic representation of HD theory at the societal level towards integrated macro-micro scales in an agent based framework. Quek et al. (2009) also design an interactive macro-micro agent based framework, which they call a spatial Evolutionary Multi-Agent Social Network (EMAS), on the dynamics of civil violence. In this paper, we focus on how advances in technology, proxied by increasing or decreasing potential agent interactions by varying network effects identified by Abdollahian and Yang (2013; Yang and Abdollahian 2014) impacts individual wealth creation and ultimately societal development paths.

In order to create a robust techno-social simulation (Solow 1956; Vespignani 2009), we instantiate a system of asymmetric, coupled nonlinear difference equations that are then empirically validated with five waves of data from the World Values Survey (2009). We then fuse this system to agent attribute changes with a generalizable, non-cooperative Prisoner's Dilemma game following Axelrod (1987, 1997a, b) and Nowak and Sigmund (1993, 1998; McPherson et al. 2001; Moyano and Sanchez 2013) to simulate intra-societal, spatial economic transactions where agents are capable of Robust Adaptive Planning (RAP). Here we specifically focus on the spatial network effects from various network sizes of heterogeneous agent interactions. Understanding macro-socio dynamics and individual agency across different sizes of emergent intra-societal transaction networks are key elements of a complex adaptive systems (CAS) approach.

Our technology proliferation results indicate that increasing agent Degree centrality in expanding communications networks drives strong individual wealth creation albeit up to a limit where competition from other agents creates a crowding effect. Similar results are obtained as Closeness centrality differs with varying communication network size, suggesting tipping points where individuals and societies can maximize wealth creation and hints towards macroeconomic conditional convergence. Overall we find strong epistatic interactions, where either social or financial networks and strategies are interdependent similar to Oh (2009), Uzzi (1996, 1999) and Zhou et al. (2003). Local social co-evolution of communication networks (Gurr 1970) help determine individual-micro and global-macro development outcomes in a particular society.

2 HD Dynamics Background

HD postulates a complex modernization process where value orientations drive an individual's level of existential security and change in predictable ways given shifts in existential security. HD theory provides a framework in which economic development, societal wealth and human needs create generalizable shifts in cultural predispositions and political behavior (Griffin 2009; Gurr 1970; Inglehart 1997; Swan 1956; Inglehart and Welzel 2005). HD theory expands upon economic drivers from neoclassical growth theory (Solow 1956; Swan 1956; Barro 1991) commonly attributed to high growth paths and convergence (Acemoglu and Robinson 2012, Axelrod 1997a). Such approaches specify detailed and interactive vectors of economic determinants, country and time-specific effects separately (Binmore 1994; Caselli et al. 1996); HD theory fuses cultural, social and political development process into economic growth (Y) dynamics.

Rational-secular (*RS*) *cultural* values correspond to individuals' growing emphasis on technical, mechanical, rational, and bureaucratic views of the world. During economic industrialization phases, cultural dispositions tend to progress from an emphasis on traditional pre-industrial values—often measured in terms of religious ceremony attendance—to secular world views, transferring authority from traditional religious figures to technological progress and bureaucratic political life.

Self-expressive (*SE*) *social* values corresponds to the post-industrial phase of economic development where the wealth and advanced welfare system generated by education, increased productivity and service-related economic activities provides individuals with an overwhelming sense of existential security (Barro 1991; Bell 1973) and the freedom to seek self-expression and demand political participation. Self-expression values promote liberal political institutions through two mechanisms. First, to the extent that there is incongruence between cultural demand for, and political supply of, liberal institutions, individuals are more or less prone to elite-challenging activity (Feng 2003; Darity 2008; Eckstein and Gurr 1975; Gurr 1970). Second, self-expression values support the social acceptance of basic democratic norms such as trust and political participation. The end result is a gradual transition toward democratization in autocratic nations and more effective political representation in democratic nations (Inglehart 1997; Inglehart and Welzel 2005).

Lastly, HD theory expects democratic (*D*) *political* values to exhibit positive feedbacks with economic progress, based on previous work on liberal institutions and economic development (Caselli et al. 1996; Bell 1973; Diamond 1992; Abdollahian et al. 2013; Acemoglu and Robinson 2012; Boix and Stoke 2003; Diamond 1992; Feng 2003). Declining economic conditions reintroduce the primacy of basic needs, fueling conditions for more traditional value orientations and less self-expression. Disequilibrium between culturally defined political expectations and political realities promotes and provides motivation for revolutionary change.

The HD perspective suggests a staged process in which rising level of existential security via economic development leads to an increased emphasis on rational-secular and self-expression values. However, these effects are neither linear nor monotonic, as we see strong reversion towards autocratic institutional preferences in survival-minded societies. Democratic norms and institutions that outpace economic progress are inherently unstable with a persistent, turbulent reversion processes, even at high levels of democratic norms and existential security. This suggests that societies experiencing democratization can frequently expect punctuated reversals and revolutions towards more autocratic institutions until more sustainable economic growth and democratic institutions re-emerge.

3 A Human Development Dynamics Model

While innovative and the first to formalize a systems approach for HD theory, a limitation of Abdollahian et al.'s (2012) work is the lack of coupling and interdependence across human scales, from individuals to institutions and finally the societal outcomes they generate. Our HDD model uniquely combines the interactive effects and feedbacks between individual human agency as well as the macro environmental constraints and opportunities that change over time for any given society. Decisions by individuals are affected by other individuals, social context, and system states. These decisions have variegated first and second order effects, given any particular system state or individual attributes. Such an approach attempts to increase both theoretical and empirical verisimilitude for some key elements of complexity processes—emergence, connectivity, interdependence and feedback—found throughout several disciplines across all scales of modernization and human development.

We maintain individual agent attribute relationships and postulated changes of *RS*, *SE*, *D* and *Y* in keeping with HD theory. These endogenously derived, individual agent attributes (RS^i, SE^i, D^i and Y^i) impact how economic transaction games occur, either increasing or decreasing individual wealth and, at increasing scales, determining societal productivity (Barro 1991; Binmore 1994). Geography and proximity are allowed to play a role by instantiating in random two-dimensional lattice worlds.

Capturing individual agent endogenous processes, we first transform Abdollahian et al.'s system of equations from differential to discrete equations for NetLogo tractability and use their empirically validated parameter values as a good first approximation. Given individual citizen attributes and HD processes at each iteration, we sum up each agent attributes across Y, RS, SE and D to find resulting societal distributions for each variable, yet are mindful of ecological correlation. This allows us to explore the interactive effects of income inequality, cultural schisms, social complexity or highly polarized political dialogues in any given society as the emergence of individual efforts and patterns of interactions (Fig. 1.1).

Social co-evolutionary systems allow each individual to either influence or be influenced by all other individuals as well as macro society (Sala-i-Martin 1996; Welzel et al. 2003; Snijders et al. 2007; Zheleva et al. 2009), perhaps eventually becoming coupled and quasi-path interdependent. Accordingly, we instantiate non-cooperative, socio-economic Prisoner's Dilemma (PD) transaction games given the similarity of agent *i*'s attribute vector (A^i) of social, cultural, political and economic preference (RS^i, SE^i, D^i and Y^i) to agent *j*'s attribute vector (A^j) for selected

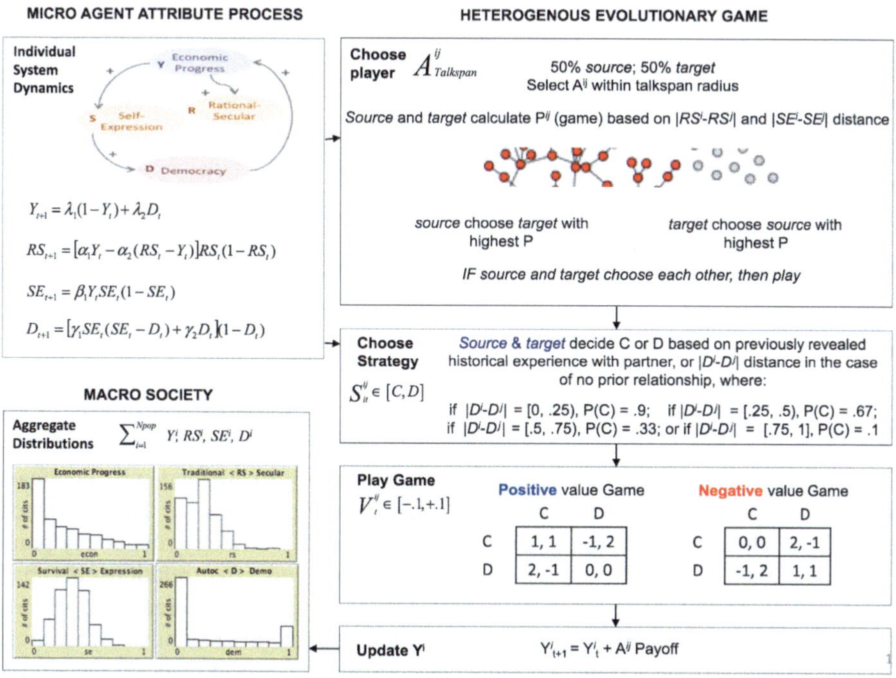

Fig. 1.1 HDD architecture (Implemented in NetLogo (Wilensky 1999))

A^{ij} pairs. Here, symmetric preference rankings and asymmetric neighborhood proximity distributions allows "talk-span," a Euclidean radius measure, to proxy for communications reach, social connectivity and technology diffusion constraining the potential set of A^{ij} game pairs. Low talk-span values restrict games to local neighborhoods among spatially proximate agents, while higher talk-span values expand potential A^{ij} pairs globally, modeling socially compressed space.

Following Social Judgment Theory, the attribute positions of two agents are conceived as a Downsian continuum (Boix and Stoke 2003; Eckstein and Gurr 1975; Darity 2008; Griffin 2009) where distance between these positions symmetrically affects the likelihood of one accepting the other's position. Agent *i* evaluates the likelihood of conducting a transaction with agent *j* based on similarity of socio-cultural preferences $|RS^i - RS^j|$ and $|SE^i - SE^j|$ within the given neighborhood. This captures communications and technology diffusion for frequency and social tie formation (Kauffman 1993; McPherson et al. 2001).

After transaction counterparties are identified, similarity is measured against an exogenous threshold to gauge compatibility. If both parties are satisfied, compatible agents, endowed with RAP cognition, enter into an engagement and search their memory for prior transactions with their period *t* counterparty. In the case of no prior transaction experience, agents individually each select strategy $S^{ij}{}_{it} \in$ [*Cooperate, Defect*] probabilistically based on similarity of political preferences as expressed by $|D^i - D^j|$ (Quek et al. 2009; Siero and Doosje 1993).

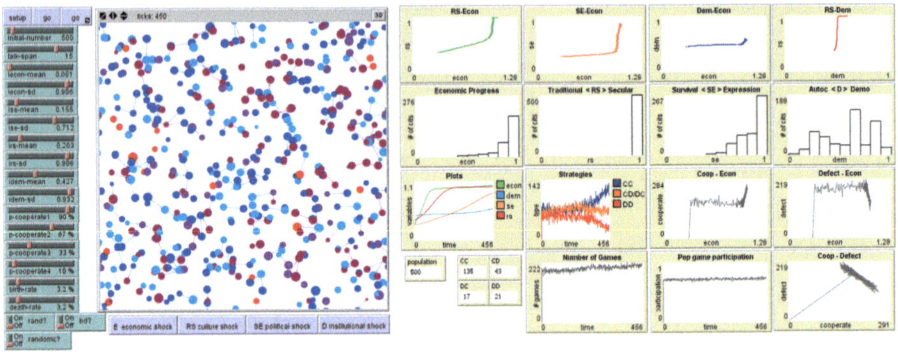

Fig. 1.2 Sample HDD run (*Source*: Abdollahian et al. 2013)

In repeat transactions, agents have perfect memory of *t-n* and will predicate their strategy in period *t* transactions on their counterparties' $t - 1$ behavior such that $S^{ij}{}_{it} = S^{ji}{}_{j(t-1)}$. Agents are unaware of counterparties' strategy rule at any point in time. This can lead to the emergence of stable productive relationships, bad relationships featuring pure defection strategies over repeated interactions, and tit-for-tat relationships, where agents alternate between strategies and never sync into a stable productive transactional relationship. This reflects recent work on the affects on co-evolution of both dynamic strategies and updating rules based on agent attributes (Inglehart and Baker 2000; Mankiw et al. 1992; Kauffman 1993; Moyano and Sanchez 2013).

Following Nowak and Sigmund (McPherson et al. 2001), we randomly assign game transaction values. However, we do not asymmetrically constrain such values; any particular game transaction value between pairs, V^{ij}, lies in between [−.1, .1]. This instantiation allows for different potential deal sizes, costs, or benefits. We specifically model socio-economic transaction games as producing either positive or negative values as we want to capture behavioral outcomes from games with both upside gains or downside losses.

In our HDD framework, A_i strategies are adaptive, which affect A_{ij} pairs locally within a proximate radius as first order effects. Other agents, within the system but outside the talk-span radius, are impacted through cascading higher orders. Agents simultaneously co-evolve as strategy pair outcomes CC, DC/CD or DD at *t* affect Y^i at $t + 1$, thus driving both positive and negative *RS, SE* and *D* feedback process through $t + n$ iterations. These shape A^i attributes which spur adaptation to a changing environment, summing Y^i, RS^i, SE^i and D^i vector values. Feedback into subsequent A^{ij} game selection networks and strategy choice yields a CAS representation across multiple scales (Fig. 1.2).

Before turning to our overall sensitivity and network results, we detail a single notional run. Here a lesser developed society, with a mean low income level but high degree of inequality, escapes the poverty trap through high growth and increasingly moderating democratic institutions. Individual productivity and wealth, driven by successful CC and DC/CD strategy outcomes of individual transactions,

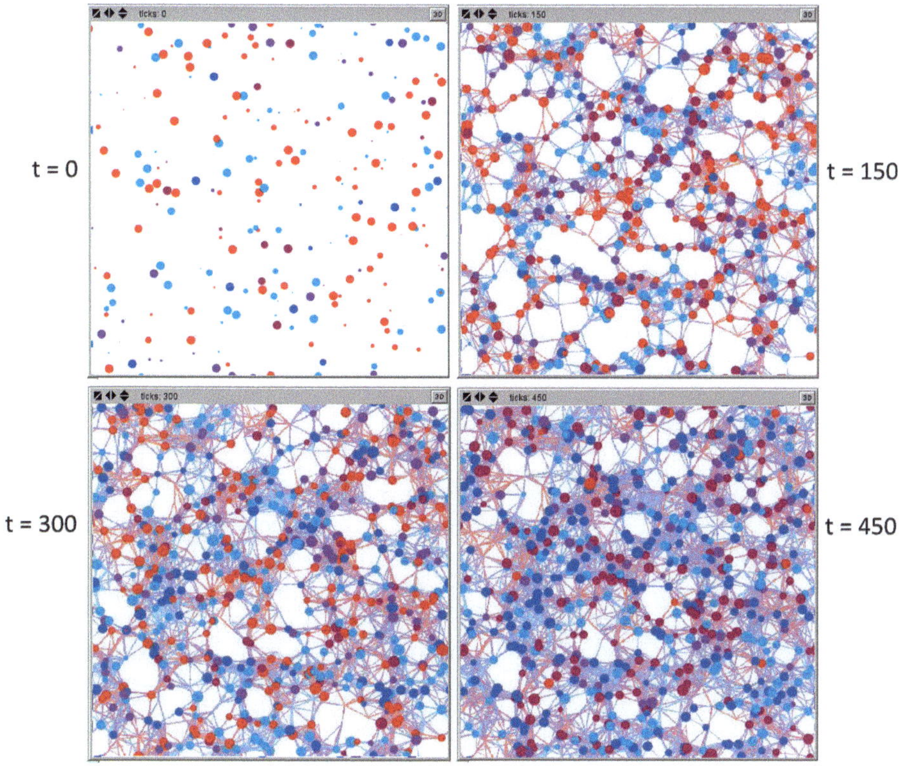

Fig. 1.3 Spatial network outcomes at t = 0, 150, 300, and 450

help accelerate the emergence of modern secular RS and expressive SE norms and values, while democratic D preferences solidify, but are not engrained throughout all of society. Figure 1.3 depicts spatialdistribution of agent wealth, preferences and the resulting communication networks from the above simulation at $t = 0$, 150, 300 and 450 snapshots. Initially, we find our low developed society with high-income inequality and polarization along autocratic and democratic preferences with no transaction networks. By $t = 150$, agents quickly increase in individual wealth as several economic transaction games are played between individuals of similar R and S preferences as shown by the emergent networks, while the strategy history shows not one dominant strategy emerges as society goes through a high growth phase of development. By $t = 300$, we see continued heterogeneously mixed populations in terms of income and democratic preferences with previously established network ties solidifying, while by $t = 400$ we see increased convergence toward democratic preferences and dense network clustering. Our resulting network structures are consistent with Gargiulo and Benassi's (2000) findings on how social capital flows impact network cohesion. Although just one particular simulation, what is critical is that co-evolutionary behavior results in path dependence of economic and cultural change networks as well as being a key determinant for development outcomes. Moreover, changes towards democratic values leads to increasing cooperative strategy pairs, which reinforce previous network connections over time.

4 Sensitivity Analysis

In order to make more generalizable model inferences, Table 1.1 detailsthe interactive parameter effects[1] on economic prosperity *Y*, as well as strategy choice pairs CC, CD/DC and DD. As all variables are relatively scaled, we can interpret

Table 1.1 Impact on economic development and strategy pairs

Model	Economic	CC	CD	DD
Economic		1.099*	0.666*	0.498*
		(0.000)	(0.000)	(0.000)
Rational secular	0.492*	−0.354*	−0.186*	−0.137*
	(0.000)	(0.000)	(0.000)	(0.000)
Self expression	−0.128*	0.156*	0.071*	0.411*
	(0.000)	(0.000)	(0.000)	(0.000)
Democracy	0.262*	0.028*	−0.209*	−0.392*
	(0.000)	(0.000)	(0.000)	(0.000)
Cooperate	0.354*			
	(0.000)			
Defect	−0.080*			
	(0.000)			
Talk-span	0.255*	−0.199*	−0.051*	−0.068*
	(0.000)	(0.000)	(0.000)	(0.000)
Time	−0.111*	−0.176*	−0.065*	−0.334*
	(0.000)	(0.000)	(0.000)	(0.000)
Threshold	−0.063*	−0.204*	−0.318*	−0.365*
	(0.000)	(0.000)	(0.000)	(0.000)
RAP	0.024*	−0.020*	−0.289*	−0.135*
	(0.000)	(0.000)	(0.000)	(0.000)
N	78,591	81,982	73,499	61,877
Prob > F	0.000	0.000	0.000	0.000
R-squared	0.946	0.809	0.472	0.412
Root MSE	0.041	0.795	0.978	0.877

Numbers in parentheses are corresponding robust standard errors
*Significance at 1 \% level

[1]Parameter setting: talk-span = 0, 1, 4, 7, 10; threshold = 0, 0.04, 0.09, 0.16, 0.25, 0.36; RAP = true, false.

magnitude and substantive effects across OLS β coefficients. The results reflect a limited, quasi-global sensitivity analysis with 500 agents in 180 runs and 700 iterations in each run, randomly down-sampled for pooled OLS tractability.

Our first model on mean societal economic development *Y* confirms HD theory that positive values of mean societal *RS* and *D* values significantly speed the pace of economic development, although *SE* is significant and slightly negative; this may relate to a loss of productivity when efforts in isolation are directed away from production and towards self-expression. Looking at the impact of evolutionary games, we see that cooperation has a stronger positive impact than defection or mixed strategies in increasing transaction value to society. Time is slightly negative, indicating that economic prosperity is not endogenous to the model. Threshold, agent willingness to engage in transactions, is slightly negative, implying that reduced trust has a slightly negative impact on growth. Lastly, RAP is slightly positive, suggesting increased cognition is beneficial in our simulated environment. Future research will investigate to what extent the RAP coefficient increases with agent analytical sophistication, and may include an endogenous education component. Talk-span spatial proximity and network creation is positive and significant, confirming priors that increasing technology and compressing potential social space also speed development processes. Next we explore in detail network formation and their potential nonlinear effects.

5 Network Effects

In order to understand the emergence of transactional clusters, we explore the impact of technology proliferation and social compression through varying communication network sizes on individual wealth creation. Running a set of experiments, simulations were conducted with talk span set exogenously and identically for the entire agent population, in environments with different numbers of agents. For populations of 100, 200, 300, 400, 500 and 600 agents, 44 simulations were run for low to high talkspan values (between 1 and 20), for a total of approximately 5,200 simulations with identical starting conditions run for 500 ticks. A cumulative transaction graph then was generated during the course of each simulation, with edges representing historical PD transactions between agents. After each simulation, node level statistics $\text{Degree}_{i,t}$, $\text{Closeness}_{i,t}$ and economic wealth *Y* for each agent *i* at each tick *t* were extracted. Combining the PD transaction history with node level statistics allowed fixed effects panel regressions on how technology proliferation and network characteristics affect individual economic outcomes.

Figure 1.4 details our node statistics on how wealth β regression coefficient means (dots) and standard deviations (bars) change across talkspan and by initial population size (color). The Degree results indicate increasing social connectivity in small populations has an immediate and positive impact on wealth creation, yet those effects become negative as both technology proliferates and population size increases. This suggests not only diminishing marginal returns to increasing

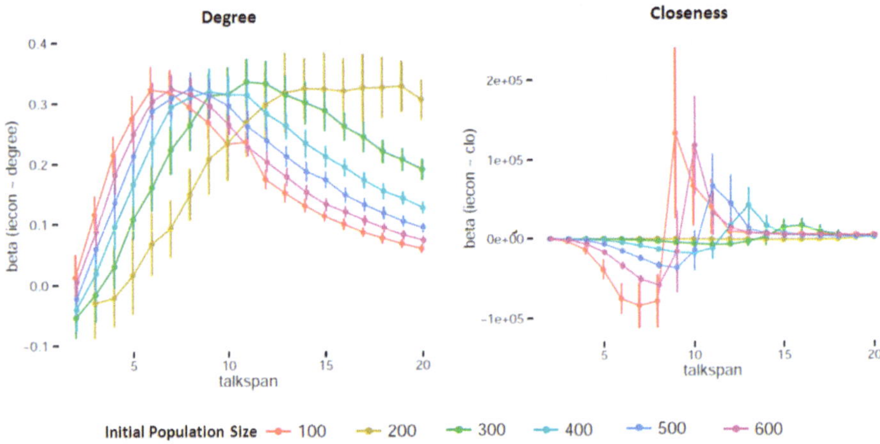

Fig. 1.4 Agent wealth elasticity with respect to technology and node level network statistics

communications' payoffs to individuals but moreover a crowding out effect. For Closeness, we find that agents with shortest path lengths, measuring the extent to which agents are near other transacting agents, is sinusoidal; negative and counter productive to wealth creation in low technology environments with a sharp phase transition to strongly positive, yet decreasing marginal returns as communications and technology proliferates.

This indicates quite different wealth maximization strategies and network placement tactics for individual agents depending on societal conditions. High connectivity via Degree or being well placed in brokering others' transactions can have a significant impact on both individual and societal wealth creation that changes over time and across societies of different sizes. As economic and social capital is created, past transaction histories tend to reinforce future success, and networks emerge and solidify at different rates depending on technology. This also suggest micro, agent level support for neo-classical macroeconomic theories of conditional convergence, where highly developed nations experience slow growth while developing nations can leapfrog more advance societies from a technology transfer perspective and converge on income levels.

6 Conclusions

Consistent with comparative political economy theory and empirical reality, our HDD model finds complexity and nonlinear path dependence in three areas: adaptive development processes, the emergence of co-evolutionary transaction networks and near equilibrium development trajectories. From a complex adaptive system perspective on HD theoretical processes, economic progress is a necessary condition for successful secularization and expressive political behavior, which are antecedents for lasting democratic institutions.

While political modernization is not inevitable, our results support empirical observations for a staged process where increasing existential security via economic development leads to increased emphasis on rational-secular and self-expressive values that results in societal development. Strategically, agents do adapt interactively with their environments as mutual cooperation does result in higher societal wealth than defection alone and is self reinforcing over time. From a network perspective, the emergence and persistence of preferred node positioning illuminates both individual wealth creation and societal development strategies. The impact of such behavior varies dramatically by both technology proliferation and population size, demonstrating social compression, competition and capital generation. Although only an initial, rough approximation at the truly complex, interdependent and highly nonlinear nature of modernization, our HDD approach provides insights into the interactivity of individual agency and societal outcomes seen through the lens of evolutionary games.

References

Abdollahian MA, Yang Z (2013) Towards trade equalization: a network perspective on trade and income convergence across the 20th century. New Polit Econ 18(3):1–27

Abdollahian MA, Coan T, Oh HN, Yesilada B (2012) Dynamics of cultural change: the human development perspective. Int Stud Q 56(4):827–842

Abdollahian MA, Yang Z, Coan T, Yesilada B (2013) Human development dynamics: an agent based simulation of macro social systems and individual heterogeneous evolutionary games. Complex Adapt Syst Model 1(1):1–18

Abdollahian MA, Yang Z, Neal PD (2014) Human development dynamics: an agent based simulation of robust adaptive heterogeneous games and social systems. In: Kennedy WG, Agarwal N, Yang SJ (eds) Social computing, behavioral-cultural modeling, and prediction: 7th international conference. Lecture Notes in Computer Science (LNCS). Springer, Switzerland, pp 3–10

Acemoglu D, Robinson J (2012) Why nations fail: the origins of power, prosperity, and poverty. Crown Business, New York

Axelrod R (1987) The evolution of strategies in the iterated Prisoner's Dilemma. In: Davis L (ed) Genetic algorithms and simulated annealing. Morgan Kaufman, Los Altos, pp 32–41

Axelrod R (1997a) The complexity of cooperation: agent-based models of competition and collaboration. Princeton University Press, Princeton

Axelrod R (1997b) The dissemination of culture: a model with local convergence and global polarization. J Confl Resolut 41:203–226

Barro R (1991) Economic growth in a cross section of countries. Q J Econ 106(2):407–444

Bell D (1973) The coming of postindustrial society. Basic Books, New York

Binmore KG (1994) Game theory and the social contract. MIT Press, Cambridge

Boix C, Stoke S (2003) Endogenous democratization. World Polit 55:517–549

Caselli F, Esquivel G, Lefort F (1996) Reopening the convergence debate: a new look at cross-country growth empirics. J Econ Growth 1(3):363–389

Darity W (2008) Social judgment theory. Macmillan Reference USA, Detroit

Diamond L (1992) Economic development and democracy reconsidered. In: Diamond L, Marks G (eds) Reexamining democracy. Sage, London

Eckstein H, Gurr TR (1975) Patterns of authority: a structural basis for political inquiry. Wiley, New York

Feng Y (2003) Democracy, governance, and economic performance: theory and evidence. MIT Press, Cambridge, MA
Gargiulo M, Benassi M (2000) Trapped in your own net? Network cohesion, structural holes, and the adaptation of social capital. Organ Sci 11:183–196
Griffin E (2009) A first look at communication theory. McGraw-Hill Higher Education, Boston
Gurr TR (1970) Why men rebel. Princeton University Press, Princeton
Inglehart R (1997) Modernization and postmodernization: cultural, economic and political change in 43 societies. Princeton University Press, Princeton
Inglehart R, Baker WE (2000) Modernization, cultural change, and the persistence of traditional values. Am Sociol Rev 65:19–51
Inglehart R, Welzel C (2005) Modernization, cultural change, and democracy: the human development sequence. Cambridge University Press, New York
Kauffman SA (1993) The origins of order: self-organization and selection in evolution. Oxford University Press, Oxford
Mankiw NG, Romer D, Weil DN (1992) A contribution to the empirics of economic growth. Q J Econ 107:407–437
McPherson M, Smith-Lovin L, Cook J (2001) Birds of a feather: homophily in social networks. Annu Rev Sociol 27:415–444
Moyano LG, Sanchez A (2013) Spatial prisoner's dilemma with heterogeneous agents. Elsevier Manuscript Atlanta, GA
Nowak MA, Sigmund KA (1993) Strategy of win-stay, lose-shift that outperforms tit-for-tat in the prisoner's dilemma game. Nature 364:56–58
Nowak MA, Sigmund KA (1998) Evolution of indirect reciprocity by image scoring. Nature 393:573–577
Oh H (2009) Using social network analysis for interpersonal comparison of utilities in behavioral games. PhD dissertation, Claremont Graduate University, Claremont
Quek HY, Tan KC, Abbass HA (2009) Evolutionary game theoretic approach for modeling civil violence. IEEE Trans Evol Comput 13:1–21
Sala-i-Martin XX (1996) Regional cohesion: evidence and theories of regional growth and convergence. Eur Econ Rev 40:1325–1352
Siero FW, Doosje BJ (1993) Attitude change following persuasive communication: integrating social judgment theory and the elaboration likelihood model. J Soc Psychol 23:541–554
Snijders TA, Steglich CE, Schweinberger M (2007) Modeling the co-evolution of networks and behavior. Longitudinal models in the behavioral and related sciences, pp 41–71
Solow R (1956) A contribution to the theory of economic growth. Q J Econ 70:65–94
Swan T (1956) Economic growth and capital accumulation. Econ Rec 32:334–361
Uzzi B (1996) The sources and consequences of embeddedness for the economic performance of organizations: the network effect. Am Sociol Rev 61:674–698
Uzzi B (1999) Embeddedness in the making of financial capital: how social relations and networks benefit firms seeking finance. Am Sociol Rev 64:481–505
Vespignani A (2009) Predicting the behavior of techno-social systems. Science 325:425–428
Welzel C, Inglehart R, Klingemann H (2003) The theory of human development: a cross-cultural development. Eur J Polit Sci 42:341–380
Wilensky U (1999) NetLogo. http://ccl.northwestern.edu/netlogo/. Center for Connected Learning and Computer-Based Modeling, Northwestern University, Evanston
Yang Z, Abdollahian M (2014) Trade networks, regional agreements and growth. In: Deese D (ed) The international political economy of trade. Edward Elgar, Cheltenham
Zheleva E, Sharara H, Getoor L (2009) Co-evolution of social and affiliation networks. In: Proceedings of the 15th ACM SIGKDD international conference on Knowledge discovery and data mining, ACM, New York
Zhou X, Zhao W, Li Q, Cai H (2003) Embeddedness and contractual relationships in China's transitional economy. Am Sociol Rev 68:75–102

Chapter 2
Exploring the Origins of Prejudice with Agent-Based Modeling

Dirk Van Rooy

Abstract Research into the cognitive origins of prejudice has largely focused on *individual* psychological processes. We introduce a novel Agent-based model that simulates both *individual-level* and *inter-personal* processes, and that allows exploring how stereotypes are shared and validated through interpersonal processes. At the individual-level, agent processes are simulated by recurrent auto-associative networks. To simulate interpersonal processes, these individual networks are combined into a "community of networks" so that they can exchange their individual information with each other by transmitting information on the same concepts from one network to another. Through simulations, it is shown how the model can account for a number of seminal findings from the empirical literature on illusory correlations, a key cognitive antecedent of prejudice. In addition, novel hypotheses in terms of the impact of interpersonal processes on the dissemination of illusory correlations were supported by the results of a small group experiment. We discuss the results and argue that agent-based models can provide a first step in integrating individual and interpersonal processes underlying stereotype formation and IC.

Keywords Agent-based modeling • Connectionism • Prejudice • Illusory correlation • Social psychology

1 Introduction

Categorizing individuals into groups, and learning about those social groups and their characteristics, is fundamental to the way people make sense of their social world. However, research has shown that people struggle to learn associations between groups and their attributes, and often perceive associations that do not exist (Hamilton and Gifford 1976). Such perceptual biases are assumed to underlie stereotyping, prejudice and minority discrimination. We will use an agent-based model (ABM) to explore the processes underlying one of the most prominent of

D. Van Rooy (✉)
Research School of Psychology, Faculty College of Medicine, Biology and Environment, The Australian National University, Australian Capital Territory, Australia
e-mail: dirk.vanrooy@anu.edu.au

Y. Nakai et al. (eds.), *Agent-Based Approaches in Economic and Social Complex Systems VIII*, Agent-Based Social Systems 13, DOI 10.1007/978-4-431-55236-9_2

these biases, illusory correlation (IC) – the perception of a correlation between a group and characteristics that does not exist. Research into illusory correlation has typically studied stereotypes as *isolated* knowledge structures within *individual* minds. However, stereotypes become relevant from the moment that they are socially shared and represented across multiple minds (Allport 1954; Lyons and Kashima 2003). Researchers have always emphasized the importance of contact and communication between individuals as a means of reducing prejudice, most notably Allport with his intergroup contact hypothesis (Allport 1954). By using an ABM, we aim to take a first step in integrating individual and interpersonal processes underlying stereotype formation and IC within one model. We start by introducing the ABM, which builds on previous work by combining a connectionist (agent) model that has been successfully applied to stereotype formation (Van Rooy et al. 2003), with a novel inter-agent process that allows agents to share and compare their information. We will then use a series of simulations to generate predictions that are compared to existing empirical findings, and then subsequently tested in a small group experiment using human participants.

2 The Model

ABM build social structures from the "bottom-up", by simulating individuals with virtual agents and stipulating rules that govern interactions among these agents. Creating computational models of social units (e.g. individuals, social groups, organizations or even nations) and their interactions, and observing the global structures that these interactions produce, has proven to provide unique insights into group phenomena. They express in clear mathematical and computational terms, how complex social structures emerge from interactions of individual agents at various distinct levels, allowing the analysis of properties of individual agents (e.g. their attributes and interactions), and the emergent group-level behavior. However, human social groups change not only through structural adaptations (i.e. social organization), but also by guiding and restructuring the behaviors and cognitions of the individuals that form them. To that extent, several modelers (Hazlehurst and Hutchins 1998; Hegselmann and Krause 2002) have argued that ABM need to incorporate relatively sophisticated models of individual agents, to allow them to adapt and change their behavior over time.

An ABM is introduced that aims at accomplishing this by using a connectionist agent model. Connectionism is an approach in the fields of artificial intelligence, psychology, neuroscience and philosophy of mind, that models mental or behavioral phenomena as the emergent processes of interconnected networks of simple units. Connectionist architectures and processing mechanisms are based on analogies with properties of the human brain, in which learning is conceptualized as a process of on-line adaptation of existing knowledge to novel information provided by the environment. The focus in this paper will be on the recurrent auto-associator (McClelland and Rumelhart 1985, 1988), a model that has been applied successfully

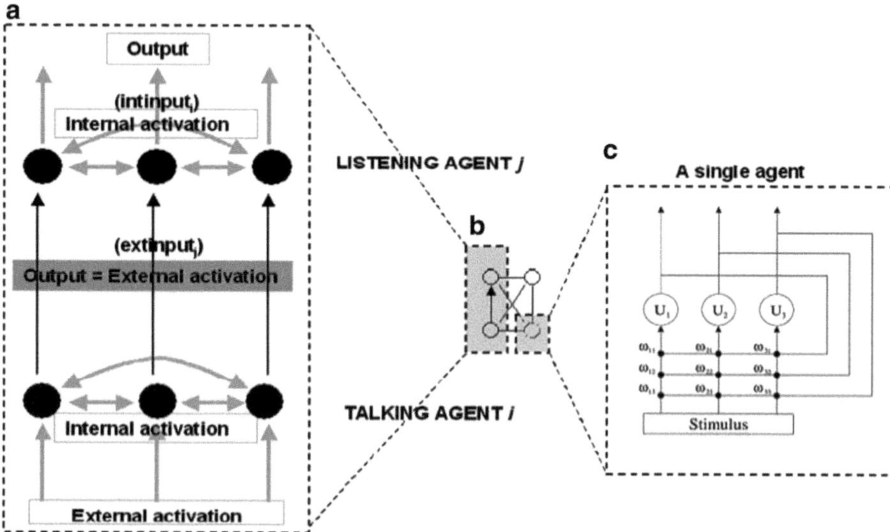

Fig. 2.1 The *left panel* (**a**) shows the transmission of information from a talking to a listening agent. The *middle panel* (**b**) shows a group of 4 agents. The *right panel* (**c**) shows a standard recurrent network representing a single agent

to group biases, causal attribution & person and group impression in social psychology (Smith and DeCoster 1998; Van Rooy et al. 2003).

2.1 Connectionist Agent

A recurrent network has three distinctive features (Fig. 2.1, panel c). First, all units within an individual agent network are interconnected, such that all units send out and receive activation. Second, information is represented by external activation (or *stimulus*), which is automatically spread among all interconnected units within an agent in proportion to the weights of their connections. The activation coming from the other units within an agent is called the internal activation. Typically, activations and weights have lower and upper bounds of approximately -1 and $+1$. And thirdly, short-term activations are stored in long-term weight changes of the connections.

The net activation of a unit is determined by the sum of the external and internal activations, after one updating cycle through the network. More specifically, every unit i in the network receives external activation, termed ext_i, in proportion to an excitation parameter E which reflects how much the activation is excited, or

$$a_i = E \times ext_i \tag{2.1}$$

This activation subsequently spreads through the auto-associative network, meaning every unit *i* receives internal activation int_i, which is the sum of the activation from the other units *j* (denoted by a_j) in proportion to the weight of their connection to unit *i*, or

$$int_i = \sum (W_{ji} \times a_j) \tag{2.2}$$

for all $j \neq i$. External and internal activation are then summed to the net activation, or

$$net_i = E \times (ext_i + int_i) \tag{2.3}$$

The updating of activation at each cycle is governed by the following equation:

$$^{\Delta}a_i = net_i - D \times a_i \tag{2.4a}$$

where *D* reflects a memory decay term. Decay (D) and Excitation (E) only play a role in non-linear recurrent networks, in which a network cycles through a number of iterations before settling in a stable state (Hazlehurst and Hutchins 1998). Our previous work has demonstrated that a simple, linear model provides a better fit of group perception phenomena like illusory correlation. So as in previous simulations (Van Rooy et al. 2003, 2013, 2014), parameter values were set to $D = E = 1$. Hence, the final activation of a unit equals the sum of the external and internal activation, or

$$a_i = net_i = ext_i + int_i \tag{2.4b}$$

After activation has been determined, the recurrent model enters the second learning phase in which the short-term activations are stored in long-term weight changes of the connections. Basically, these weight changes are driven by the difference between the internal activation received from other units in the network and the external activation received from outside sources. This difference, also called the error, is reduced in proportion to the learning rate that determines how fast the network changes its weights and learns. This error-reducing mechanism is known as the delta algorithm (McClelland and Rumelhart 1988). In mathematical terms, the delta algorithm strives to match the internal predictions of the network int_i as closely as possible to the actual state of the external environment ext_i and stores this information in the connection weights. This error-reducing process is formally expressed as (McClelland and Rumelhart 1988)

$$^{\Delta}w_{ji} = \varepsilon \times (ext_i - int_i) \times a_j \tag{2.5}$$

where Δw_{ji} is the change in the weight of the connection from unit j to i, and ε is a learning rate that determines how fast the network learns. An implication of this learning algorithm is that when an object and its feature co-occur frequently, then their connection weight gradually increases to eventually reach an asymptotic value of $+1$.

2.2 *Socially Distributed Network & Communication*

A number of authors have illustrated how auto-associative networks can be naturally extended to allow communication between them (Hazlehurst and Hutchins 1998; Van Overwalle and Heylighen 2006). It basically involves creating an ABM such that individual recurrent networks or agents are linked in an adaptive network structure. Any agent can (in principle) interact with any other agent, but the impact of the interaction will adapt to experience. Different adaptation rules have been used in previous simulations, to explore the impact of trust on communication (Van Overwalle and Heylighen 2006) and persuasiveness of information on the development of knowledge structures (Hazlehurst and Hutchins 1998). In the current simulation, communication involves the transmission of information from one agent's network to another, along connections whose adaptive weights reflect the mutual social influence between agents (see Fig. 2.1, panel a). During a simulated interaction, "listening" agents compare their information (as represented by internal activation of their own network) with the information they receive from "talking" agents (represented by the external activation received from talking agents). The stronger the connection between agents, the more influence they have on each other. As such, a group of agents functions as an adaptive, socially distributed network in which information and knowledge are distributed among and propagated in function of the social influence between different individual networks. The listening agent sums all information received from other talking agents in proportion to the inter-agent weights, and then processes this information internally (according to the standard recurrent approach). Or, in mathematical terms:

$$ext\_a_j = \sum_j w_{kl}^* a_i \tag{2.6}$$

where ext_a_j represents the external activation received by the listening agent l; w_{kl} is the inter-agent weight from the talking agent k to the listening agent l; and a_i denotes the final activation (which combines the external and internal activation received) expressed by the talking agent i.

2.3 *Social Adaptation*

An important aspect of the model is that the network in which the agents are situated is adapted to the outcomes of the comparisons between agents. Inter-agent weights are updated driven by the error between the external information, representing the attitude expressed by the talking agent, and the internal activation, representing the listening agents' attitude:

$$\delta_i = \text{extinput}_j - \text{intinput}_i \tag{2.7}$$

where $extinput_j$ is the final activation send out by the talking agent and $intinput_i$ is the internal activation of the listening agent. When agents share the same attitude, the weight of the links between them is adjusted upwards. If they disagree on an issue, the weights are adjusted downwards. This is expressed mathematically as:

$$\begin{aligned} &\text{If } \left|\text{ext\_a}_j - \text{int\_a}_j\right| < \text{Tolerance} \\ &\quad \text{then } \Delta\, w_{ij} = \eta \times \left(1 - w_{ij}\right) \times |a_i| \\ &\quad \text{else } \Delta\, w_{ij} = \eta \times \left(0 - w_{ij}\right) \times |a_i| \end{aligned} \tag{2.8}$$

where ext_a_j represents the external activation received (from the talking agent i) by the listening agent j and int_a_j the internal activation generated independently by the listening agent j; η is the rate by which the weights are adjusted. When agents largely share the same attitude (i.e. the difference is below the Tolerance threshold), the links between them are strengthened. Otherwise, the links between them are weakened. This constitutes an adaptive social process, in which agents learn from interacting with each other: Agents that consistently confirm each other's attitudes will be connected by stronger links than agents that consistently disagree. The social experience acquired in this way is represented in a distributed manner, in patterns of weighted links across the whole network.

The simulations below use the same recurrent network and follow similar simulation procedures used by Van Rooy and colleagues in previous work (Van Rooy et al. 2003). This allows us to explore the unique contribution of the newly implemented social comparison process on the development of shared stereotypes. In addition, several simulation runs using default parameter ranges (Van Rooy et al. 2003, 2013) produced similar results.

3 Modeling Illusory Correlation

In this section, we focus on illusory correlation (or IC), a cognitive antecedent of prejudice that is very much at the heart of the group perception literature and has received both extensive modeling and empirical attention (Van Rooy et al. 2003). By applying our model to IC, we can compare our simulations and experimental data to an extensive literature, and also explore the unique contribution of the social interaction that an ABM brings to the table. In the following simulations, agents are first trained according to a design that closely mimics a standard IC experiment: They are presented with patterns of information about two fictional social groups, with the aim of learning the underlying stereotypes (or prototypes). We subsequently introduce an extension to the classic IC paradigm, by allowing agents to interact and share their information during a *group* phase. This will allow us to model both the development of a stereotype by individual agents, but also how the agents share their information about the 2 groups, and how that affects their initial attitudes. Overall, the key aim of simulations and associated experiment is to establish our ability to simulate individual-level information processing and interpersonal communication processes that contribute to IC.

3.1 Simulation 1: Illusory Correlation

We simulated the illusory correlation effect in the Hamilton and Gifford (1976) paradigm: Participants in their seminal experiment read statements describing a member of either a majority or minority group (A or B) engaging in either a desirable (positive) or an undesirable (negative) behavior (i.e. "John, a member of Group A, helped an old lady across the street"). Statements were presented one at a time, and participants were asked to develop an overall attitude towards the two groups. The ratio of positive to negative behavior statements (2:1) was the same for the two groups. However, participants were exposed to twice as many statements about people in Group A than about people in Group B (Group A: 18A+:8A−; Group B: 9B+:4B−). Despite the fact that the overall probability of a positive or negative behavior given membership of Group A and Group B was equal, participants rated the minority group (i.e., B) as more negative than the majority group (i.e., A). The same result has been replicated using a variety of stimulus material and distributions, as long as the ratio of positive to negative stayed approximately 2:1 (Mullen and Johnson 1990).

Table 2.1 represents the simulated learning history for a generic IC design, where participants receive statements in a 2:1 positive to negative ratio (i.e. 20A+, 10A−, 10B+ and 5B−). Each line in the top panel of Table 2.1 represents a pattern of external activation at a trial that corresponds to a statement presented to

Table 2.1 Simulation of the Hamilton and Gifford paradigm

	Group		Valence	
Trial	A	B	+	−
	Experimental phase			
Group A	1	0	1	0
Group A	1	0	0	1
Group B	0	1	1	0
Group B	0	1	0	1
	Test phase			
Evaluation of group A	1	0	?	−?
Evaluation of group B	0	1	?	−?

Note: A value of "+1" indicates the unit is activated, while "0" means inactive. Network: A = Group label, + = positive attribute, − = Negative attribute

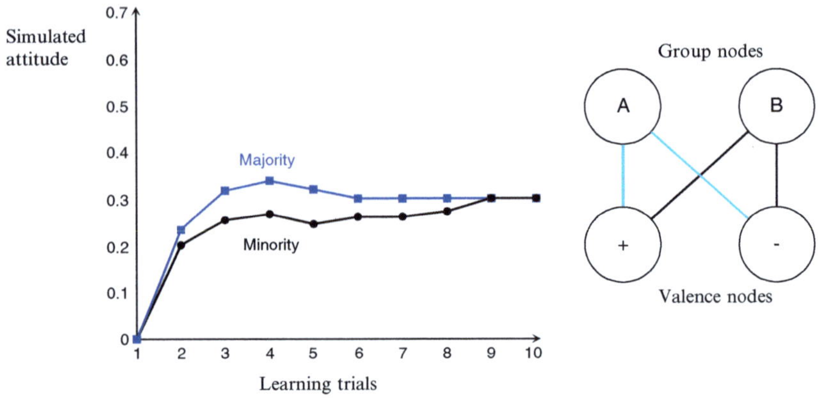

Fig. 2.2 *Left panel*: Simulation of the illusory correlation paradigm (Hamilton and Gifford 1976). On the Y-axis, the simulated average attitude towards the group (with higher numbers representing more positive attitudes). On the X-axis, each step represents a block of 10 trials. *Right panel*: Stereotypes of Group A & B as represented in a network

a participant. The first two cells represent the group label present in each statement, the next two cells denote the valence of the statement (see Fig. 2.2 for a graphical representation of an agent network). In the test phase of the simulation, to measure the traditional evaluative judgments on the groups (i.e., likability ratings), the group nodes were turned on and the difference between the resulting activations of the evaluative nodes was read off (denoted by question marks, see bottom panel of Table 2.1). Figure 2.2 shows the resulting differential activation from the desirable and undesirable node, representing the average attitudes towards Group A (Majority) and B (minority) for 50 agents, trained on the generic IC design in Table 2.1. We used several sets of parameters and training trials to illustrate the effect, but the basic effect remains similar: The model predicts that, initially, Group A will have a stronger positive association than Group B. More precisely, the illusory correlation effect is initially absent, gradually emerges with increasing amounts of learning, but diminishes and disappears as learning continues. This is very much in line with the empirical literature, which suggests that the illusory correlation effect reflects incomplete learning rather than a bias due to information loss in judgments or distinctiveness (Mullen and Johnson 1990; Van Rooy et al. 2003). The model thus suggests that negative minority stereotypes are not an inevitable final product of general learning processes.

3.2 *Simulation 2: Interpersonal Communication*

The second simulation explores the impact of interpersonal processes on IC. This is important, as the intergroup contact hypothesis (Allport 1954) predicts that

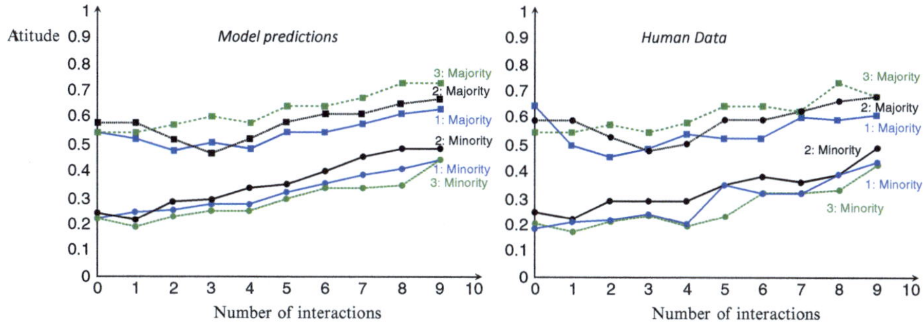

Fig. 2.3 *Left Panel*: Simulated average attitudes towards majority and minority group of 15 groups of 3 agents in function of amount of interaction cycles. Each step represents 4 interactions between all three agents. *Right panel*: Attitudes towards majority and minority group averaged across all groups for participants 1, 2 and 3 within each group of 3 (Pilot study). Each step represents a block of 4 positive and negative traits

increased contact between individuals should reduce prejudice. We decided to explore some of these issues in the following simulation and a pilot study.

3.2.1 Model Hypotheses

The simulation focuses on how individuals validate their attitudes by listening to arguments that support their initial attitude position. We simulated groups of 3 agents, each with the same network structure and learning as in the previous simulation (i.e. two group nodes and two valance nodes – see Fig. 2.2). Agents were individually trained and started the simulation with a more positive attitude towards the majority group, i.e. IC (see step 0 in left panel of Fig. 2.3). Agents were then allowed to exchange their information with all other agents during interaction cycles. During each cycle, each agent interacted 4 times with every other agent. After each cycle, we measured the agents' attitude towards the majority and minority groups, by priming the group node and reading off the difference between the positive and negative valence units.

In total, 15 groups of 3 agents were simulated, to correspond closely to the experiment below. The average simulated attitudes for agents 1 through 3 across those 15 groups are shown in the left panel of Fig. 2.3. The figure shows that the model predicts that under these conditions, the IC effect will begin to diminish, as even after a few interaction rounds, agents' attitudes towards the Majority and Minority groups start to converge towards each other. However, it also shows a polarization effect – attitudes towards both groups shift to a more extreme position. This simulation thus seems to capture an important group dynamic through which real social groups create, validate and maintain socially shared knowledge (Haslam et al. 1999; Hardin and Higgins 1996): The agents organize themselves around a shared norm or attitude, and with every interaction, the connection weights between them increase, reflecting increased social influence. The gradually strengthening links between agents act as positive feedback loops that further reinforce attitudes. This produces the polarization effect, in which all agents end up with more extreme, and also more consensual norms after the interaction. We set out to test these hypotheses in a small group experiment.

3.2.2 Pilot Study

Forty-two psychology undergraduate students (18 men, 24 women; mean age = 20.43) participated in the study. Participants arrived in the lab and were informed that they would be receiving information about individuals who belonged to one of two groups (Group A & B). They were asked to form an impression of these groups, and told that they would afterwards share their impressions with other participants. Individual participants were then presented with written information describing members of the two groups in the form of statements. The stimulus material was developed and tested in a preliminary study, as part of larger study (Van Rooy & Van Overwalle 2001; Van Rooy et al. 2013). An experimenter led the group session. Each trial involved the experimenter reading out either positive or negative traits (e.g. "Good", "Lazy", "Intelligent", ...) and then asking each participant to indicate on a 9-point rating scale the degree to which they considered each statement to be representative of both group A & B. Importantly, they were asked to voice their judgment by reading aloud the number they assigned (i.e. "Eight" to indicate it was very representative). The order in which participants answered was randomized across trials. On finishing the study, participants were debriefed and thanked for their participation.

3.2.3 Results

Participants were presented with 36 positive and 36 negative traits. For each participant, we calculated an average attitude towards both the majority and minority group per block of 4 traits. Figure 2.3 (Right panel) shows the results averaged across participants and groups. The 2 main predictions of the model were confirmed: The illusory correlation effect did in fact diminish as participants exchanged information. At the same time, there was a polarization effect, although not as outspoken as predicted by the model – participants' final attitudes ended more positive than their initial ones. In sum, the model not only correctly predicted the gradual disappearance of IC, it also predicted the polarization effect we found in the pilot study.

4 Conclusion and Future Studies

The simulations and the study in this paper are the first in which the interactive impact of individual and interpersonal processes on IC were investigated. Existing models make no precise predictions about learning curves, the emergence and

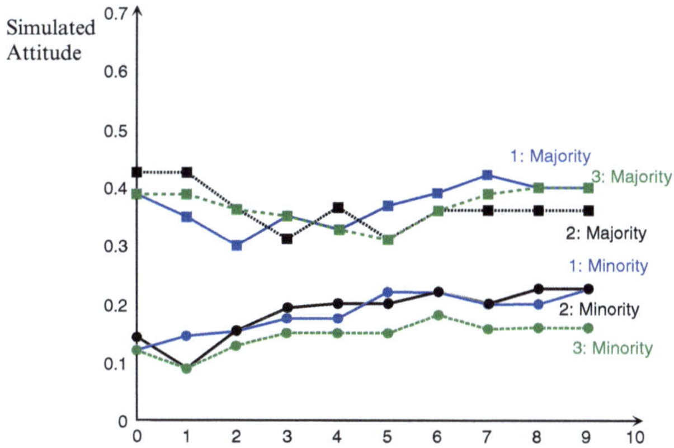

Fig. 2.4 Simulated average attitudes towards majority and minority group of 3 agents in function of amount of interaction. Each step represents only one interaction between all three agents

disappearance of illusory correlation in function of learning, and have not explored the impact of social interaction on the phenomenon. All of these issues are worth exploring in detail, and clearly merit further investigation. Our model can drive such research: By creating a community of networks, new parameters appear that are not present when we only consider an individual network. Small group studies, like the one described above, allow us to validate and inform the most psychologically plausible values of these parameters. In this process, simulations provide guidance for empirical research as well as sufficient depth to support interactive modification of the underlying theory (Wolfram 2002).

The model also allows to revisit existing research issues in novel ways. For instance, previous simulation work has suggested that deviant minorities are protected against majority influence by the spatial distance between the groups. This can be tested in our model by repeating the simulation above, but this time restrict the amount of information exchange between the agents (i.e. only one interaction instead of 4). Figure 2.4 shows that the model predicts less polarization, and a stable IC effect, which would be consistent with the literature – people are less influenced by others that are distant, not only in physical terms, but also socially (i.e. part of different cultural groups, status differences – for an overview, see (Isenberg 1986)).

Overall, this paper makes a number of new contributions. It introduces a more psychologically plausible agent model by implementing social comparison processes in a recurrent, connectionist network. Agents are embedded in a network structure that adapts in function of agent experiences. And finally, it illustrates how a tight coupling of an ABM and empirical tests can aid research. This last aspect is uncommon in an ABM literature that tends to focus on large scale simulations (economies, societies) and typically uses very simple agent models. The SCM provides an integrated framework that allows investigating key issues relating to the origin and maintenance of prejudice in ways that previous generations of social scientists, such as Allport, never could.

References

Allport GW (1954) The nature of prejudice. Addison-Wesley, Reading

Hamilton DL, Gifford RK (1976) Illusory correlation in intergroup perception: a cognitive basis of stereotypic judgments. J Exp Soc Psychol 12:392–407

Hardin C, Higgins ET (1996) Shared reality: how social verification makes the subjective objective. In: Sorrentino RM, Hig-gins ET (eds) Handbook of motivation and cognition: foundations of social behavior, vol 3. Guilford, New York, pp 28–84

Haslam SA, Oakes PJ, Reynolds KJ, Turner JC (1999) Social identity salience and the emergence of stereotype consensus. Pers Soc Psychol Bull 25(7):809–818

Hazlehurst B, Hutchins E (1998) The emergence of propositions from the co-ordination of talk and action in a shared world. Lang Cogn Process 13:373–424

Hegselmann R, Krause U (2002) Opinion dynamics and bounded confidence: models, analysis and simulation. J Artif Soc Soc Simul 5(3) http://jasss.soc.surrey.ac.uk/5/3/2.html.

Isenberg DJ (1986) Group polarization: a critical review and meta-analysis. J Pers Soc Psychol 50:1141–1151

Lyons A, Kashima Y (2003) How are stereotypes maintained through communication? The influence of stereotype sharedness. J Pers Soc Psychol 85(6):989–1005

McClelland JL, Rumelhart DE (1985) Distributed memory and the representation of general and specific information. J Exp Psychol 114:159–188. Library Holdings

McClelland JL, Rumelhart DE (1988) Explorations in parallel distributed processing: a handbook of models, programs and exercises. Bradford, Cambridge, MA

Mullen B, Johnson C (1990) Distinctiveness- based illusory correlations and stereotyping: a meta-analytic integration. Br J Soc Psychol 29:11–28

Smith ER, DeCoster J (1998) Knowledge acquisition, accessibility, and use in person perception and stereotyping: simulation with a recurrent connectionist network. J Pers Soc Psychol 74:21–35

Van Rooy D, Van Overwalle F (2001) A connectionist account of illusory correlation. Int J Psychol 35(3–4):24–24

Van Overwalle F, Heylighen F (2006) Talking nets: a multiagent connectionist approach to communication and trust between individuals. In: 7th international conference on cognitive modeling, American Psychological Association/Educational Publishing Foundation, Trieste, pp 606–627. doi:10.1037/0033-295x.113.3.606

Van Rooy D, Van Overwalle F, Vanhoomissen T, Labiouse C, French R (2003) A recurrent connectionist model of group biases. Psychol Rev 110:536–563

Van Rooy D, Vanhoomissen T, Van Overwalle F (2013) Illusory correlation, memory and group size. J Exp Soc Psychol 49(6):1159–1167

Van Rooy D, Wood I, Tran E (2014) Modeling the emergence of shared attitudes from group dynamics using an agent-based model of social comparison theory. Systems Research and Behavioral Science. Article published online: 13 Oct 2014 doi:10.1002/sres.2321

Wolfram S (2002) A new kind of science. Wolfram Media, Champaign

Chapter 3
Globalization May Cause Cultural Accumulation in the Whole Population

Shiro Horiuchi

Abstract We constructed an agent-based model (ABM) that tested how globalization, frequent movements of individuals between local societies, affects the accumulation of cultures. In the model, multiple groups were connected as a circular stepping-stone formation without boundaries. Agents copy cultural traits of others in their groups; agents may gain or lose their cultural traits through the process, depending on the traits of opponents, which is called within-boundary communication. Agents periodically migrate between adjacent groups. Agents also visit adjacent groups, copy the cultural traits in those groups, and return to their group, which is called cross-boundary communication. The model indicates that cultural traits may accumulate in the whole population even if they migrate frequently. The necessary conditions are that agents also frequently communicate cross-boundary by finding an appropriate group.

Keywords Globalization • Cultural traits • Try and error • Migration • Groups

1 Introduction

Individuals transmit cultural traits through teaching and learning, which is different from biological inheritance through DNA (Cavalli-Sforza and Feldman 1973). Here cultural traits are languages, rituals, festivals, clothes, cuisine, art, and social norms maintained in local societies. Cultural phenomena are found in many vertebrates, particularly in our closest relative, the chimpanzee (Whiten et al. 1999). However, cumulative characteristics are only found in human cultures. The metaphor "ratchet" is often assumed to be a cumulative characteristic of human culture (Tomasello 1999).

Humans have created complex cultures due to these ratchet effects. Due to the cumulative features of human culture, a variety of local cultures are found around the world. Individuals gain local culture by learning from others, who are residents

S. Horiuchi (✉)
COC Promotion Office, Yamagata University, Yamagata, Japan
e-mail: horiuchi.shiro@gmail.com

Y. Nakai et al. (eds.), *Agent-Based Approaches in Economic and Social Complex Systems VIII*, Agent-Based Social Systems 13, DOI 10.1007/978-4-431-55236-9_3

of their local society. Local cultures usually do not directly contribute to the utility of the carriers. Nevertheless, residents maintain their local culture to ensure group identity. Each local society has grown and preserved its original local culture, by which the society is distinguished from other local societies.

Now many local societies have lost their culture due to the effects of globalization. In the age of globalization, individuals have been freed from local society restraints. They no longer require group identities for their social life. Local cultures now provide few benefits to their carriers. Additionally, mass migration has caused serious damage to local cultures since the great explosion of the fifteenth century. Immigrants from most cultures do not usually respect the local cultures of minorities; thus, it is difficult for residents of a minority culture to preserve their local culture. In fact, they may abandon their minority culture to conform to the majority culture. The influx of tourists also leads to negative effects on local culture, and local residents often relinquish their traditional local culture due to the impact of large numbers of tourists. Hence, globalization has seriously damaged local culture.

Globalization may not only result in negative effects on local cultures. Particularly, we should note the existence of certain individuals as keepers of local culture. They are often outsiders, who may be immigrants or visitors to the local society. Freed from the boundaries of local societies, some individuals seek identities shared with others. By learning about different local cultures, they may revive the local cultures of their targeted local societies. Thus, they contribute to maintaining local cultures that might otherwise disappear. A new culture, revived by outsiders, may fascinate others beyond the boundary of a local society. Actually, Horiuchi (2012) found that many visitors emotionally and financially support local artists; some immigrants or visitors participate in performing local arts, and local arts become media through which the local society is activated, with local residents and outsiders acting together. Young residents, eager to succeed in a local culture, can encounter depopulation and aging in the local society. Thus, globalization may also contribute to maintaining local cultures.

Accordingly, it is an open and important question whether globalization has negative or positive effects on local cultures (Cowen 2004). Sociology should elucidate the process of how interaction among individuals at the micro level affects local cultures at the macro level, following the idea of the Coleman boat (Coleman 1990). Interactions among individuals are nonlinear and complex. It is difficult to fully grasp such interactions and effects on local cultures only by observation and intuition.

The agent-based model (ABM) is an efficient tool when interactions among individuals are complex and difficult to grasp intuitively. Several ABM studies have modeled culture as a cumulative real number to analyze the cumulative features of cultures (Powell et al. 2009; Premo and Kuhn 2010; Lewis and Laland 2012). They predict that a large population size has positive effects on cultural accumulation. In contrast, Axelrod (1997) modeled culture as vectors, with each element representing an independent cultural trait. This model predicts that large population size has negative effects on cultural diversity. Following Axelrod's study, later studies tested the effects of global information flow (Shibanai et al. 2001), the range of local communications (Greig 2002), complex networks (Klemm et al. 2005), or communication links constructed by agents (Centola et al. 2007) on cultural traits.

These studies did not fully model the complex features of culture. Culture is cumulative and, at the same time, different aspects within cultures can be contradictory. Thus, culture should be modeled as a vector, and each element can be summed up. Individuals evaluate the summed values. Lehman et al. (2011) or Horiuchi and Kubota (2013) modeled culture as being composed of independent multiple traits. If an agent knows or does not know a cultural trait, the trait is given a 1 or 0, respectively. Multiple cultural traits may be summed, and large numbers represent an elaborate culture. These modeling assumptions are valid for testing both the cumulative and contradictory features of a culture. In this study, we constructed an ABM to study the effects of an agent's interactions on diversity and accumulation of culture following these ideas.

2 Simulation Method

We constructed a simple ABM to elucidate how interactions among agents affect culture. The ABM assumed N agents and G groups. The G groups were arranged as circular stepping-stones without boundaries. N/G agents belonged to each group under the initial conditions. The model assumes N to be a multiple value of G, so the number of members is initially the same integer value for all groups. A number from 1 to N was denoted for each agent and for each group from 1 to G.

Each agent had their own culture, represented by the vector $(p_{i,1}, p_{i,2}, \ldots, p_{i,K})$ for agent i. If the agent knows or does not know the kth cultural trait $(1 \leq k \leq K)$, $p_{i,k}$ was 1 or 0, respectively. P_i is denoted as the total number of cultural traits that agent i knows, or $P_i = \sum_k p_{k,i}$. Additionally, the vector $(q_{g,1}, q_{g,2}, \ldots, q_{g,K})$ is denoted for group g $(1 \leq g \leq G)$. If one or more agents knows or no agents know the kth cultural trait in the group, $q_{g,k}$ is 1 or 0, respectively. Q_g denotes the total number of cultural traits remaining in the group g, or $Q_g = \sum_k q_{g,k}$. The range is $0 \leq P_i$, $Q_g \leq K$ for any agent and any group (Fig. 3.1).

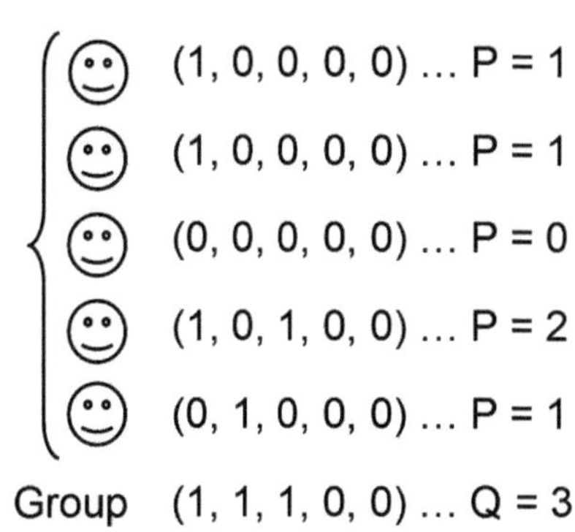

Fig. 3.1 *P* and *Q* calculated for each agent and their group

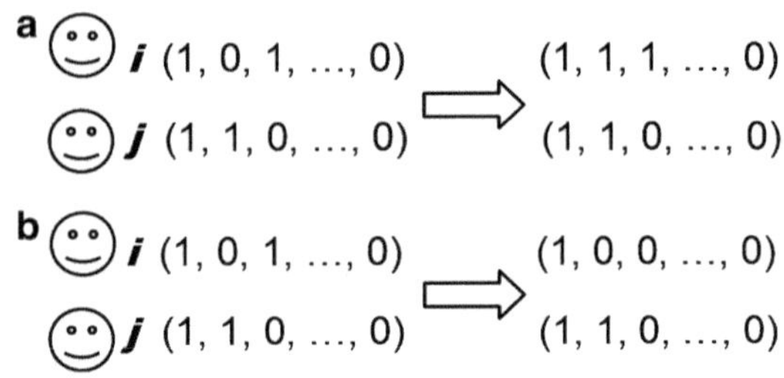

Fig. 3.2 The process of within-boundary communication. (**a**) Agent *i* gains the second cultural trait by copying a cultural trait of agent *j*, (**b**) but loses the third cultural trait by copying another cultural trait

Under the initial conditions, agents of group *g* know only the *g*th cultural trait, so $P_i = 1$ for all agents and $Q_g = 1$ for all groups. Here, a cultural trait *g* is the endemic knowledge of group *g*. The model assumes that the total number of groups equals the total number of cultural traits, or $G = K$, for simplicity. Hence, the set of all groups is matched against the set of all cultural traits.

At each turn, agents learn the cultural traits of others within their group, which is called within-boundary communication. Agent *i* is selected randomly during this process. Another agent, *j*, is selected randomly from the same group as agent *i*. A cultural trait, *k*, is randomly selected. The cultural trait *k* of agent *i* becomes equivalent to that of agent *j*: $c_{i,k}$ equals $c_{j,k}$. As a result, agent *i* may gain a new cultural trait (Fig. 3.2a) or lose her original cultural trait (Fig. 3.2b). The same agent may be selected twice, or $i = j$, in which case social learning does not occur, but it is likely to occur when the number of members is small in that group.

A randomly selected agent migrates to one of the two adjacent groups for each R_m turn. The range of R_m is $1 \leq R_m \leq 10^6$. Lower values of R_m indicate that agents migrate between groups more frequently. The agent emigrates into a group with probability S_m, where Q is larger in the two adjacent groups. The agent misses the group with probability $1 - S_m$, where Q is larger; and randomly emigrates into one of the two groups.

A randomly selected agent visits an adjacent group and learns the cultural traits of another agent there for each R_c turn. This process is called cross-boundary communication. The range of R_c is $1 \leq R_c \leq 10^6$. Lower values of R_c indicate that agents communicate cross-boundary more frequently. The agent finds a group with probability S_c, where Q is larger in the two adjacent groups. He visits the group and randomly selects an agent *j* in that group with cultural trait *k*. After copying the cultural trait, *k*, the agent returns to his own group. The cultural trait *k* of the agent *i* becomes equivalent to that of agent *j*: $c_{i,k}$ equals $c_{j,k}$, like within-boundary communication. The agent misses the group with probability $1 - S_c$ where Q is larger; he randomly visits one of the two groups and copies a cultural trait *k* from an agent *j*.

After enough turns, the total number of cultural traits remaining in the whole population, *U*, is the index of culture that remains. A larger value of *U* suggests that more cultural traits remain in the whole population. We checked the average number of cultural traits for each agent, *V*, which equaled $\sum P_i / N$. Larger values of *V* suggest that agents know more cultural traits on average. We also checked the diversity of local cultures, W, which equals $\sum\sum_{g\neq h}\sum_{k}|q_{g,k} - q_{h,k}|/\{G\ (G-1)\}$. A larger value of W suggests that different local cultures are maintained in different groups. The ranges are, $0 \leq U,\ V,\ W \leq K$.

3 Results of the Simulation

We first fixed these values: $N = 200$, $G = K = 20$. The simulation investigated the values of U, V, and W at each (R_m, R_c, S_m, S_c). We determined how the U, V, and W values changed as time passed to examine how many iterations was sufficient for the system. At equilibrium, U and V should match each other and W should be 0. By testing the simulation with several values of R and S, we concluded that 300,000 turns was sufficient (Fig. 3.3). Note that we did not need to wait for the simulation to reach equilibrium. If agents rarely migrate or visit, a variety of different local cultures are more likely to persist, as the system does not reach equilibrium, which is an important point to be elucidated. Hereafter, we show the results after 300,000 turns had passed.

We set the parameters $S_c = 0$ and $S_m = 0$. In this case, the agent randomly migrated and randomly communicated cross-boundary with one of the two adjacent groups. Figure 3.4 shows a box plot of U, V, and W along the value of $\log_{10}R_c$ when $\log_{10}R_m = 3$ (Fig. 3.4a–c) or $\log_{10}R_m = 0$ (Fig. 3.4d–f); we ran the simulation 30 times for each condition. The figure suggests that, as the value of R_c decreased, U and W decreased significantly, but V did not change. Figure 3.5 shows a box plot of U, V, and W along the value of $\log_{10}R_c$ when $\log_{10}R_m = 3$ (Fig. 3.5a–c) or $\log_{10}R_m = 0$ (Fig. 3.5d–f), when the parameters $S_m = 0.5$ and $S_c = 0$. In this case, the agent migrated to a group with a larger Q with a probability of 0.5 but randomly communicated cross-boundary with one of the two adjacent groups. The figure shows a similar trend for U, V, and W with that of Fig. 3.4. Figure 3.6 shows a box plot of U, V, and W along the value of $\log_{10}R_c$ when $\log_{10}R_m = 3$ (Fig. 3.6a–c) or $\log_{10}R_m = 0$ (Fig. 3.6d–f), when the parameter $S_m = 0$ and $S_c = 0.5$. In this case,

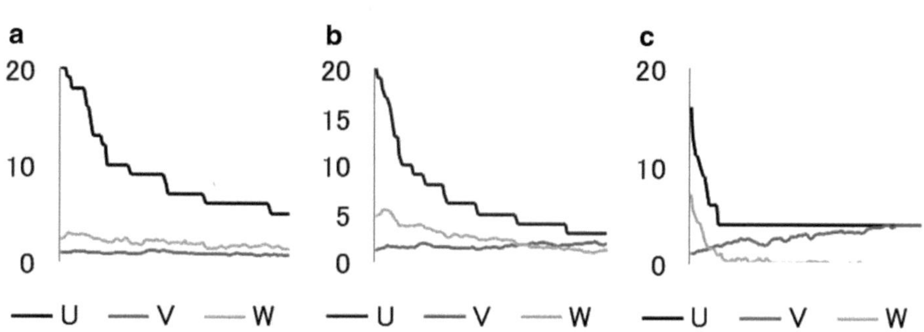

Fig. 3.3 The values of U, V, and W over time ($0 \leq \mathrm{T} \leq 10_6$). (**a**) $R_m = 10_3$, $R_c = 10_3$, $S_m = 0$, $S_c = 0$. (**b**) $R_m = 102$, $R_c = 102$, $S_m = 0.5$, $S_c = 0$. (**c**) $R_m = 1$, $R_c = 1$, $S_m = 0$, $S_c = 0.5$

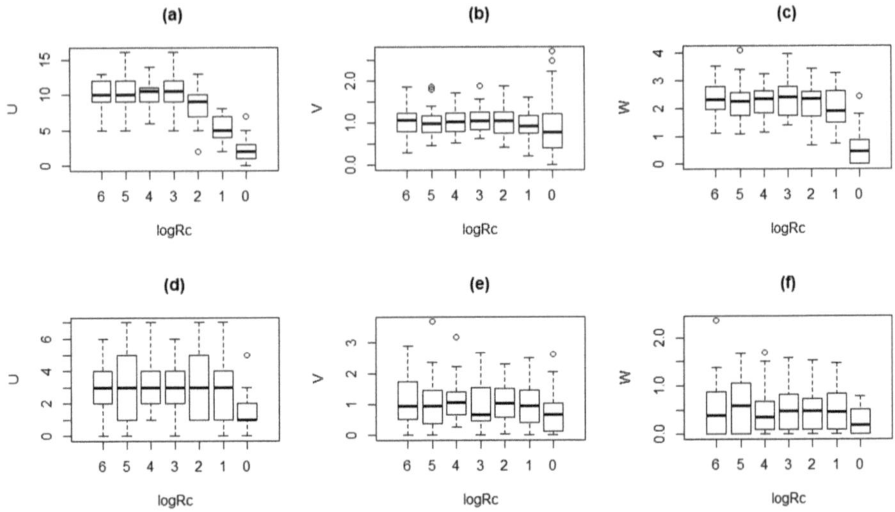

Fig. 3.4 A box plot of U, V, and W from 30 trials with the value of $\log_{10}R_c$ when $S_m = 0$ and $S_c = 0$. (**a–c**) $\log_{10}R_m = 3$. (**d–e**) $\log_{10}R_m = 0$

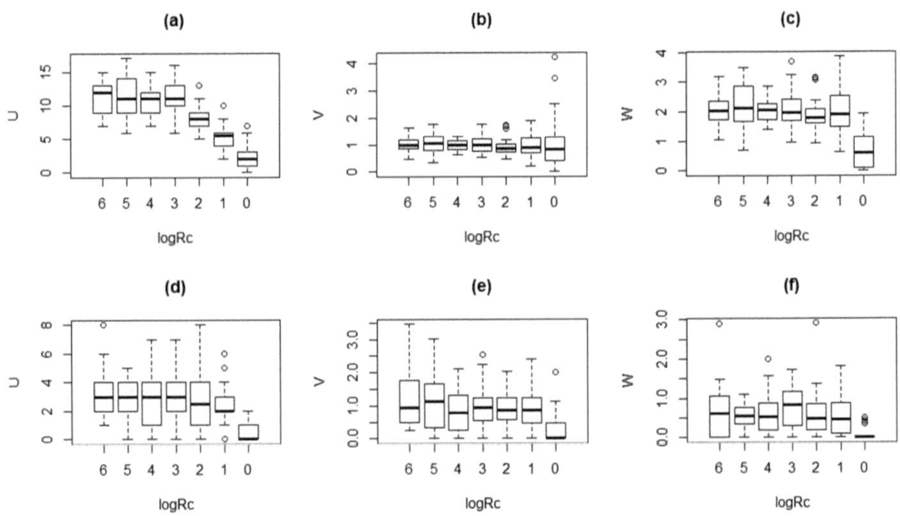

Fig. 3.5 A box plot of U, V, and W from 30 trials with the value of $\log_{10}R_c$ when $S_m = 0.5$ and $S_c = 0$. (**a–c**) $\log_{10}R_m = 3$. (**d–e**) $\log_{10}R_m = 0$

the agent randomly migrated to one of the two adjacent groups and communicated cross-boundary with a group with a larger Q and probability of 0.5. The figure suggests that when the value of $\log_{10}R_m = 0$, U increased significantly as the value

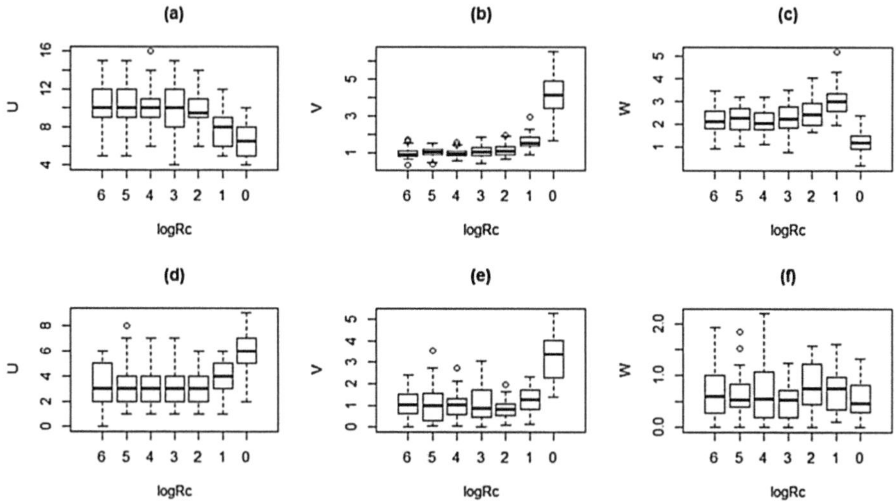

Fig. 3.6 A box plot of *U*, *V*, and *W* from 30 trials with the value of $\log_{10}R_c$ when $S_m = 0$ and $S_c = 0.5$. (**a–c**) $\log_{10}R_m = 3$. (**d–e**) $\log_{10}R_m = 0$

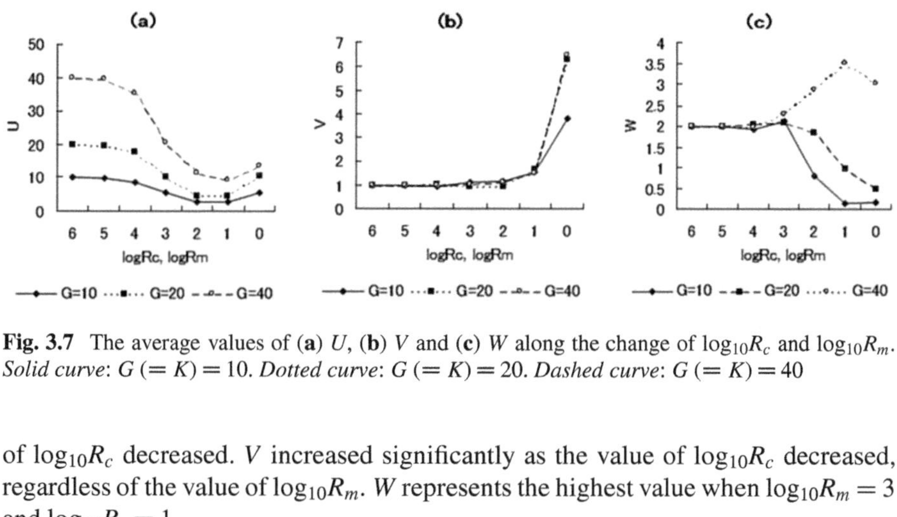

Fig. 3.7 The average values of (**a**) *U*, (**b**) *V* and (**c**) *W* along the change of $\log_{10}R_c$ and $\log_{10}R_m$. *Solid curve*: $G\ (= K) = 10$. *Dotted curve*: $G\ (= K) = 20$. *Dashed curve*: $G\ (= K) = 40$

of $\log_{10}R_c$ decreased. *V* increased significantly as the value of $\log_{10}R_c$ decreased, regardless of the value of $\log_{10}R_m$. *W* represents the highest value when $\log_{10}R_m = 3$ and $\log_{10}R_c = 1$.

Now we set $R_c = R_m$, as both values should decrease at the same time as globalization proceeds. Figure 3.7 shows the average values of *U*, *V*, and *W* along the value of $\log_{10}R_c$ (= $\log_{10}R_m$), when the parameter $S_m = 0$ and $S_c = 1$. We set the value of $G = K$ as 10, 20, or 40. In the simulation, the value *N* was fixed at 200, as different values of *N* require different simulation times for equilibrium. Accordingly, the number of agents at the local society was 20, 10, and 5, respectively, for each $G = K$ is 10, 20, and 40. We ran the simulations 30 times under each condition. Regardless of the value of *K* or *G*, the values of *U* showed U shaped curves and those of *V* showed increasing curves along the change of $\log_{10}R_c$

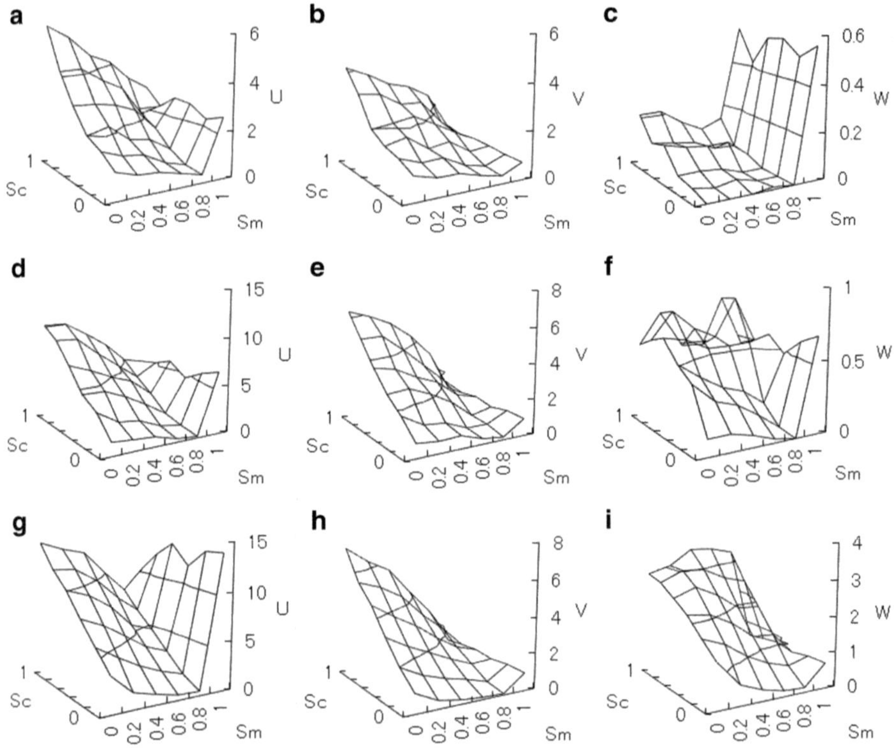

Fig. 3.8 The average values of U, V, and W of 30 simulations at each (S_m, S_c) when $R_c = R_m = 1$. (**a–c**) $G = (K =)$ 10. (**d–f**) $G = 20$. (**g–h**) $G = 40$

and $\log_{10}R_m$. In contrast, the values of W showed different curves depending on the value of G or K along the change of $\log_{10}R_c$ and $\log_{10}R_m$.

Finally, we set the value of $R_m = R_c = 1$, most frequent migration and cross-boundary communications, and changed the values of S_m and S_c from 0 to 1. We ran the simulation when the value of G $(= K) = 10$, 20, or 40, respectively; the number of agents was 20, 10 and 5, respectively at each G and K. Figure 3.8 shows the average values of U, V, and W along the values of S_m and S_c; we ran the simulation 30 times for each condition. Depending on the value of G or K, the values of U and W showed different curves along the change of S_m and S_c.

4 Discussion

The present model clarified how the movement frequency of agents affects cultural accumulation in the whole population. If agents migrate between groups or communicated cross-boundary frequently, the total number of cultural traits remaining

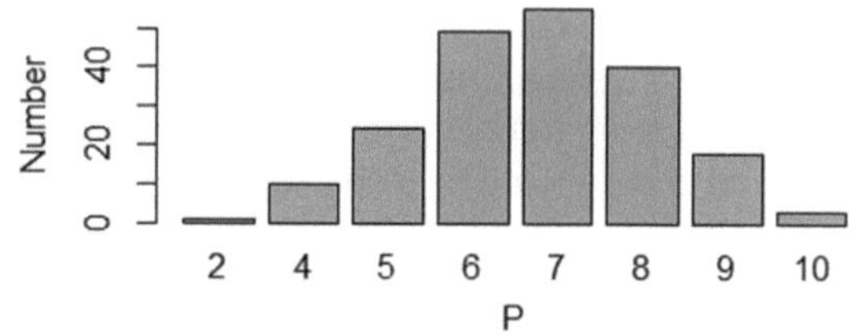

Fig. 3.9 The number of agents with P when $(R_m, R_c, S_m, S_c) = (1, 1, 0, 1)$

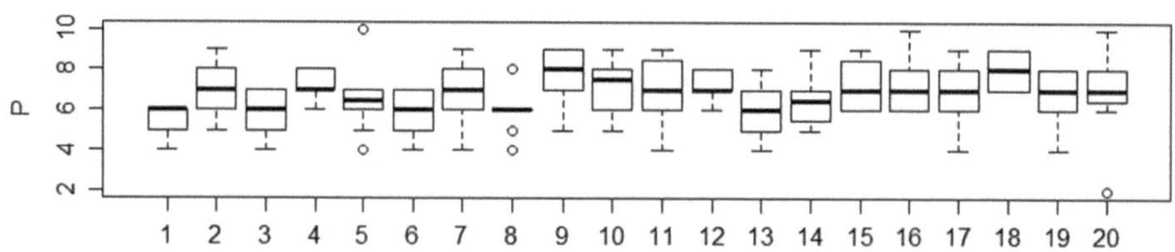

Fig. 3.10 A box plot of P at each local society when $(R_m, R_c, S_m, S_c) = (1, 1, 0, 1)$

should decrease in the whole population, which is due to the negative effects of globalization. The simulation certainly showed such expected results as long as S_m and S_c were low; U decreased as the value of R_m or R_c decreased, or as agents moved more frequently. The simulation thus followed naïve intuition that, as individuals are freed from local societies and move between groups more frequently, or as globalization proceeds, the total number of cultural traits remaining should decrease more. On average, only one cultural trait should remain in the world, or $U = 1$, as $K/G = 1$ is the modeling assumption ($K = G$).

However, the simulation also showed that frequent movements of agents might result in a high U value or more cultural traits remaining in the whole population. The results arise depending on the value of S_m and S_c. When S_c is large, or agents are likely to visit groups with rich cultural traits and engage in cross-boundary communications, more cultural traits will remain in the whole population as agents communicate cross-boundary frequently. That should be natural as some groups with rich cultural traits attract many agents for social learning, who are likely to relay their learned traits to their original local societies. When agents engage in cross-boundary communication with a group of higher Q, some agents maintain their original cultural traits as well as the new cultural traits. Agents who are equipped with many cultural traits are "cultural elites". Figure 3.9 shows the existence of cultural elites who have more cultural traits than average; a few agents with the value of $P = 10$ can be the cultural elites.

Cultural elites should scatter at all local societies if the values of R_m and S_m are small. Cultural elites with the largest P may appear in any local society (Local societies 5, 16, and 20 in Fig. 3.10). As long as many agents communicate cross-boundary around local societies that include cultural elites, cultural traits will accumulate in the world. Thus, random frequent migration and non-random cross-boundary communication result in a high value of U, or more remaining cultural traits. Accordingly, we should encourage cultural elites to work across boundaries of local societies to maintain and accumulate various cultural traits. In other words, as long as we cannot stop frequent migration of individuals between local societies, we should also promote their frequent and selective cross-boundary communication. Cultural elites should be respected as holders of many cultural traits.

The results depend on the number of groups or cultural traits (G and K). If there are few local societies or few cultural traits, fewer cultural traits will remain in the whole population as agents selectively migrate between groups (large S_m). In this case, some local societies, which are accidentally rich in cultural traits, attract many agents, and the immigrant agents should loss their original cultural traits. If there are many local societies or cultural traits, more cultural traits may remain in the whole population as agents selectively migrate between groups. In this case, quite a few local societies function as cultural refugees, in which sufficient cultural traits remain. Multiple cultural refugees are more likely to be distantly distributed, as there are more local societies. So, the number of cultural traits in the world, as well as the diversity of local cultures, is more likely to be maintained due to high S_c and high S_m in this case. This result follows my previous study in which frequent but selective migration by agents causes cultural diversity (Horiuchi 2011). If agents are assumed to migrate or communicate cross-boundary far away from their original groups, by assuming complete, small world or scale free graphs (Albert and Barabasi 2002), such effects may hardly appear. We should also note that individuals usually copy not only the cultural traits of others but also innovate new cultural traits that are unknown by others (Lehman et al. 2011). If agents innovate new cultural traits, cultural traits are more likely to accumulate. Future studies should test how the distance of an agent's movements and innovation affect cultural accumulation and diversity.

Culture is not only a characteristic of humans but is also expressed by other animals such as birds, monkeys, and apes. However, even chimpanzees, who have various cultures, cannot accumulate culture as much as humans. Archaeological studies also show that the Neanderthals could not accumulate culture like modern humans (Mellars 1989). We accumulate our culture partly because we engage in cross-boundary communication, which was not common among the Neanderthals (Marwick 2003). Cross-boundary communication, coupled with migration, contributed to our cultural accumulation and made us homo sapiens.

Acknowledgments I thank comments of the reviewers on this paper. This research was financially supported by the MEXT KAKENHI. No. 21710051, 23101505 and 25101707.

References

Albert R, Barabasi AL (2002) Statistical mechanics of complex networks. Rev Mod Phys 74:47–97

Axelrod R (1997) The dissemination of culture. J Confl Resolut 41:203–226

Cavalli-Sforza LL, Feldman MW (1973) Cultural versus biological inheritance: phenotypic transmission from parents to children (A theory of the effects of parental phenotypes on children's phenotypes). Am J Hum Genet 25:618–737

Centola D, Gonzalez-Avella JC, Eguiluz VM et al (2007) Homophily, cultural drift, and the co-evolution of cultural groups. J Confl Resolut 51:905–929
Coleman JS (1990) Foundations of social theory. Belknap, Cambridge
Cowen T (2004) Creative destruction: how globalization is changing the world's cultures. Princeton University Press, Princeton
Greig JM (2002) The end of geography? Globalization, communications, and culture in the international system. J Confl Resolut 46:225–243
Horiuchi S (2011) Diversity of local cultures maintained by agents' movements between local societies. The 7th conference of the European Social Simulation Association CD-ROM. Montpellier
Horiuchi S (2012) Community creation by residents and tourists via Takachiho Kagura in Japanese rural area. Sociol Mind 2:306–312
Horiuchi S, Kubota S (2013) The effects of cross-boundary rituals on cultural innovation. In: Akazawa T, Nishiaki Y, Aoki K (eds) Dynamics of learning in neanderthals and modern humans, vol 1. Springer, Tokyo, pp 229–236
Klemm K, Eguîluz VM, Toral R et al (2005) Globalization, polarization and cultural drift. J Econ Dyn Control 29:321–334
Lehmann L, Aoki K, Feldman MW (2011) On the number of independent cultural traits carried by individuals and populations. Philos Trans R Soc B 366:424–435
Lewis HM, Laland KN (2012) Transmission fidelity is the key to the build-up of cumulative culture. Philos Trans R Soc B 367:2171–2180
Marwick B (2003) Pleistocene exchange networks as evidence for the evolution of language. Camb Archaeol J 13:67–81
Mellars P (1989) Major issues in the emergence of modern humans. Curr Anthropol 30:349–385
Powell A, Shennan S, Thom MG (2009) Late Pleistocene demography and the appearance of modern human behavior. Science 324:1298–1331
Premo LS, Kuhn SL (2010) Modeling effects of local extinction on culture change and diversity in the Paleolithic. PlosOne 5:e15582
Shibanai Y, Yasuno S, Ishiguro I (2001) Effects of global information feedback on diversity: extensions to Axelrod's adaptive culture model. J Confl Resolut 45:80–96
Tomasello M (1999) The human adaptation for culture. Annu Rev Anthropol 28:509–529
Whiten A, Goodall J, McGrew WC et al (1999) Cultures in chimpanzees. Nature 399:682–685

Chapter 4
Topos Modeling of Social Conflict: Theory and Methods

David L. Sallach

Abstract Category theory and, more specifically, topos categories provide a more expressive type of mathematical modeling and, thereby, open the door to social models that are both rigorous and expressive. The present analysis draws upon four views of topos categories to construct a rich model of a logic based on recognition theory. The topos initially provides support for: (1) set theory (and classical logic), (2) topological regions dualism. The resulting structures support: (3) a local intuitionist logic that can vary by situated circumstances and actor types, and (4) the specification of regions that are defined by finely-differentiated classifiers. These tools construct an integrated topos category of social recognition that supports diverse forms of local logic. The latter are then explored regarding their contributions to a mathematical model of social conflict. Categorial analysis of historical patterns, as well as a complementary simulation model, is used to illustrate the advantages of such an approach.

Keywords Category theory • Topos theory • Recognition theory • Local logic • Truth granularity • Notional truth attribution • Social conflict • Social model of war

1 Introduction

Arguably, for centuries, mathematical tools were not sufficiently expressive to support social models. Accordingly, rigorous social analysis has focused on counting and measuring, including the application of ever more powerful statistical techniques, while continuing to lack the mathematical capacity to represent dynamic interaction, evolving relations, and the pervasive fluidity of social processes. During the past century, however, dramatic progress has been made in higher mathematics.

D.L. Sallach (✉)
Argonne National Laboratory, University of Chicago, Chicago, IL, USA
e-mail: sallach@anl.gov

Y. Nakai et al. (eds.), *Agent-Based Approaches in Economic and Social Complex Systems VIII*, Agent-Based Social Systems 13, DOI 10.1007/978-4-431-55236-9_4

Nonetheless, the range, complexity, and abstraction of these innovations make it challenging to identify and apply emerging insights and techniques to the modeling of social phenomena.

Mathematical contributions are constituted through a formal discourse that, in recent decades, has advanced dramatically, and continues to expand at a prodigious rate. In addition to being abstract, the areas in which recent advances have been achieved are diverse, and their prospective implications are not easy for non-specialists from other disciplines to identify. This is unfortunate since various innovations have the potential to support new and productive research strategies in a variety of substantive disciplines. The subject of the present paper is to illustrate ways in which the emerging richness of mathematical formalisms provides innovative and expressive representations for theoretical modeling in the social sciences.

Potential contributions of category theory in the social sciences have been addressed in previous papers. The focus has been on: (1) the use of adjoint functors to represent social structures in classical social theory (Sallach 2012a), (2) prospective categorical contributions to social methods, including the mapping of qualitative concepts to equivalence classes (Sallach 2012b), and (3) the propagation of cross-scale social propensities (Sallach 2012c).

The present paper is more specialized and detailed. From within the extensive range of categories that have been defined, topos categories are quite expressive, and seem likely to be especially productive in the social sciences. The focus of the present discussion is on summarizing what topos theory may be able to contribute to social analysis, and to illustrate ways that these capabilities can be applied.

2 Category Theory

During the last 70 years, category theory has arisen as a rich formalism capable of tying many research domains together (Awodey 2010). It first emerged as a means of embellishing topological surfaces with algebraic operators. However, soon it was being applied in other areas, first within mathematics and later to: logic (Jacobs 1999), computer science (Pierce 1991), physics (Crane and Yetter 1993; Flori 2013), biology (Rosen 1991) and neurology (Ehresmann and Vanbremeersch 2007).

Whereas set theory has (1) focused on mathematical *objects* (sets), (2) privileged the member relation above other potential relations of interest, and (3) emphasized functions that manipulate a single object type (e.g., union, difference, intersection), category theory focuses on relations and morphisms that transform mathematical objects of widely varying types. It has developed a framework by which to shift to ever-higher levels of abstraction (e.g., to functors, natural transformations and higher categories).

Among the strengths of category theory that make it particularly relevant to social modeling are, first, that support for equivalence relations allows an *expressiveness* of qualitative concepts to be retained while allowing them to be translated into a more *precise* form (Sallach 2012a). Second, categorical models can apply duality analysis in a way that provides a means of integrating coupled processes. Together, such capabilities make rigorous theoretical integration feasible.

2.1 Topos Theory

Topoi[1] are categories that combine the strengths of topology and set theory. This blending makes them a powerful source of rich and variegated representations. Joyal and Johnstone provide a comprehensive set of descriptions of topoi that have emerged over the decades,[2] but explicating and/or elaborating them is outside of the scope of the present discussion. To begin, we will draw upon the definitions provided by Borceux (1994) and Johnstone (2002). Borceux defines topoi as "the categorical framework for studying those structures [that] behave like sets (1994: 288). Somewhat more technically, Johnstone (2002: 68) defines a topos as "a properly Cartesian closed category with a subobject classifier."

Borceux identifies three representative examples (1994: 288–289): (1) a topos of sets (the 'classical' formulation); (2) a topos of sheaves on a locale, "where elements exist at various levels and can be glued or restricted to produce elements at other levels"; and (3) a topos of G-sets, for a Group G, where "the sets of elements are provided with some structure, namely, an action of the group G." The first two Borceux examples are of particular interest because they illustrate the constructive interaction between the set-theoretic and topological aspects of topos theory.

In moving from generic definitions to topoidal capabilities that can readily contribute to social science representation and modeling, the present discussion will focus on four topos characteristics: (1) determinate objects and the sets they form, including set-theoretic functions and the (classical) predicate logic with which they are associated; (2) topological spaces, including stalks, presheaves, sheaves, locales, écales, pretopoi and, ultimately, topoi; (3) intuitionist logic (Bell 1988: 162–219), a 'local' logic that does not assume the principle of the excluded middle; and (4) subobject classification, a structured way of providing graduated, indexed

[1]Toposes and topoi are both used as a plural of topos. In this discussion, the latter is preferred.

[2]To show how mathematically expressive definitions of topoi have become, Johnstone (2002: vii–viii) lists the seven descriptions of topoidal categories first assembled by André Joyal): (1) a category of sheaves on a site, (2) a category with finite limits and power objects, (3) an intuitionistic higher-order theory, (4) a first-order (infinitary) geometric theory, (5) a totally cocomplete object in the meta-2-category of Cartesian categories, (6) a generalized space, and (7) a semantics for intuitionistic formal systems. He then notes that six additional definitions have been formulated since the initial list was formulated: (8) a Morita equivalence class of continuous groupoids, (9) the category of maps of a power allegory, (10) a category whose canonical indexing over itself is complete and well-powered, (11) the spatial manifestation of a Giraud frame, (12) a setting for synthetic differential geometry, and (13) a setting for synthetic domain theory. Formally, these definitions overlap each other to some extent, but they also illustrate how diverse are the contributions that topoi can make.

and/or spectral distinctions within a stable set of values. The first characteristic makes available all of the familiar concrete entities that are measured, counted and subjected to statistical analysis. The second can be used to define synthetic geometries, but also to create cultural and ideational spaces. All topos contributions make the resulting analysis more systematic (cf., Takahara & Takai 1985; Takahashi & Takahara 1995).

By providing a local logic, the third example allows the introduction of a *social reference frame,* relative to which social actors can draw distinctive inferences. Bell (1988: 239–242) notes an analogy with relativity theory, which also has reference frames (coordinate systems) that define local patterns. Since it does not assume the 'law' of the excluded middle (cf., Godel 2004; Dummett 1977: 17–21), it has the potential of supporting partial, qualified and probabilistic inferences, as well as varying types of inference in diverse relationships or scenarios. Finally, the fourth characteristic allows either an analyst or a simulative agent to assess the effects of incremental differences in spaces or structures of interest.

Since these four characteristics are alternative ways of viewing a common model, and may interact with each other in structured ways, these core mechanisms can represent complex and subtle dynamics. The expressiveness of a topos category, including the additional capabilities implicit in footnote one, have the potential to provide the underpinnings of a new generation of social science methodologies.

2.2 Point-Set Topologies

Further regarding the interaction of multiple topoidal aspects, point (and set) distributions are often used to define topological regions while, conversely, spatial characteristics can influence the characteristics of a point (or discrete actor). Figure 4.1 provides a generic example of one form that such codefinition (and coevolution) can take, and one way that point distribution and spatial shapes can operate together to address ambiguities. Specifically, Fig. 4.1 uses point sets to generate shapes by applying a moving least squares (MLS) algorithm (Amenta and Kill 2004).[3] The generated relationship provides the basis for an interpretive result, i.e., diverse regions of a shape can have a distinctive significance relative to the problem at hand.

When a topos consists of sheaves on a locale, it is possible for elements to exist at various levels, in which case they can be *glued* or *restricted* to produce newly integrated elements, or processes that are coupled across levels. Figure 4.2 shows a system of two sheaves that have been joined at two structurally similar sites. As categories, topoi naturally express such reciprocal part-whole influences (Goldblatt 1984; Bell 1988; McLarty 1996; Marquis 2009), which is one reason why they are of interest in social modeling.

[3]The pattern generated in Fig. 4.1 (Amenta and Kil 2004) is shown only for illustrative purposes. Other than the recognition theory examples, none of the figures in this paper are intended to imply an empirical social process.

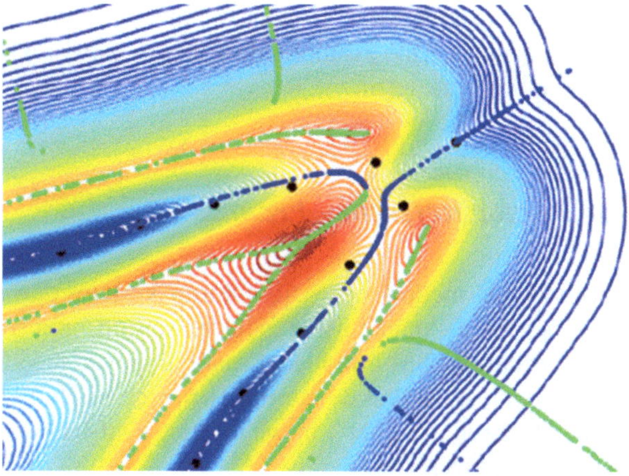

Fig. 4.1 Points, sets and spaces codefine each other

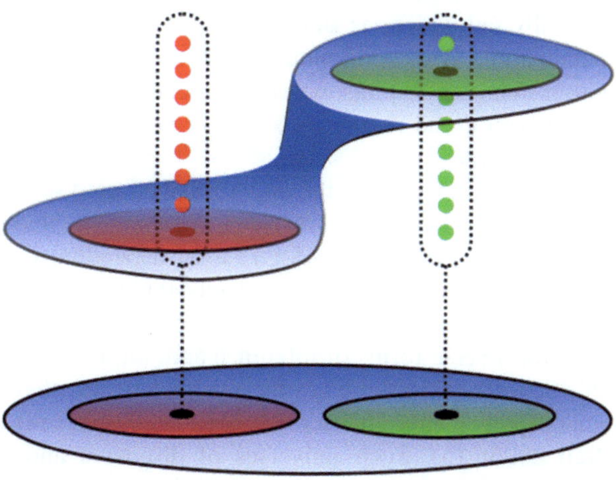

Fig. 4.2 Gluing sheaves at two points (Image from http://en.wikipedia.org/wiki/File:2_point_sheaf_gluing.svg under the GNU Free Documentation License)

2.3 Cross-Scale Influences

In topoi, categories with morphisms that are entirely invertible (and thus, groupoids) can "send moving frames to moving frames according to the underlying structure ...", making sure that it is done coherently (Marquis 2009: 258).

Sewell (2005: 168–172) notes that different cultures often have a logic of their own, and this is what the dual cross-scale relations inherent in topoi provide. In particular, Sewell (2005: 339) describes how discourses are *jointed* or *sutured* together. This can emerge on a tacit basis but, in other cases, there is an intentional process, sometimes involving multiple actors in order to achieve coupled discourse.

As an example, he describes (2005: 340) professional basketball as a game that simultaneously integrates semiotic conventions regarding on-floor physical performance, the technical analysis of coaches and players, the physical codes of urban honor, media attentional priorities, an advertising focus on sports celebrity, the financial strategies of owners and investors, the substrate of legal hermeneutics, and many more. This example illustrates a case for which Sewell considers *suturing* as the appropriate term.

2.4 Actor Reference Frames

Set-theoretic models of socio-cultural systems have been limited by a lack of expressiveness. An exclusive focus on sets, as opposed to their relations (including transformations) has provided a spare, impoverished foundation for the representation of complex social dynamics. However, as Bell (1988: 49) notes, "a topos is a 'generalization' of a set", in which its (sheaf-based) locales provide much greater expressive power.

In sheaf categories, both the axiom of choice and the axiom of well-pointedness generally fail which, as Bell (2006: 14) observes, shows that "both principles are incompatible with continuous variation." However, in addition to being located within complex settings, actors in social conflicts continuously adapt and adjust their position and responses and, therefore, require the expressiveness that topos theory provides.

Nor is expressiveness the only contribution to social modeling that topos theory makes. Like relativity theory, topos theory can be understood in terms of reference frames (Bell 1988: 239–245). That is, depending upon its specific axioms, each sheaf within a topos, is defined by a local logic as well. If local axioms are regarded as held by social actors, whether explicitly or implicitly, they can provide a formal basis for diverse forms of inference and, ultimately distinct universes of discourse (cf., Sewell 2005). Among other characteristics, their granularity can range from binary (polar), through discretely graduated (indexed), and continuous, to 'smooth' (Bell 2006: 15). Such universes of discourse and inferential practices can be implemented computationally, and further refined, incorporating *types* (Martin-Löf 1984; UFP 2013), and type classes, as provided by Haskell (O'Sullivan et al. 2009: 135–164; Lipovača 2011: 109–152), and other computer languages.

Social actors in their reference frames exist across many scales. Such influences may arise from positive or negative affect (Heise 1979; Collins 1993; Sallach 2008), common interests, shared strategies (Sallach et al. 2011), the elicitation of cooperation (Sallach 2012c) or persuasion (Perloff 2010).

3 Recognition Theory

The relationship among cross-scale actors is pertinent to a number of social theories and models. Recognition theory provides an important example. Honneth (1996) distinguishes among three patterns of recognition: love, rights and solidarity. The affinity relation that Honneth calls 'love' gives rise to beneficent strategies,

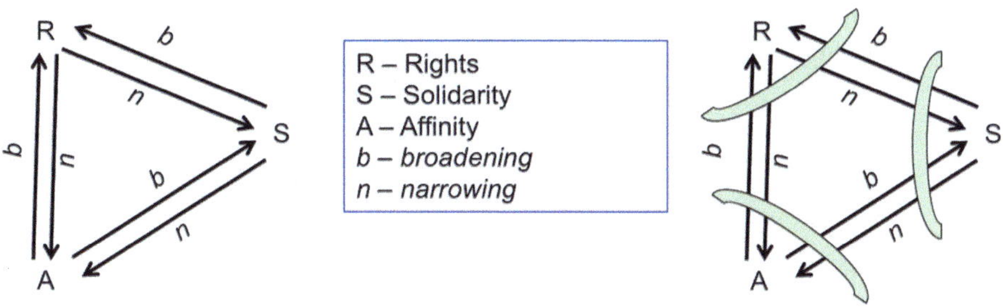

Fig. 4.3 Adjoint recognition systems with (RHS) and without (LHS) collars

calibrated by a selected response to the particular situation. The legal recognition relationship ('rights') is primarily instrumental in nature, where various actors agree to support legal rights for all as a means of securing their own (1996: 109).

Groups based on solidarity (and its diverse bases) may draw upon multiple strategies, depending on their historic and current relationships. Groups can view each other as: (1) allies (with whom there is a mutual affinity), (2) competitors and/or actors with asynchronous dependencies (cf. Emerson 1962) (who engage each other in a pragmatic or instrumental way), or (3) enemies (toward whom they attribute the necessity to be coerced, or threatened with coercion). In each case, the calibration of particular moves will depend upon the specific situation, and the actors' comprehension of it.

Recognition theory can be formulated categorically. As Fig. 4.3 illustrates, each of the poles of the theory (affinity, solidarity and rights) can be treated as ideal types, invariant within the system, approached but never fully realized. They codefine an adjoint system by providing the means of binding (up to isomorphism) the affinity, homophily or generalized groups in question.

Broadening and narrowing are defined in terms of the scope of the group, with affinity groups being the narrowest, and generalized groups being the broadest. They define progressions that consist of a net balance between two coupled orders.

The left hand system (LHS) seems to imply that the specific ideal must be (nearly) realized before a reversal or alteration of a progression becomes possible. In contrast, for the right hand system (RHS), 'collars' define the size of regions in which progressions can reverse, or shift to an alternate coupling. It is posited that, over time, there is an alternation among the three focal poles. Overall, recognition dynamics will be shaped by the exploitation, and/or exploration of the current or possible forms of binding (cf., March 1991; Gupta et al. 2006).

Figure 4.4 and the immediately preceding paragraphs illustrate how a category-theoretic analysis provides an approach to modeling that is both rigorous and expressive. However, the focus of the present paper is to (also) demonstrate how topos theory can be applied within the social sciences. To provide the basis for this analysis, we will focus on the attribution of truth, or falsehood, toward third-party actors who are sources of information, albeit mediated by their recognition level.

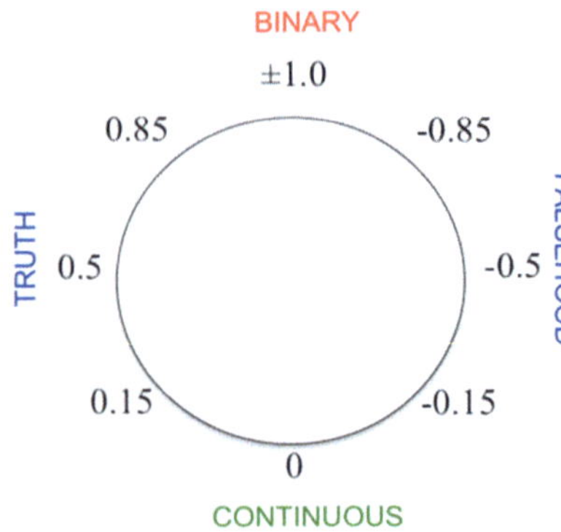

Fig. 4.4 Representing truth-attribution with a unit circle

Now, prior to such an analysis, what should be noted about recognition level is that the binding effect for each type of recognition is phenomenologically distinct. Affinity binding is based on extensive personal knowledge and interaction. Solidarity binding is based on similarity *and* the salience of that type of similarity. Generalized binding is based on an ideational (theory, theology or ideology) perspective or calculation that the recognition of rights is either normatively required, in the long-term interests of the actor, or both.

Reviewing the distinct bases of the bindings shows that, in practice, there are distinct differences in their bases. Therefore, individuals, groups and multiscale actors may have divergent bases for the attribution of truth (or falsehood) to differently situated actors. Figure 4.4 shows one way of representing these differences. The unit circle is used to combine representation of two dimensions: (1) the distinction between the attribution of truth and the attribution of falsehood, and (2) the distinction between a binary (polar) definition of truth, as with the law of the excluded middle, and a graduated, continuous and/or probabilistic notion of truth.

Because, within a topos, the concept of truth may be defined locally, each social actor of whatever scale can have a private method of attributing truth. Moreover, it may differ by recognition level, power differentials, in-group/out-group status, or a variety of other contingencies. For present purposes, the discussion will confine itself to differential practices in the logical style of the actor attributions based on role and recognition.

Table 4.1 shows one way that truth-attribution factors can be summarized. Specifically, the three styles of truth-attribution are (potentially) applied differentially, based on the role and recognition level of an alter. Here it is presumed that smooth attribution is preferable to binary, with indexed or incremental in an intermediate position. Therefore, is a continuous or probabilistic attribution of truth more likely based upon personal contact, similarity or an inclusive worldview? And, similarly, is a continuous or probabilistic attribution of truth more likely based upon the actor's characterization of an alter's role (friend, neutral or enemy)? Historically, of course, a wide range of patterns has been empirically effective. What the application of topos theory allows us to do, in a systematic way, is to explore, via simulation or

Table 4.1 Notional truth-attribution style by recognition level

	Affinity	Solidarity	Rights
Enemy	75 % Binary 25 % Indexed	Binary	Binary
Neutral	75 % Smooth 25 % Indexed	25 % Smooth 75 % Indexed	Indexed
Friend	Smooth	50 % Smooth 50 % Indexed	Indexed

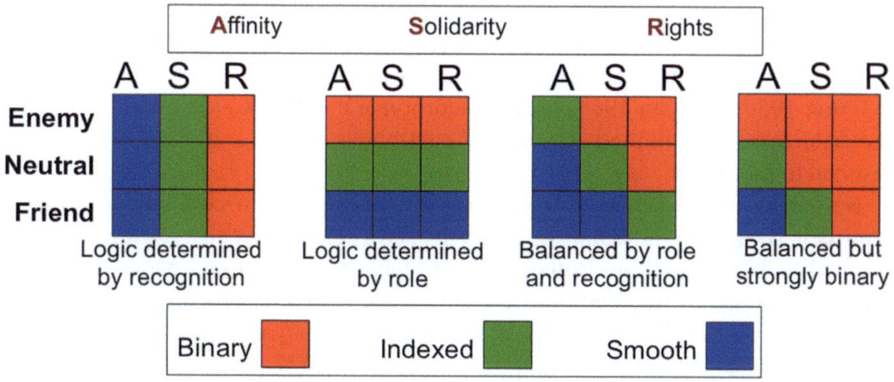

Fig. 4.5 Truth granularity by role and recognition levels

extended analysis, the effects of diverse truth-attribution practices of a collection of actors, regarding these practices as an actor reference frame that is sometimes shared.

Figure 4.5 shows the same dimensions as Table 4.1, with various assumptions regarding truth-attribution styles and/or practices. As the truth-attribution key indicates, binary logic (e.g., true or false, but also, in particular circumstances: "all or nothing", "life or death", "kill or be killed", "fish or cut bait", "win or lose", "laugh now or cry later") is indicated by the color red. The finest-grained attribution of truth or falsehood (e.g., in the conundrum expressed by Oscar Hammerstein's lyric in the *King and I*: "Some things *nearly* so, others *nearly* not ...". [Asch 2008: 348]) is indicated by the color blue, with green representing the indexed or incremental position. The two actors on the left attribute truth strictly by recognition or role, respectively, while the third actor has a balanced style and the fourth, on the far right, is overwhelmingly binary. The examples are hypothetical, but the representation of diverse forms of logical practices will be a great benefit for those constructing computational models of social processes under varying assumptions. Of course, it will also be possible to shape distributions of truth-attribution practices based upon additional considerations.

4 Theories of Conflict

During the decade following World War II, a single sociological theory came to define the dominant paradigm of the discipline. Referred to as functionalism, or structural-functionalism (Parsons 1953; Parsons and Smelser 1956), the theory, which focused on the sources of social order, and synthesized a number of classical social theories, became regarded as definitive.

In the later 1950s, however, the theory was subject to extensive criticism. The basic objection was that functionalism failed to adequately address social conflict and change (Lockwood 1956; Dahrendorf 1958, 1959; Horton 1966). Functional theorists attempted to respond by showing how the theory could account for change (Merton 1957; Cancian 1960) and/or incorporate conflict (Coser 1964, 1967), but they addressed only limited conflict and continuous change and, thus, did not fully respond to the critics.

Several efforts were made to synthesize consensual and conflictual processes (van den Berghe 1963; Johnson 1966; Buckley 1967), but the results were not deemed to be compelling. Rather than producing an integrated paradigm, social theory continued to fragment into ever more specialized forms including separate theories of conflict (Collins 1975, 1986). While a variety of scholars made significant progress in conflict theory, *per se* (see, Collins 1994: 47–120), these advances have not produced a general theory. Not even Collins' unique prediction of the collapse of the USSR (1986) brought conflict models to the forefront of social theorizing. More generally, the failure to define an integrated theoretical paradigm weakened the explanatory power of subsequent social science.

4.1 Social Model of War

More recently, Clausewitz's theory of war is serving as a catalyst for the rearticulation of social conflict theories, in this case emerging from the disciplines of political science and international relations (cf., Echevarria 2007; Herberg-Rothe 2007; Strachan 2007). Several characteristics of this theory contribute to its centrality to a more general theory of conflict. First, Clausewitz's analysis of war is inherently multi-scale. Its focus ranges from the most detailed historical cases to the most abstract theory. Because social phenomena are high-dimensional and manifest great fluidity, their scope makes the identification of unambiguous generalization difficult (as Clausewitz acknowledged). When it is achieved, the ability to effectively model multi-scale interactions will greatly strengthen social theory and analytical tools based on it.

Second, Clausewitz recognized the need to break down false distinctions. Perhaps, the best-known example is his characterization of war as a continuation of politics by additional means. Rather than trying to limit the complexity of his theory by treating war as a separate, *sui generis* phenomena, he accepted the more challenging task of conceptualizing how politics and war co-define (and co-refine) each other. Sharma (2008) calls this a "social theory of war", which seems apt, as long as we also recognize that the social theory of war (and conflict) continues to evolve.

Sharma suggests that, in a social theory of war, no distinction should be made between international and civil wars. Certainly, throughout history, each type of war has repeatedly transmogrified into the other. Thus, a second potentially misleading distinction has been identified, with the focus shifting to more inclusive forms of interaction.

Third, as a means of identifying historical reference points, Clausewitz reasons by using pure or ideal concepts (which he often calls extreme or absolute). Examples include absolute war, in which pure violence (as a reference point) has become detached from political purpose. As Sharma (2008) suggests, patterns of empirical violence can be assessed relative to a state of pure violence that has no logical limit. While Clausewitz is not as methodologically rigorous in the formulation of ideal types as Weber (1949; Burger 1987), he nonetheless lays a foundation for a more systematic analysis. Ideal types, such as those introduced by Clausewitz, point toward the identification of social invariants, relative to which theories can be cogently formulated.

Sharma's social theory of war advances the prospective Clausewitzian contribution to a theory of social conflict by asserting that the scale and intensity of warfare, whether international or domestic, is related to the amount of institutional upheaval that is sought or implied. Sharma summarizes this as the difference between 'who rules' (suggesting limited restructuring) versus 'what rules' are appropriate (implying increasing levels of transformation). This formulation can be further extended by observing that, when empirical patterns approach absolute violence (as occurs in genocidal situations), the question becomes 'who lives'. In each case, the scale of conflict is defined by observed patterns of violence and the degree of mobilization.

The 'what rules' question can be addressed in fine-grain logic that topos theory makes available. Specifically, the established power will have a particular configuration of logics based on affinity, group and generalized criteria.

5 Conclusion

The innovations of abstract mathematics have many prospective applications in social analysis. The present paper introduces and illustrates that potential, especially through the use of topos theory in the representation of social theory with applications of computational models.

When topoi are used to model social phenomena, they provide the expressiveness to address subtle structures and dynamic processes. The area of social recognition theory has been used to show that topos theory can provide rich articulation of complex social theories that include various kinds of subtlety.

Such representational capabilities have the potential to increase the effectiveness of computational social modeling. The fact that these representations provide a basis for formal validation is an additional advantage for the use of category-theoretical methods in the social sciences.

References

Amenta N, Yong JK (2004) The domain of a point set surface. In: Alexis M, Rusinkiewicz S (eds) Eurographics symposium on point-based graphics, pp 139–147. http://graphics.cs.ucdavis.edu/~yjkil/pub/domain.html

Asch A (ed) (2008) The complete lyrics of Oscar Hammerstein II. Alfred A. Knopf, New York

Awodey S (2010) Category theory. Oxford University Press, New York

Bell JL (1988) Toposes and local set theories: an introduction. Oxford University Press, New York

Bell JL (2006) Abstract and variable sets in category theory. In: Sica G (ed) What is category theory? Polimetrica, Monza, pp 9–16

Borceux F (1994) Handbook of categorical algebra 3: categories of sheaves. Cambridge University Press, New York

Buckley W (1967) Sociology and modern systems theory. Prentice Hall, Englewood Cliffs

Burger T (1987) Max Weber's theory of concept formation: history, laws and ideal types. Duke University Press, Durham

Cancian F (1960) Functional analysis of change. Am Sociol Rev 24(December):818–827

Collins R (1975) Conflict sociology: toward an explanatory science. Academic, New York

Collins R (1986) The future decline of the Russian empire. In: Collins R (ed) Weberian sociological theory. Cambridge University Press, New York, pp 186–201

Collins R (1993) Emotional energy as the common denominator of rational choice. Ration Soc 5(April):203–230

Collins R (1994) Four sociological traditions. Oxford University Press, New York

Coser L (1964) The functions of social conflict. MacMillan, New York

Coser L (1967) Social conflict and the theory of social change. In: Coser LA (ed) Continuities in the study of social conflict. Free Press, New York, pp 17–35

Crane L, Yetter D (1993) A categorical construction of 4D topological quantum field theories. In: Kauffman LH, Baadhio RA (eds) Quantum topology. World Scientific, River Edge, pp 120–130

Dahrendorf R (1958) Out of utopia: toward a reorientation of sociological analysis. Am J Sociol 64(September):115–127

Dahrendorf R (1959) Class and class conflict in industrial society. Stanford University Press, Stanford

Dummett M (1977) Elements of intuitionism. Oxford University Press, New York

Echevarria II, Antulio J (2007) Clausewitz and contemporary war. Oxford University Press, New York

Ehresmann AC, Vanbremeersch J-P (2007) Memory evolutive systems: hierarchy, emergence, cognition. Elsevier, Amsterdam

Emerson RM (1962) Power-dependence relations. Am Sociol Rev 27(February):31–41

Flori C (2013) A first course in topos quantum theory. Springer, New York

Godel K (2004) On intuitionistic arithmetic and number theory. In: Davis M (ed) The undecidable: basic papers on undecidable propositions, unsolvable problems and computable functions. Dover, Mineola, pp 75–81

Goldblatt R (1984) Topoi: the categorial analysis of logic. Dover, Mineola

Gupta AK, Smith KG, Shalley CE (2006) The interplay between exploration and exploitation. Acad Manag J 49(August):693–706

Heise DR (1979) Understanding events: affect and the construction of social action. Cambridge University Press, New York
Herberg-Rothe A (2007) Clausewitz's puzzle: the political theory of war. Oxford University Press, New York
Honneth A (1996) The struggle for recognition: the moral grammar of social conflicts. MIT Press, Cambridge, MA
Horton J (1966) Order and conflict theories of social problems as competing ideologies. Am J Sociol 71(May):701–713
Jacobs B (1999) Categorical logic and type theory. Elsevier, New York
Johnson C (1966) Revolutionary change. Little, Brown, Boston
Johnstone PT (2002) Sketches of an elephant: a topos theory compendium, Two vols. Oxford University Press, New York
Lipovača M (2011) Learn you a Haskell for great good! No Starch Press, San Francisco
Lockwood D (1956) Remarks on *the social system*. Br J Sociol 7(June):134–146
March JG (1991) Exploration and exploitation in organizational learning. Organ Sci 2(February):71–87
Marquis J-P (2009) From a geometrical point of view: a study of the history and philosophy of category theory. Springer, New York
Martin-Löf P (1984) Intuitionistic type theory. Grafitalia, Naples
McLarty C (1996) Elementary categories, elementary toposes. Oxford University Press, New York
Merton RK (1957) Social theory and social structure. Free Press, New York
O'Sullivan B, Goerzen J, Stewart D (2009) Real world Haskell. O'Reilly Media, Sebastopol
Parsons T (1953) The social system. Free Press, New York
Parsons T, Smelser NJ (1956) Economy and society. Free Press, New York
Perloff RM (2010) The dynamics of persuasion: communication and attitudes in the 21st century. Routledge, New York
Pierce BC (1991) Basic category theory for computer scientists. MIT Press, Cambridge, MA
Rosen R (1991) Life itself. Columbia University Press, New York
Sallach DL (2008) Modeling emotional dynamics: currency versus field. Ration Soc 20:343–365
Sallach DL (2012a) Socio-cultural structures: a categorical synthesis. Paper presented to the Midwest Sociological Society, Minneapolis
Sallach DL (2012b) Categorial social science: theory, methodology and design. In: Proceedings of the World Congress on Social Simulation, Taipei
Sallach DL (2012c) Social coordination: toward a category-theoretical synthesis. In: Proceedings of the World Congress on Social Simulation, Taipei
Sallach DL, North MJ, Tatara E (2011) Multigame dynamics: structures and strategies. In: Bosse T, Geller A, Jonker CM (eds) Multi-agent-based simulation XI. Springer, Berlin, pp 108–120
Sewell WH (2005) Logics of history: social theory and transformation. University of Chicago Press, Chicago
Sharma V (2008) A social theory of war: Clausewitz and war reconsidered. Presented at the comparative politics workshop, Yale University
Strachan H (2007) Clausewitz's on war. Grove Press, New York
Takahara Y, Takai T (1985) Category theoretical framework of general systems. Int J Gen Syst 11:1–33
Takahashi S, Takahara Y (1995) Logical approach to systems theory. Springer, New York
Univalent Foundations Program (UFP) (2013) Homotopy type theory: univalent foundations of mathematics. Institute for Advanced Study, Princeton
van den Berghe P (1963) Dialectic and functionalism: toward a theoretical synthesis. Am Sociol Rev 28(October):695–705
Weber M (1949) The methodology of the social sciences. Free Press, New York

Chapter 5
Emergence of Peace Resulting from TFT Strategy Observing a Limited Number of Agents

Masayoshi Muto, Fumiaki Kawachi, and Yutaka Nakai

Abstract The various reputation theories that proposed to solve the problem of social order have an unrealistic assumption that all agents observe what occurred in all other agents. To improve this situation, Nakai and Muto (2008) proposed us-Tit For Tat (TFT) strategy that requires an agent to regard as a friend one who did not attack himself/herself and his/her "friends", and they found a resultant peaceful state. They assume that the us-TFT agent must observe only what occurred in himself/herself and his/her friends. However, when all agents become mutual friends, they observe all other agents, hence us-TFT suffers from the same weakness of related studies. To overcome the weakness, we propose a new us-TFT strategy with which an agent observes a limited number of other agents. A limited number of other agents are selected based on how peacefully they act toward the new us-TFT agent. We performed evolutionary simulations with this strategy and found the emergence of a peaceful state. It means that a peaceful state can emerge without observing all other agent's actions. In addition, we find that the more the limited number is, the less frequently a peaceful state emerge.

Keywords Hobbesian state • Friend selection strategy • us-TFT • Complete information

1 Introduction

How does social order emerge among individuals acting freely? Parsons (1937) named this fundamental question in sociology as the "problem of order." For example, if people, as selfish individuals, can freely choose to attack or not to attack others, society will inevitably become a "battling state" (Hobbesian state: a "war of all against all"). However, actual society is not in this state and seems to have order. As is well known, many different solutions to this problem have been proposed, such as "central authority and social contract" (Hobbes 1651), "institutionalization

M. Muto (✉) • F. Kawachi • Y. Nakai
Faculty of Systems Engineering and Sciences, Shibaura Institute of Technology,
307 Fukasaku, Minuma-ku, Saitama, Japan
e-mail: muto@shibaura-it.ac.jp

Y. Nakai et al. (eds.), *Agent-Based Approaches in Economic and Social Complex Systems VIII*, Agent-Based Social Systems 13, DOI 10.1007/978-4-431-55236-9_5

and internalization of norms" (Parsons 1937), "system rationality and reduction of complexity" (Luhmann 1968), "mutual understanding based on communicative reason" (Habermas 1981), and "trust based on rational expectation" (Coleman 1990).

Recently, researchers have proposed solutions based on reputation, including "in-group altruistic strategy" (Takagi 1996),"image scoring strategy" (Novak and Sigmund 1998),"standing strategy" (Leimar and Hammerstein 2001), and "strict discriminator strategy" (Takahashi and Mashima 2003). These studies share the common strategy that an agent helps only agents who have helped a "good man," and thus, they are sometimes called "discriminator strategies" (DISCs). Moreover, DISC share the common assumption that each agent knows all of every other agent's actions ("complete information assumption"), sometimes criticized as unrealistic.

To overcome the weakness, we assume incomplete information and propose a more realistic DISC strategy in which the agent observes a limited number of other agents (his/her friends) and evaluates whether a third agent is a friend or an enemy based on whether the third agent took a friendly or a hostile action against him/her and his/her friends. We examined whether a Hobbesian state can become a peaceful state as a result of our new DISC.

2 Battle Game Paradigm and Friend Selection Strategy (Nakai and Muto 2008)

In a closely related study, Nakai and Muto proposed another DISC strategy that does not require an agent to observe all other agents. Let us examine their model and results in detail. In preparation, to describe a Hobbesian state, they introduced the battle game paradigm based on the giving game (Takagi 1996), as follows.

2.1 Battle

(B1) N agents play the game.
(B2) Each agent has a friend list of who is a "friend" or an "enemy."
(B3) In one battle game, each agent (agent A) meets M other agents at random. (M stands for the agent's number of matches in one game.) Each agent (agent A) interacts with the other agent (agent B) one by one.
(B4) Agent A (as a performer) chooses whether or not to attack agent B (as a performed) according to A's own friend list. Agent A attacks agent B if B is A's enemy, and A does not attack B if B is A's friend.
(B5) If agent A attacks agent B, A obtains a payoff of 0.5 and B loses a payoff of 1.0. Conversely, if agent A does not attack agent B, both obtain nothing. (Fig. 5.1)
(B6) In one battle game, there are $N \times M$ times interactions described above.

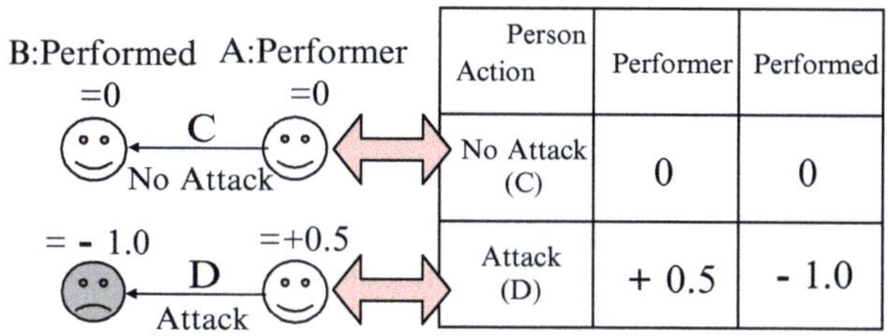

Fig. 5.1 Payoffs in battle game

Fig. 5.2 Battle game's payoff matrix

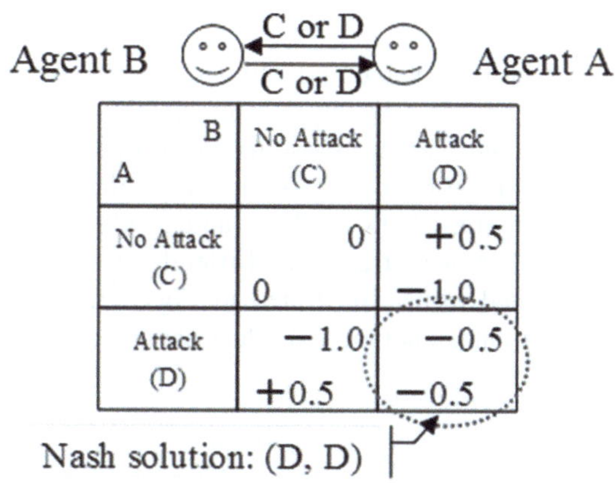

In Nakai and Muto, the "friend" is defined as the other agent whom an agent decides not to attack. His/her decision is fully independent of the other's intention. That is, the expression "friend" does not mean a close friend but simply persons to whom he/she pays attention without mutual agreement.

When two agents interact with each other reciprocally, their states can be described by the payoff matrix illustrated in Fig. 5.2, which is derived from the assumed payoffs in Fig. 5.1. Obviously, Fig. 5.2 presents a typical payoff matrix of a two-person Prisoners' Dilemma, which causes a society to fall into a battling state.

The Nakai and Muto study introduced "friend selection strategies" (FSSs). First, they assume an agent evaluating third agents on the basis of their direct actions toward the agent himself/herself ("me"). They name these strategies "my friend selection strategies" (MFSSs). They further assume an agent evaluating third agents on the basis of their actions toward the agent and his/her friends ("us" rather than "me"). They name these "our friend selection strategies" (OFSSs). OFSSs consist of, for example, 2×2 theoretical versions of strategies because a third agent who attacked "us" can be regarded as a friend or an enemy, and a third agent who did not attack "us" as a friend or an enemy. If the term "us" in OFSSs' definitions is replaced with "me," we obtain the MFSS definitions.

2.2 OFSSs

(O1) us-ALL_C: the agent regards anybody who interacted with his/her "us" as a friend.
(O2) us-Tit-for-Tat (TFT): the agent regards a third agent who attacked his/her "us" as an enemy and a third agent who did not as a friend.
(O3) us-coward (CWD): the agent regards a third agent who attacked his/her "us" as a friend and a third agent who did not as an enemy.
(O4) us-ALL_D: the agent regards anybody who interacted with his/her "us" as an enemy.

Obviously, Nakai and Muto's agent does not observe all other agents but only his/her friends (incomplete information assumption). To clarify what strategies survive and whether those result in a peaceful state, they constructed an artificial society and conducted evolutional simulations with six strategies: ALL_C, ALL_D, me-TFT, me-CWD, us-TFT, and us-CWD. Each agent in their artificial society has his/her own strategy and friend list. One simulation run comprises a sequence of iterated turns. Illustrated in Fig. 5.3, one round consists of four phases: (1) perception, (2) action, (3) selection, and (4) mutation.

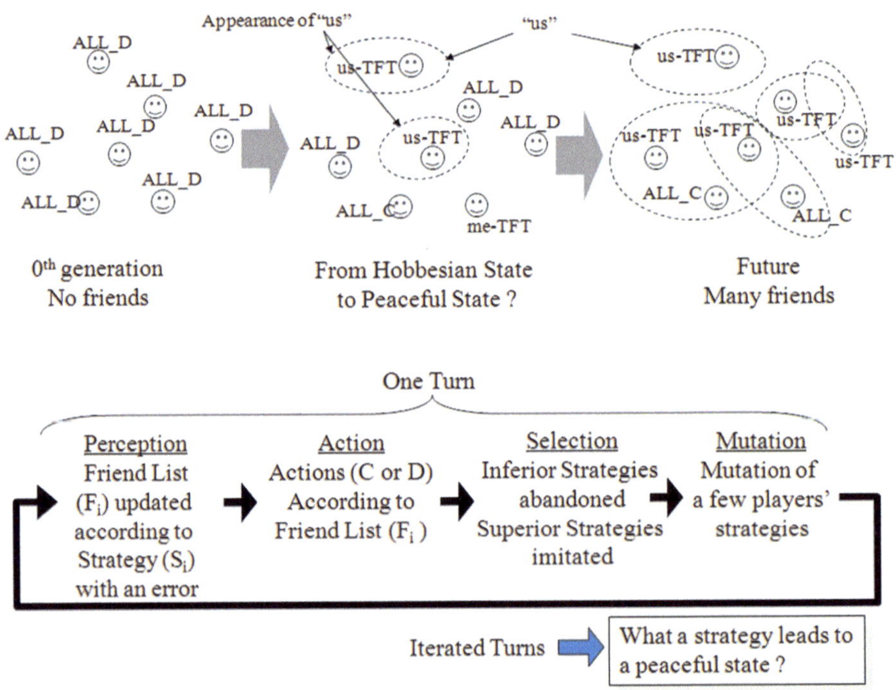

Fig. 5.3 Evolutionary simulation of peace

(1) In the perception phase, each agent updates his/her friend list based on his/her strategy and information on third agents' preceding actions. The updating suffers from a perception error (μ_p: perception error rate).
(2) In the action phase, each agent plays the battle game according to the updated perception. After all agents finish playing one game, each agent sums all payoffs that he/she earned as a performer and performed during the iteration.
(3) In the selection phase, inferior agents surrender their strategies and imitate the superior agent's strategy. The lower $R\%$ agents in payoff abandon their strategies (R: a reflection ratio).
(4) In the mutation phase, a few agents' strategies mutate by a mutation rate μ_s. In the 0th turn, all agents are assumed to have an ALL_D strategy and a friend list with all other agents as enemies, which express the "war of all against all" state. After many iterated turns, superior strategies survive and inferior strategies disappear. Their results are as follows.

2.3 Nakai and Muto's Remarks

(NM1) A peaceful state is not established by me-TFT but by us-TFT.
(NM2) A small us-TFT group, where members are mutually friendly, accidentally appears in a battling state. The us-TFT group increases and establishes a peaceful state.
(NM3) After that, me-TFT, me-CWD, and us-CWD invade the us-TFT group and gradually make the state weaker against ALL_D.
(NM4) ALL_D invades the population and eventually establishes a battling state.

As is well known, the collapse of social order is sometimes triggered by the ALL_C. That is, after ALL_C increases as a result of the TFT's umbrella protection against the ALL_D, ALL_D exploits the ALL_C, which eventually destroys social order. In contrast, Nakai and Muto demonstrated in new scenarios that all strategies except ALL_C could trigger the collapse of social order.

Now let us focus on the weak point of the us-TFT strategy in a large population. An us-TFT agent is assumed to observe his/her friends and act based on a third agent's actions toward him/her and his/her friends. He/she does not observe all other agents. Therefore, the fewer the number of friends (the more limited the information), the more easily an agent can manage the information. Thus this assumption is valid particularly in the transition phase from Hobbesian state to peaceful state. However, once a peaceful state is established, all agents become friends and an agent must observe all other agents. Nakai and Muto (2008) model thus suffers from the same weak point as previous studies because of which they said that us-TFT works well in a small-scale population.

3 us-TFT Strategy to Observe a Limited Number of Agents

To solve this problem, we introduce a new us-TFT. An us-TFT agent observes all his/her friends. In contrast, an agent with the new strategy observes only a limited number of agents. The agent pays attention to K observed agents, who are selected based on their higher order of peaceful attitude. We call the new strategy "us-TFT to observe a limited number of agents" (us(K)-TFT). For an example of five observed agents, we denote it as us(5)-TFT. Illustrated in Fig. 5.4, the algorithms of the perception phase are as follows.

3.1 *Perception Phase*

(PP1) At the T th round, agent i has his/her own strategy $S^T{}_i$, which is one of ALL_D, ALL_C, and us(K)-TFT.

(PP2) Agent i has a friend list $F^T{}_i$, described as a vector. If agent j is agent i's friend, the element j of $F^T{}_\mathrm{i}$ is set to 1. Conversely, if agent j is agent i's enemy, the element j of $F^T{}_i$ is set to 0.

(PP3) Also, Agent i has a list $O^T{}_i$ of observed agents, described as a vector. If agent j is i's observed agent, the element j of $O^T{}_\mathrm{i}$ is set to 1. Conversely, if agent j is not agent i's observed agent, the element j of $O^T{}_i$ is set to 0. The i's K observed agents are selected in the descending order of i's friend total scores (cf. PP2 and Fig. 5.4).

(PP4) Each agent updates his/her friend list. Specifically, each agent updates his/her preceding list $F^{T-1}{}_i$ to the present one $F^T{}_i$ using his/her present strategy $S^T{}_i$ and information on the $T-1$ th third agents' actions toward himself/herself and K observed agents.

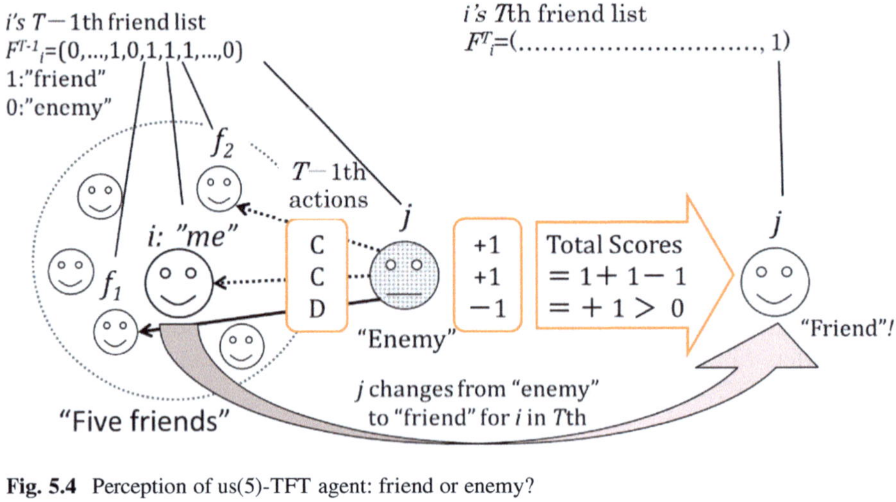

Fig. 5.4 Perception of us(5)-TFT agent: friend or enemy?

(PP5) An us(K)-TFT agent assigns +1.0 to a peaceful agent toward himself/herself and his/her K friends. He/she assigns −1.0 to a militant agent against himself/herself and his/her K observed agents.

(PP6) When an us(K)-TFT agent evaluates a third agent, he/she must take into account the agent's all actions toward himself/herself and his/her K observed agents. Specifically, he/she sums all scores assigned to the agent and evaluates the agent as a friend if the total score is positive, and as an enemy if negative. If the total score equals 0, the agent does not evaluate the other agent and simply retains his/her preceding perception of the agent.

4 Peaceful State Resulting from us(K)-TFT Strategy

We conducted evolutionary simulations of us(K)-TFT strategy with a variety set of parameters to verify whether a peaceful state emerges or not. In Fig. 5.5, we suppose a number of agents is twenty ($N = 20$), so that a number of observed agents K and a matching number M vary from 0 to 19 and from 1 to 19 respectively, by an increments of 1.0, where $M = 19$ means round-robin situation. Figure 5.5 (left) shows how frequently a peaceful state emerges corresponding to a variety of K and M. Figure 5.5 (right) is an aerial view of Fig. 5.5 (left).

The figures shows clearly emergence of a peaceful state even if a number of observed agents is limited. We can see that the more K is, the less frequently a peaceful state emerges. The frequency of emergence of a peaceful state is the highest in case of $K = 2$. In other words, a peaceful state is easily to emerge when agents pay attention to himself/herself and his/her two observed agents.

Previous researches have a common assumption that all agents observe all other agents, which are sometimes criticized as a strong one. In contrast, our result shows that a peaceful state can emerge without observing all other agents' actions.

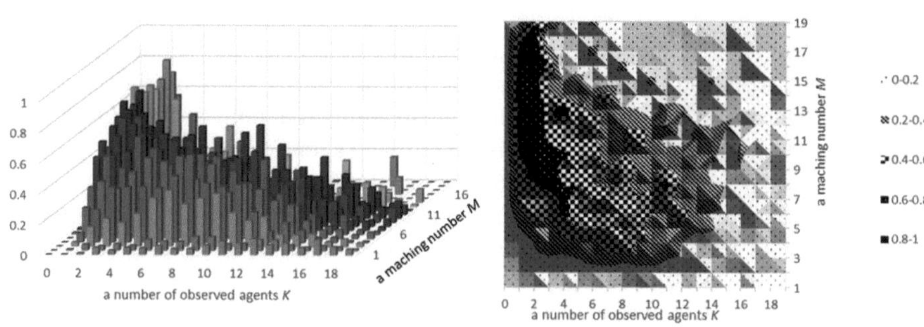

Fig. 5.5 Frequency that a peaceful state emerges in each number of M and K (3D Graph/*Left* and an Aerial View/*Right*) (*Number of Agents: N = 20 agents, Reflection Ratio: R = 10, Strategy's Mutation Rate: $\mu s = 0.5$ %, Number of Rounds is 20,000)

5 Discussions

Let us examine typical mechanism bringing about a peaceful state. In the Hobbesian state, because all agents regard all other agents as enemy, only militant agents can survive. In the state, the best strategy is ALL_D or us(K)-TFT which acts equivalently to ALL_D. In a Hobbesian state, the society is composed of ALL_D or us(K)-TFT agents.

At this time, if an ALL_C agent emerges by mutation and acts peacefully, us(K)-TFT agents will regard the ALL_C agent as a friend at next round, and change their action to the ALL_C agent from a militant one to a peaceful one. However, since the ALL_C agent suffers from many unilateral attacks by ALL_D and us(K)-TFT agents, the ALL_C agent cannot survive. Here note that the selection may replace the ALL_C agent with an us(K)-TFT agent.

The relationships between the us(K)-TFT agent changed from the ALL_C agent and the other us(K)-TFT agents are not so peaceful. Since at previous round the other us(K)-TFT agents were peacefully acted to by the ALL_C agent but he/she was militantly acted to by them, at the present round they act peacefully to the us(K)-TFT agent changed from the ALL_C but he/she acts militantly to them. Therefore at next round they will act militantly to him/her but he/she will act peacefully to them. These alternately unilateral peaceful acts are called "echoes". Therefore we have to examine other mechanism such that we discuss next.

First, we discuss emergence of a peaceful pair of us(K)-TFT agents who regard each other as a friend. Second, we show that the peaceful us(K)-TFT pairs will compose a "star-like" network of friends, which bring about the expansion of friends network and prepare a peaceful state.

For understanding the emergence of a peaceful pair of us(K)-TFT agents and the process from the Hobbesian state to a peaceful one, we pick up the case of $K = 1$ illustrated by Fig. 5.6 because the case is the easiest for understanding. In Fig. 5.6, actions and observations of agents are depicted at the same column (as the same round). Suppose a number of agents is four ($N = 4$) for the meantime. C1 denotes that agent1 is ALL_C. T2 and T3 denote that agent2 and agent3 are us(1)-TFTs. D4 denotes that agent4 is ALL_D. Suppose that these four agents meet each other, which is round-robin case. A solid line with arrow denotes an agent's peaceful action to the arrowed agent: no solid line means militant action. A dotted line with arrow denotes an agent's observation to the arrowed agent.

Now suppose that at round0 there only existed a lot of us(1)-TFT agents and a few ALL_D agents who acted militantly each other. Then at round1, suppose an us(1)-TFT or ALL_D agent mutates into an ALL_C that is C1. C1 acts peacefully to all agents at round1.

Therefore at round2 all agents observe agent1 (by PP3) who is now probably T1 changed from C1, because at round1 C1 had less payoffs than others (due to be attacked by T2, T3, D4) and us(1)-TFT agents were majority. At the same round2, T2 occasionally mutate into C2 who can be called "second ALL_C agent". In short we suppose that two ALL_C agents happen to appear by mutations at two continuous rounds respectively. However, C2 at round2 will probably change into T2 at round3, similarly.

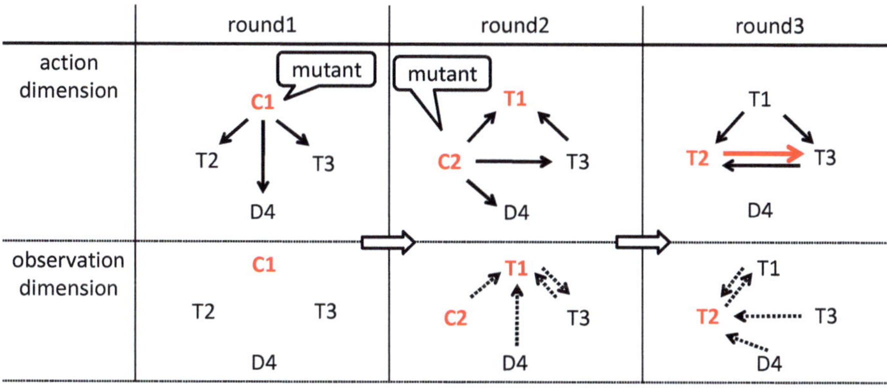

Fig. 5.6 Action and observation dimensions of friends expanding mechanism in K = 1 case (*The observations of agents are omitted at round1, because those do not influence agents' acts at round2 and round3)

Although agent3 (T3) acted *militantly* to agent2 (C2) at round2, agent2 (T2) acts *peacefully* to agent3 (T3) at round3. Because at round2 agent3 (T3) acted peacefully to agent1 (T1) observed by agent2 (C2), then at round3 agent2 (T2) takes over his/her round2's scores of agent 3 that is "friend" resulting from the total score being 0 (by PP6). At round3, a peaceful pair of us(1)-TFT agents (T2 and T3) emerges, who regard each other as a friend, which can be called a "mutual friendship".

By the way, T3 can be any us(1)-TFT agent (e.g. T5, T6, ...) if a number of agents is more than 4 ($N > 4$). After all, through the above process the us(1)-TFT agent who was the second ALL_C agent can succeed in having mutual friendships with other us(1)-TFT agents that looks like a "star-like" network. It is almost obvious that the star-like network can remain because of its formation. Us(1)-TFT agents composing a star-like network have more payoffs than other agents, so that us(1)-TFT agents will increase and ALL_D agents will decrease. In the course of time, if other ALL_C mutant occasionally appears and his/her star-like unilateral peaceful acts may overlap the existing star-like friends network, then the friends network will expand. In this way, the friends network expands on the occasion of ALL_ C mutant appearance. After this iterated process a peaceful state will ever come, where all agents act peacefully to all agents.

In addition we can find another friends expanding mechanism by "echoes" that is, above mentioned, alternately unilateral peaceful acts by the ALL_C agent's heritage. If the second ALL_C agent (C2) at the round2 did not appear in the above example (Fig. 5.6), the echoes by the ALL_C agent (C1) at the round1 remain. We can find the "star-like" echo by agent1 and us(1)-TFT agents around him/her. If the new (second) ALL_C mutant appears for the time that the star-like echo remains, some mutual friendships between the new ALL_C agent and some us(1)-TFT agents may rise depending on their observations. Of course attacked by the ALL_D or other us(1)-TFT agents, the new ALL_C agent will soon change into us(1)-TFT, but the mutual friendships between us(1)-TFT agents remain. The mutual friendships can earn more payoffs than the other agents and so they prepare a peaceful state.

However, the larger K is, the worse the above two friends expanding mechanisms doesn't work. If $K > 0$, the larger K is, the more hardly a peaceful state emerges. The reason is that the larger K makes it more difficult for an us(K)-TFT agent to act peacefully. For example, let us suppose the case of $K = 18$. For an us(18)-TFT agent to regard a third agent as a friend, it is necessary for the third to act peacefully to more than 10 agents among the us(18)-TFT agent and his/her 18 observed agents. In short a third agent has to act peacefully to a lot of agents to be regarded as a friend if K is large. In contrast, in the case of $K = 2$, an us(2)-TFT agent regards a third agent as a friend if the third acts peacefully to only *two* agents among the agent and his/her *two* observed agents. In addition If $K = 0$, since agents have to decide their actions based on only their own experience, they don't have any observed agents, which results in no expansion of a network of friends.

References

Coleman JS (1990) Foundations of social theory. Cambridge University Press, Cambridge
Habermas J (1981) Theorie Des Kommunikativen Handelns. Suhrkamp Verlag, Frankfurt/Main
Hobbes T (1651) Leviathan, printed for Andrew Crooke
Leimar O, Hammerstein P (2001) Evolution of cooperation through indirect reciprocity. Proc R Soc Lond Ser B Biol Sci 268:743–753
Luhmann N (1968) Zweckbegriff und Systemrationalität: über die Funktion von Zwecken in sozialen Systemen. Suhrkamp, 1977
Nakai Y, Muto M (2008) Emergence and collapse of peace with friend selection strategies. J Artif Soc Soc Simul 11(3)
Novak MA, Sigmund K (1998) Evolution of indirect reciprocity by image scoring. Nature 393:573–577
Parsons T (1937) The structure of social action. McGraw Hill, Boston
Takagi E (1996) The generalized exchange perspective on the evolution of altruism. In: Liebrand WBG, Messick DM (eds) Frontiers in social dilemmas research. Springer, Berlin, pp 311–336
Takahashi N, Mashima R (2003) The emergence of indirect reciprocity: is the standing strategy the answer? Center for the Study of Cultural and Ecological Foundations of the Mind: Working Paper Series No. 29, Hokkaido University, Japan

Part II
Public Issues and Economy

Chapter 6
Agent-Based Simulation of Citizens' Channel Choice of Public Services Based on Social Learning

Shuang Chang, Manabu Ichikawa, and Hiroshi Deguchi

Abstract Different from social network of practice that emphasizes relations among members with weak ties, community-based learning more focuses on the competence and practice of individuals connected by strong ties. With respect to the E-government service adoption, we assume that learning within communities is more common than that via social network. On the other side, the spread of information/knowledge on E-government might also influence the learning process, and further affect the adoption behaviour indirectly. Understanding such dynamic learning mechanism is crucial to the investigation of divergent citizens' adoption behaviour of E-government services, thus potentially important to the evaluation and design of supporting policies as well. In order to investigate the influence of learning within communities that are composed of citizens with different characteristics, and to explore the effectiveness of supporting policies in a long-term perspective, agent-based modelling is applied. This model could enable the understanding of a wide range of possible adoption behaviours under different scenarios, and the exploration of to what extent the variant supporting policies are effective.

Keywords Community-based learning • E-government service system • Agent-based simulation

1 Introduction

Web technology based public services such as E-government services have enabled citizens to take up public services in a more efficient and convenient way. Citizens are liberated from the labour of traffic to traditional service counter and the restriction of office hour benefited by Internet's 24/7 services. Through years of development, services provided by E-government have evolved to be more flexible

S. Chang (✉) • M. Ichikawa • H. Deguchi
Department of Computational Intelligence and Systems Science,
Tokyo Institute of Technology, Yokohama, Kanagawa, Japan
e-mail: chang11@cs.dis.titech.ac.jp; ichikawa@dis.titech.ac.jp; deguchi@dis.titech.ac.jp

Y. Nakai et al. (eds.), *Agent-Based Approaches in Economic and Social Complex Systems VIII*, Agent-Based Social Systems 13, DOI 10.1007/978-4-431-55236-9_6

to satisfy citizen's needs (Gil-Garcia and Luna-Reyes 2003; Venkatesh et al. 2012). However according to a survey conducted by Hong Kong Government (Census and Statistics Department 2009), although the adoption rate of easy-going E-government services such as information provision is increasing, the one of more complex transactional service is still relatively low, especially for social groups who are not favoured by E-government, such as ageing people (Sebie and Irani 2005).

In literature, few extant empirical research works focus on citizens' preference of using E-government services over other traditional means such as visiting the government service counter (Reddick and Turner 2012). Besides, many research works only aim at exploring the factors that could affect citizens' adoption decision of E-government, but not the underlying dynamic adoption process and the particular social context (Venkatesh et al. 2012; Hossain et al. 2011; Schaupp et al. 2010; Lean et al. 2009; Gunasekaran and Ngai 2008). However citizens from divergent background might have various needs, demands and preferences of those services, which might further impact their adoption behaviour and the choice of channel to take up different governmental services (Maruping et al. 2009; Venkatesh et al. 2012). In this sense, modelling individual's characteristics and involved interactions during the process might be inspiring and important. In addition, social influence and social learning involved in the individual's adoption process of E-government is seldom considered, although it has been studied extensively in other fields (Sunitiyoso and Matsumoto 2009). Different from social network of practice that emphasizes relations among members with weak ties; community-based learning more focuses on the competence and practice of individuals connected by strong ties (Lave and Wenger 1991). With respect to the E-government services adoption, we assume that learning within communities is more common than that via social network. This assumption makes sense in the way that in daily life, a citizen probably will not learn how to use E-government from someone loosely connected. Rather he/she is more prone to be influenced by someone more closely associated, such as family members or colleagues. As a result, with respect to social learning, the effectiveness of learning and its influences on the adoption behaviour might depend on the community in which citizens reside. On the other side, the spread of information/knowledge on E-government might also influence the learning process, and further affect the adoption behaviour indirectly (Deguchi 2004; Yucel and van Daalen 2011).

Therefore understanding such dynamic learning mechanism across different social groups is crucial to the investigation of divergent citizens' adoption behavior of E-government services, and potentially important to the evaluation and design of E-government supporting policies as well. In order to investigate the influence of learning within communities that are composed of citizens with different characteristics, and to explore the effectiveness of supporting policies in a long-term perspective, agent-based modelling is applied (Gilbert 2008). In this work, by simulating the dynamic channel selection behaviours of citizens from different social groups, and considering the social learning occurred within communities, we aim to understand citizens' preference of channel to utilize governmental services over time. In addition, by evaluating different public strategies such as E-government educational program and E-government promotion, we aim to identity what kind of strategies could be more effective to attract citizens taking up E-government services in the long term. This agent-based model could enable the understanding of a wide range of possible adoption behaviours under different scenarios, and the exploration of to what extent the variant supporting policies are effective.

This paper is organized as follows: The detailed agent-based model is introduced and discussed in Sect. 2, while simulation model and scenario analysis are shown in Sect. 3. Conclusion and future work are discussed in the last section.

2 Modelling

There is a set of assumptions embedded in our agent-based model as follows,

- There are two types of public service provision channel: traditional counter service and E-government service. Only general public services that involve complex procedures and require more time and effort to complete, such as on-line tax-filing services, are considered.
- The basic service provision procedures are similar on both channels. Technical support is only provided for E-government in order to facilitate the service provision process.
- Citizens are categorized into two general social groups, one is favoured by E-government (as *ordinary group*) and the other is not (as *preferential group*), such as elderly people or people with less education.
- We assume that citizens are closely associated with each other within communities (5–15 citizens per community, such as family and friends circle). They will be influenced by the information prevailing in the community, and learn from others who have adopted E-government within the same community.

2.1 *Formal Modeling of Agents*

In this work, we define three types of agents, which are Service provider agent, Community agent and Citizen agent. In the following we will explain the agents in details.

2.1.1 Service Provider Agent

Basically the service channel enabled by the government is defined as a static agent that provides public services in terms of time and effort required to complete the process, as well as the provided technical support. The rationale behind this abstraction is that three major aspects can evaluate the governmental services: easier service, faster service and better service (Gouscos et al. 2007). Easier service refers to the citizens' effort to complete the service. Faster service refers to the time that citizens may need until obtain the service result. Better service refers to the technical support received during the service provision process. Those indicators are rather objective in the sense that they address particular attributes, which can be controlled by the service provider.

Therefore the service provider agent is abstracted as $Service = \{S_1, S_2\}$. S_1 indicates the traditional counter service and S_2 represents the E-government service. Each of S_i, $i \in \{1, 2\}$ will be defined as $<T_S, TS_S, E_S>$, where T_S, $E_S \in R^+$. T_S represents the total time of service provision, including the time from locating the service until obtaining the result. E_S represents the total effort required to complete the process, including effort needed to get familiar with the location, to know where to submit the request and how to obtain the result. TS_S stands for technical support provided. Three kinds of technical support are identified, which are Help website (such as FAQ), Email contact and direct communication (such as face to face communication or phone call). Each type of technical support TS_S is defined as $<T_{TS}, E_{TS}>$, where T_{TS}, $E_{TS} \in R^+$. T_{TS} indicates the time required for technical support, and E_{TS} refers to the effort saved by receiving technical support. The value of T_S and E_S is different between the traditional counter service S_1 and E-government service S_2 respectively. Intuitively the effort consumed by using traditional counter is lower than the one by using E-government and time is just the opposite case (Tables 6.1 and 6.2).

2.1.2 Community Agent

We let community be the unit within which citizens are closely associated. Each community could consist either one kind of citizens or mixed kinds. Citizens will obtain information of E-government or learn how to use it from the community in which he/she currently reside. Community set is defined as $Community = \{1, 2, \ldots, k\}$, where k is the number of communities. For each of the community $i \in \{1, \ldots, k\}$, a set of variables is defined as shown in Table 6.3.

Table 6.1 Value table of T_S and E_S

T_S/E_S	Public service
Traditional counter	High/Low
E-government	Low/High

Table 6.2 Value table of T_{TS} and E_{TS}

	T_{TS}	E_{TS}
Help website	High	High
Email contact	Low	Low
Direct communication	Low	High

Table 6.3 Explanation of Community agent variables

H_i	A set of citizens who are currently involved in community $i \in \{1,\ldots,k\}$
$K_i \in R^+$	Correct knowledge of E-government spread in community i
$K_i \in N$	Number of citizens currently involved in community i
$K_i \in N$	Number of E-government adopters in community i
$K_i \in N$	Number of Non-E-government adopters in community i

Table 6.4 Explanation of Citizen agent variables

$Util_{S1} \in R^+$	Evaluated utility of traditional counter service at each iteration
$Util_{S2} \in R^+$	Evaluated utility of E-government service at each iteration
T_C, $E_C \in R^+$	Total time and effort consumed to complete the service respectively
$Pref_T$, $Pref_E \in R^+$	How citizens weight time and effort respectively, while we require $Pref_T + Pref_E = 1$
L_{exp}	A binary list of using history of E-government. 1 as success, 0 otherwise
P_E	Probability of choosing E-government at each iteration

2.1.3 Citizen Agent

A citizen is an active agent who might take up public service through different channels, as he/she needs. Citizen set is defined as $Citizen = \{C_1, C_2, \ldots, C_n\}$, where n is the number of citizens. Each citizen is abstracted as $C_i = <Util_{S1}, Util_{S2}, Pref_T, Pref_E, T_C, E_C, L_{exp}, P_E>$. Detailed explanation of the variables is given in Table 6.4. Total time T_C includes the time to complete the process plus the time of technical support received, while total effort E_C includes the effort to complete the service process, while received technical support would help decrease the effort. Besides, the weight $Pref_T$ and $Pref_E$ should be different for citizens coming from different groups. The larger the value, the more citizens emphasize the attribute. For instance, a citizen who thinks time is more important than effort will be with a larger value $Pref_T$ compared with $Pref_E$. Here we assume $Pref_E$ for ordinary group is smaller than the one for preferential group, while $Pref_T$ is set in the opposite way.

2.2 Decision Making of Citizens

At each iteration, the channel selection behaviour of each citizen is illustrated in Fig. 6.1 Joining learning groups and trying self-learning machine are optional activities based on policy implemented, which will be introduced in Sect. 3. Based on previous experience or communities' learning environment, each citizen will choose either traditional counter or E-government to take up the services. Through the process, he/she will update the time and efforts consumed during the process and calculate the utility value by the end of each iteration. At each

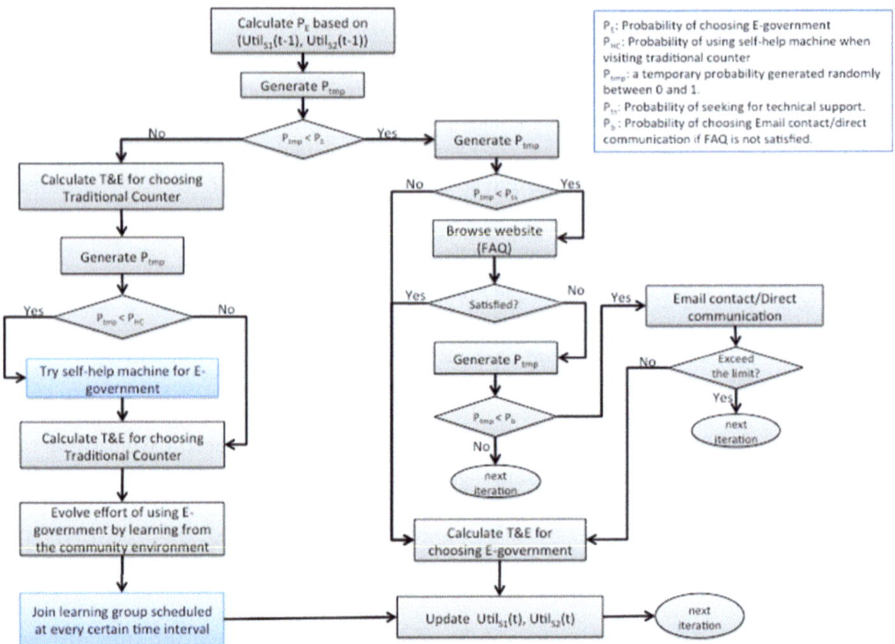

Fig. 6.1 Selection behavior of citizens at each iteration

discrete time unit $t \in T = \{1, 2, \ldots, N\}$, the utility value of channel S_i is updated *as* $Util_{Si}(t) = Pref_T * T_C(t, S_i) + Pref_E * E_C(t, S_i) + \varepsilon, i \in \{1, 2\}$, where ε is a random noise uniformly distributed between 0 and 1. Detailed explanation of the equations will be discussed in the following subsections.

For traditional counter, we assume that citizens do not need any technical support since they can communicate with the office staff directly during the process. Therefore the time and effort consumed at time t by choosing traditional counter S_1 equal to the time and effort defined in Service provider agent, as $T_C(t, S_1) = T_S$ and $E_C(t, S_1) = E_S$.

2.3 Effort Evolvement of E-Government Adopters

For E-government, utility value will be calculated in the same way, but the value of time and effort consumed will be updated differently. For E-government adopters already, the effort of using E-government will be evolved based on their past experience and technical support received, thus the value at time *t* will be updated as follows.

$$T_C(t, S_2) = T_S + \gamma * T_{TS} \quad (6.1)$$

$$E_C\,(t, S_2) = E_C * P_{EST} - \gamma' * E_{TS} \tag{6.2}$$

γ and γ' are uniformly distributed random number ranging between 0 and 1, and multiplied to adjust the time and effort required by technical support. From time to time, the time consumed to complete the service process T_C will not be changed significantly, but the effort of utilizing E-government service will be evolved. E_C will be evolved based on citizens' previous corresponding experience. In the following the way to update the evolved effort rate P_{EST} for E-government at each iteration is explained (Ahn 2010). Basically the value depends on whether the previous w tries of E-government are successful or not. For each citizen he/she will keep a list to record the history of using E-government service, denoted as L_{exp}. We let *Num* indicate the length of the list, *NoW* indicate the number of success of last *w* tries, and *NoS* represent the total number of successful tries, while *w*, *Num*, *NoW*, *NoS* $\in N$, and $P_{EST} \in R^{+}$. Then P_{EST} will be updated at each iteration as follows,

$$P_{EST} = \begin{cases} 1 - Est, & \textit{If the current try is successful} \\ 1 + Est, & \textit{Otherwise} \end{cases} \tag{6.3}$$

$$Est = \begin{cases} NoW/w, & if\ Num \geq w \\ (w - Num + NoS/Num)/w, & if\ Num < w \end{cases} \tag{6.4}$$

2.4 *Social Learning of E-Government Non-adopters*

For citizens who haven't adopted E-government yet, they will learn from the community until their ability of using E-government converges to the same level within the same community, and the effort will be updated accordingly. For instance, E_C of citizen $Ci \in H_l$, while $i \in \{1, \ldots, n\}$ and $l \in \{1, \ldots, k\}$ will be updated as follows,

$$E_C\,(t, S_2) = E_C\,(t-1, S_2) * \left(1 - \beta * \left(E_C\,(t-1, S_2) - AVG_E^l\,(t, S_2)\right) * ADJ\right) \tag{6.5}$$

$$AVG_E^l\,(t, S_2) = \left(\sum_{\forall C_j \in H_l}^{j \neq i} E_C^j\,(t-1, S_2) \right) / N_l(t) \tag{6.6}$$

$$ADJ = \frac{NE_l(t)}{N_l(t)} + K_l\,(t, Freq_t) \tag{6.7}$$

$$K_l\,(t, Freq_t) = K_l\,(t-1, Freq_t) + K_l\,(t-1, Freq_t) * (1 - K_l\,(t-1, Freq_t)) \tag{6.8}$$

AVG_E^l indicates the average effort level of citizens within community l, in other words the average ability of using E-government of citizens within the same community. Here we assume citizens within the same community will not directly interact with each other, but be influenced by the status of the community indirectly. ADJ is a parameter considering the influences of the number of E-government adopters and prevailing E-government knowledge within communities. The knowledge/information of E-government $K_l(t)$ will be updated only when $t \bmod Freq_t \equiv 0$, where $Freq_t \in N$. Otherwise the value will remain as the same.

2.5 Probability of Choosing Channels

At each iteration, the probability of choosing E-government P_E will be updated and the probability of choosing traditional counter is defined as $1 - P_E$. For non-adopters of E-government, this probability will depend on the properties of the community he/she currently resides in. For instance, the probability of choosing E-government f citizen $C_i \in H_l$, while $i \in \{1, \ldots, n\}$ and $l \in. \{1, \ldots, k\}$ will be updated as follows,

$$P_E(t) = P_E(t-1) + \alpha * P_E(t-1) * \frac{W_l(t-1) - Util_{S2}(t-1)}{W_l(t-1)} \tag{6.9}$$

$$W_l(t) = \left(\sum_{\forall C_j \in H_l}^{j \neq i} Util_{S1}^j(t-1) + \sum_{\forall C_j \in H_l}^{j \neq i} Util_{S2}^j(t-1) \right) / N_l(t) \tag{6.10}$$

For citizens who are E-government adopters already, the probability will not be influenced by other members within the same community, but this citizen's own previous experience. As a result, $W(t) = P_E * Util_{S1}(t) + (1 - P_E) * Util_{S2}(t)$.

The value of α and β are both positive real numbers ranging between 0 and 1, and because of the lack of empirical data, they are set as constant in this work. α is used to adjust the influences of community properties when choosing E-government and β is used to adjust the impact of community-based learning. The above social learning and channel selection algorithm are adopted from Deguchi's social learning dynamics and support commitment model (Deguchi 2004).

2.6 E-Government Supporting Strategies

Basically we assume there are two general kinds of strategy to increase the E-government adoption rate, one is to promote E-government via public media (spread information/knowledge of E-government) and the other is to educate citizens how to use E-government, such as organizing workshop and setting self-help machine in traditional counter such that every time when citizens visit traditional counter, they could try E-government with certain probability. Each of the strategies is bore with an implementation cost at each iteration, $Ct_i \in R^+$ and the frequency of implementation, $Freq_i \in N$ while $i \in \{1, 2, 3\}$. We assume the total cost of each strategy $Ct_i*N/Freq_i$ will be the same during the simulation, where N is time unit. Different scenarios will be carried out on the basis of different compositions of the strategies. E-government promotion strategy will update the knowledge spread in each community, thus indirectly influence citizens' effort of using E-government, whereas educational strategy will help mitigate citizens' effort of using E-government, in other words, they will decrease the value of E_C in certain degree directly.

3 Simulation Model

In the simulation model, we have 1,000 citizens divided into two social groups evenly, one is favoured by E-government and the other is not. All citizens will be allocated to one of the 100 communities defined randomly at the outset of simulation. We will run 2,000 iterations and all the results displayed below are the average value of 10 runs. We do not intend to interpret the number of iterations at social level as the actual number of using public services; rather it is defined from the simulation perspective to be long enough to examine the learning dynamics. As a result, 2,000 iterations are necessary to find the stable state of the learning dynamics. The frequency $Freq_1$ for organizing learning group will be 50, and $Freq_3$ for public promotion will be 30. Self-help machine will always be available at traditional counter, thus $Freq_2$ will be 1. The initial value of average effort level and knowledge of each community are fixed at the outset of simulation because of the lack of relevant empirical data. The scenario settings are listed in Table 6.5.

3.1 Community Scenarios

In these scenarios, we will simulate how social learning influences the E-government adoption rate in closed community and open community respectively.

Table 6.5 Scenario setting

Scenario	Learning group	Self-help machine	Promotion
0	Yes	No	No
1	Yes	Yes	No
2	No	Yes	No
3	No	No	No
4	Yes	No	Yes
5	Yes	Yes	Yes
6	No	Yes	Yes
7	No	No	Yes

Here closed community indicates the community that only consists of one kind of citizens, i.e. either *ordinary group* or *preferential group*. In contrast open community indicates the community within which different kinds of citizens are mixed.

3.1.1 Closed Community

In Fig. 6.2, we will show the adoption rate of both ordinary group and preferential group under the closed community setting in eight different scenarios.

We could observe that in closed community, without any strategies (Scenario 3), preferential group's adoption rate of E-government is relatively low (Fig. 6.2a). While with different strategies, the adoption rate will be improved in various degrees over time. Compared with Self-help desk, the learning group will improve the adoption rate more. Comparing Fig. 6.2 (a) with (c) in which public promotion is considered, we could observe that the adoption rate will increase more obviously and achieve a better converging point with information spread considered. On the other side, ordinary group's adoption rate will increase steadily in all scenarios with no significant difference among different strategies.

3.1.2 Open Community

In Fig. 6.3, we will show the adoption rate of both ordinary group and preferential group under open community setting.

We could observe that in open community, even without any strategy (Fig. 6.3a, Scenario 3) the adoption rate of preferential group will increase steadily to certain degree through the learning from ordinary groups within the same community. With public propaganda considered as shown in Fig. 6.3c, the increase of adoption rate for preferential group will be more obvious. For ordinary group, without any strategy considered the adoption rate will increase slower compared with the case of closed community, which may indicate that even ordinary group needs an environment for E-government learning and adoption.

3.2 Policy Scenarios

The cost-effectiveness of policies will be evaluated in terms of different social group's adoption rate of E-government per cost invested at each time unit. In other words we will consider the cost of each strategy and their resulting adoption rate for each social group. Due to lack of empirical data, we will set the total cost of three strategies equally in the simulation.

From Fig. 6.4, we could observe that for preferential group in closed community, the most cost-effective strategy is Scenario 0 that implements learning group only. In contrast for preferential group in open community, the cost-effectiveness of

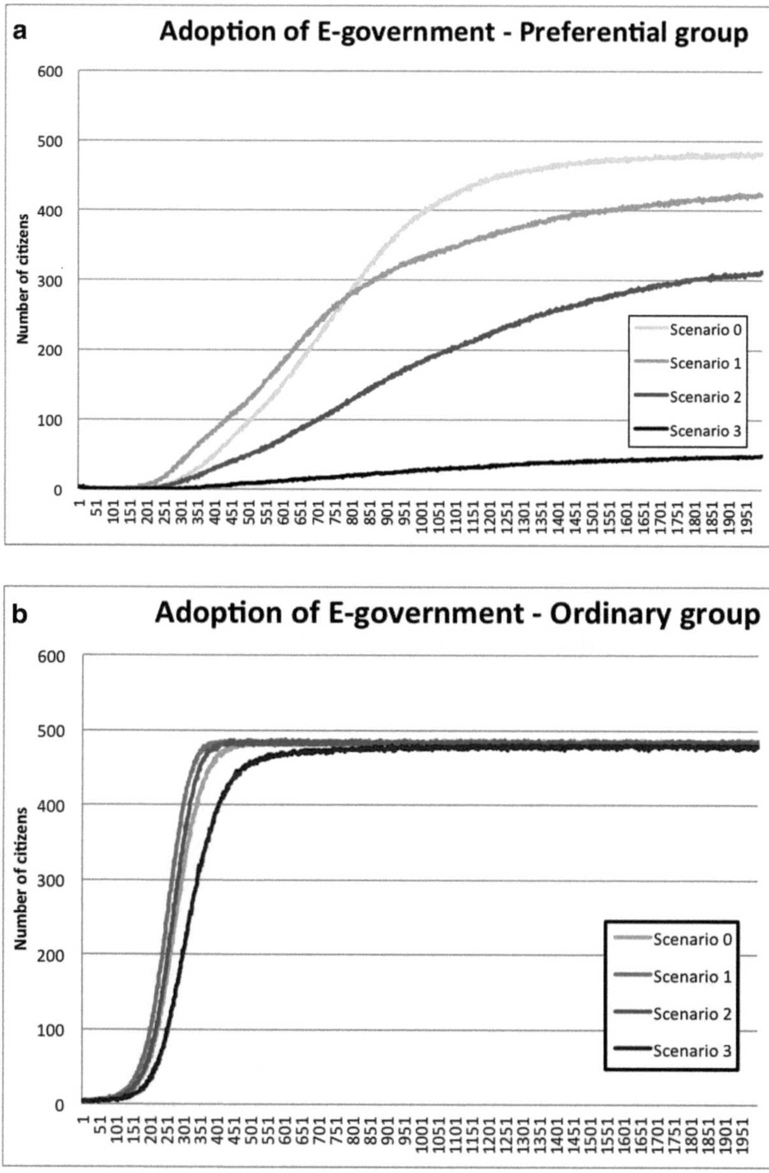

Fig. 6.2 Channel choice – Closed community. (**a**) Preferential group; Scenario 0–3 (**b**) Ordinary group; Scenario 0–3 (**c**) Preferential group; Scenario 4–7 (**d**) Ordinary group; Scenario 4–7

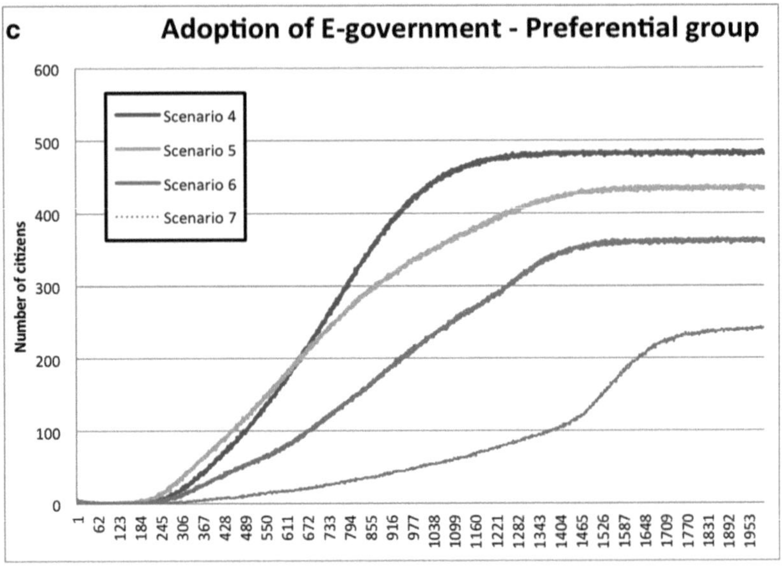

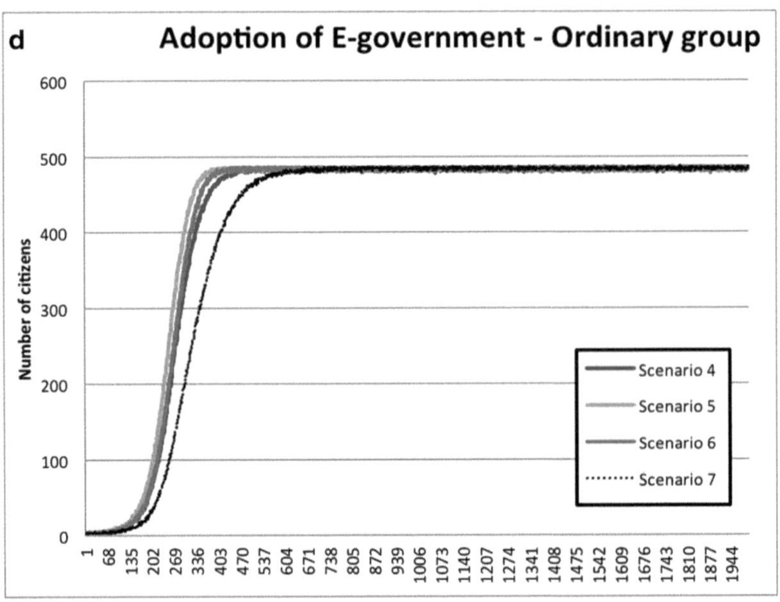

Fig. 6.2 (continued)

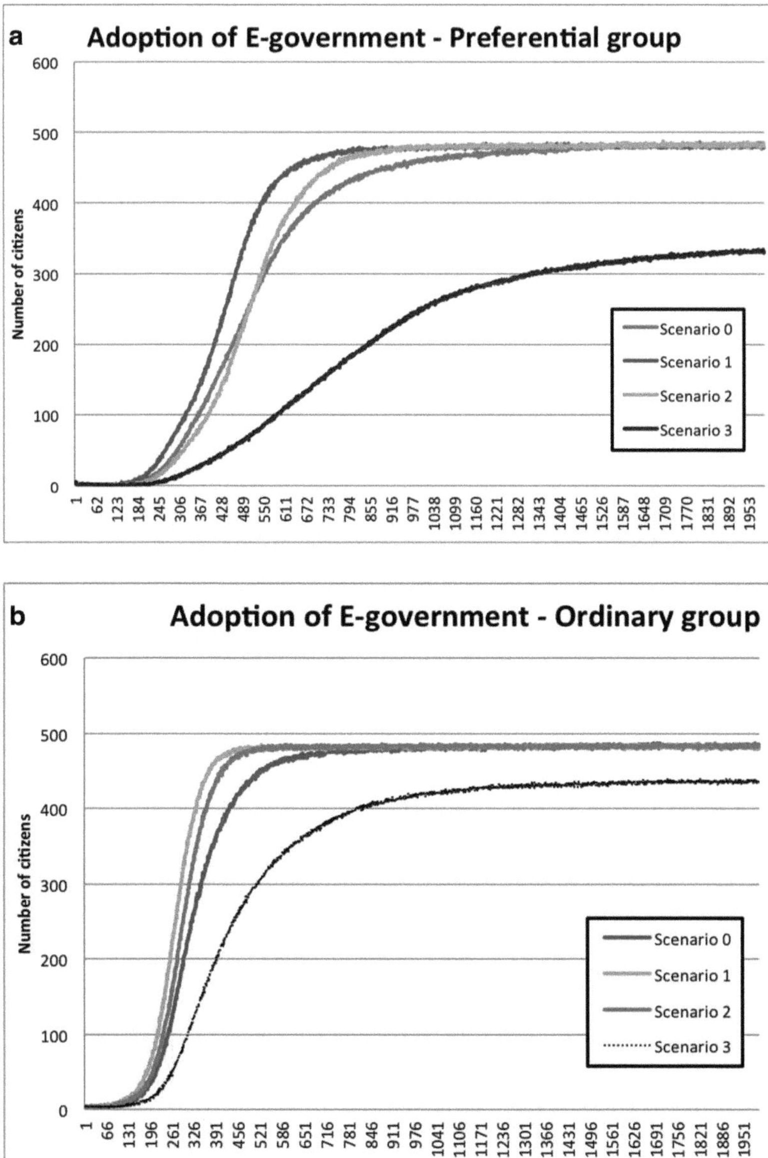

Fig. 6.3 Channel choice – Open community. (**a**) Preferential group; Scenario 0–3 (**b**) Ordinary group; Scenario 0–3 (**c**) Preferential group; Scenario 4–7 (**d**) Ordinary group; Scenario 4–7

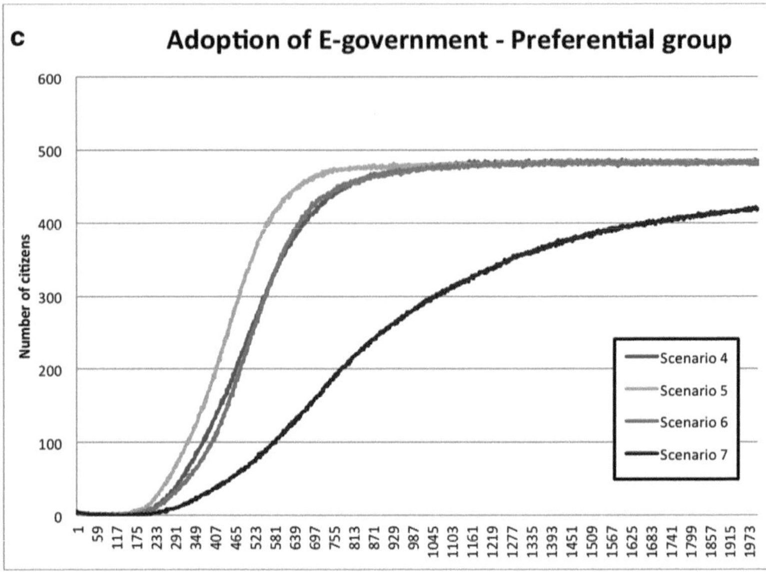

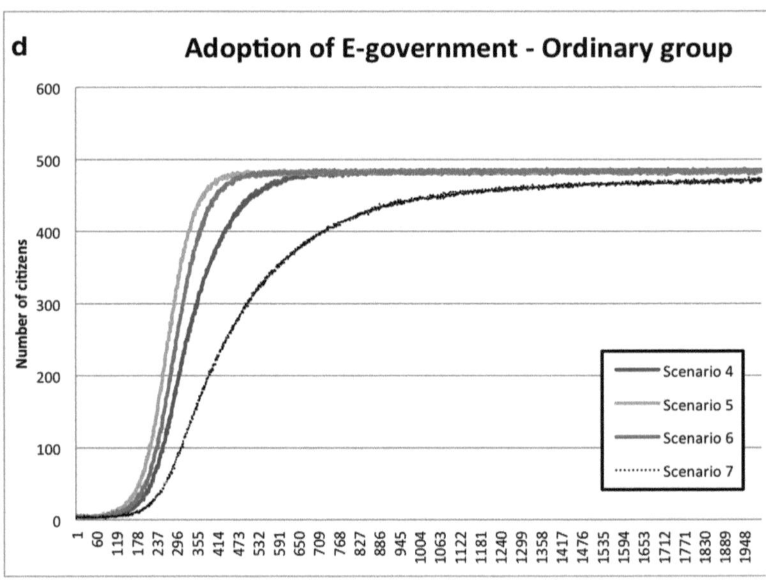

Fig. 6.3 (continued)

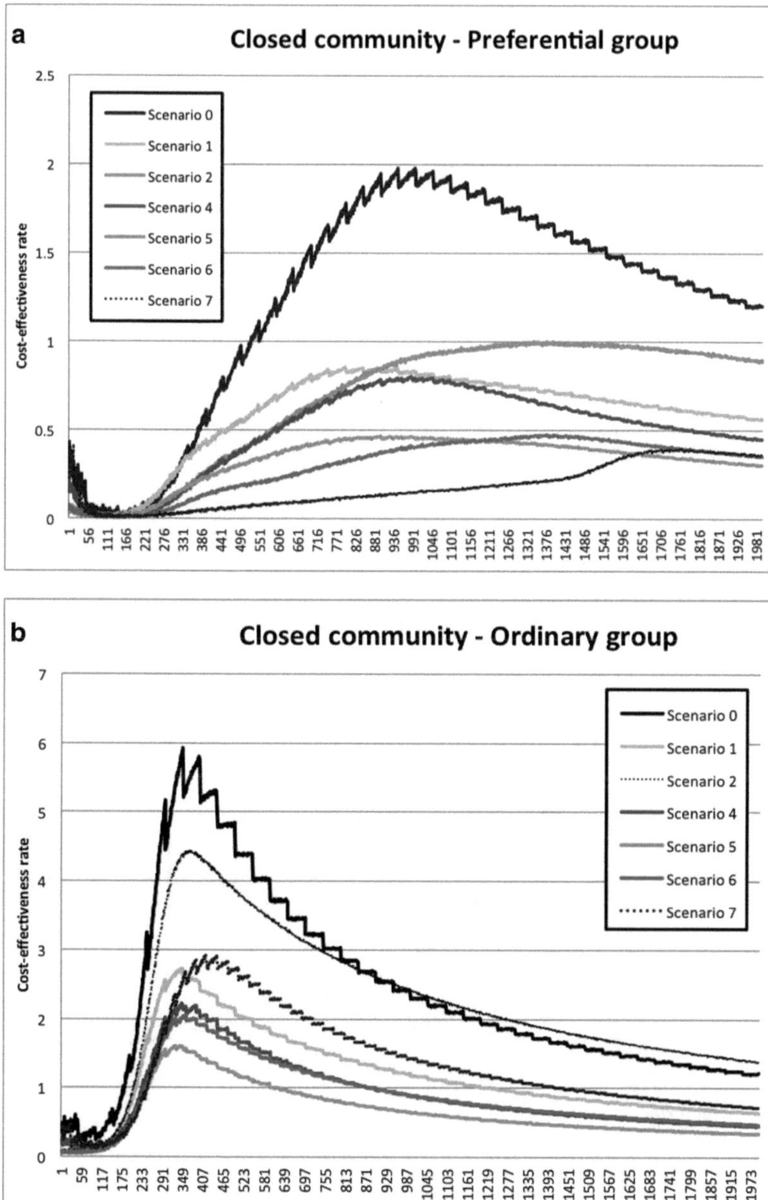

Fig. 6.4 Cost-effectiveness of strategies. (**a**) Preferential group; Closed community (**b**) Ordinary group; Closed community (**c**) Preferential group; Open community (**d**) Ordinary group; Open community

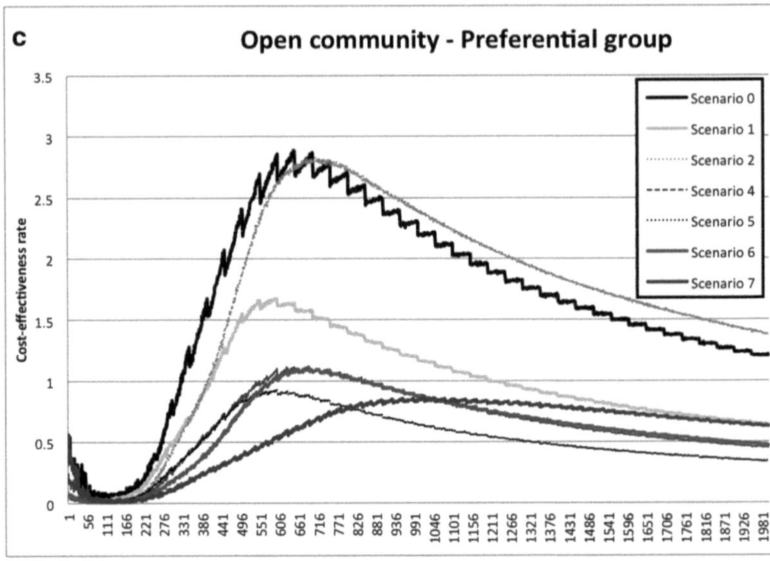

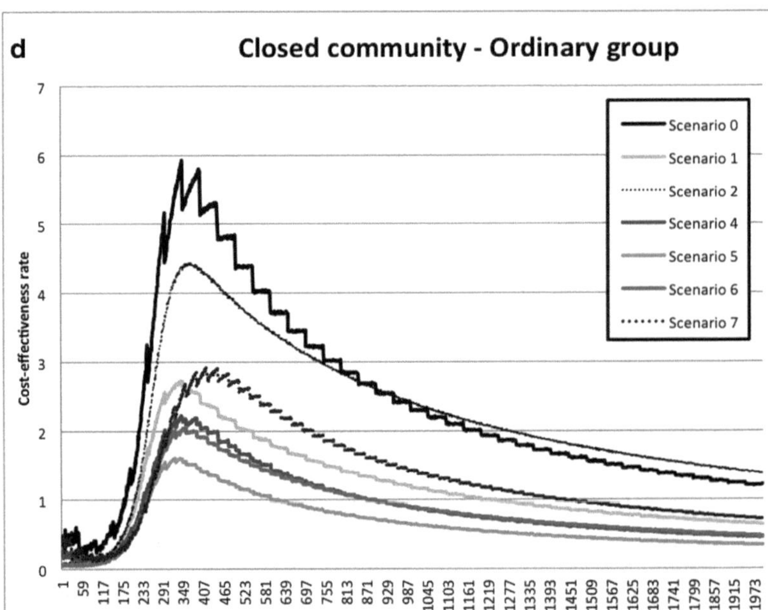

Fig. 6.4 (continued)

strategy that implements learning group and the one sets Self-help machine are relatively the same. For ordinary group, we could observe a similar result to the one for preferential group that the most cost-effective strategy is organizing learning group only. Without considering the public propaganda, implementing both other strategies is the least cost-effective one in the long term for both preferential group and ordinary group, which may indicate resources waste in both cases. In general, although public propaganda improves the adoption rate in all cases, the cost-effectiveness is relatively low when implementation cost is considered. At the outset, all strategies will experience a slump, which makes sense that strategies need time to become effective. When the adoption rate of E-government increases slowly with time going, the effectiveness of all strategies will decline. For ordinary group, the effectiveness of strategies will change swiftly compared with the one for preferential group.

In general, open community in which ordinary group and preferential group could communicate with each other is a better environment for E-government adoption, especially for preferential group. Besides, learning group is a much more cost-effective strategy for both ordinary group and preferential group under the parameter setting in this model.

3.3 Community-Level Analysis

From the above macro-level analysis, we could observe the aggregated adoption trend for all communities in long term under different scenarios. However, the adoption rate and learning dynamics down to each community are still missing. In the following, we will analyse the micro-level (community-level) result and treat each community as the unit of case study. Applying agent-based approach enables the micro-level analysis due to the inherited nature of ABM.

There are several steps to identify special cases (unit of analysis). First, we check the adoption rate for all communities at the final iteration through which we could identify the communities with relatively lower adoption rate, as shown in Figs. 6.5a and 6.6a (x-axis: community number; left y-axis: average ability of using E-government; right y-axis: adoption rate of E-government). Second, we go into details of those communities, i.e., community composition and average effort, as shown in Figs. 6.5b and 6.6b (x-axis: time unit; y-axis: average ability of using E-government of each community).

In Fig. 6.5, we take the scenario of which there are 40 % of preferential group in the whole population (open community), and no supporting strategy is carried out. Therefore, the only way through which preferential groups could improve their ability to use E-government is from the community environment. Figure 6.5a shows the adoption rate of E-government and the average ability of using E-government for all 100 communities at the final iteration (i.e. 2,000). We could see that for

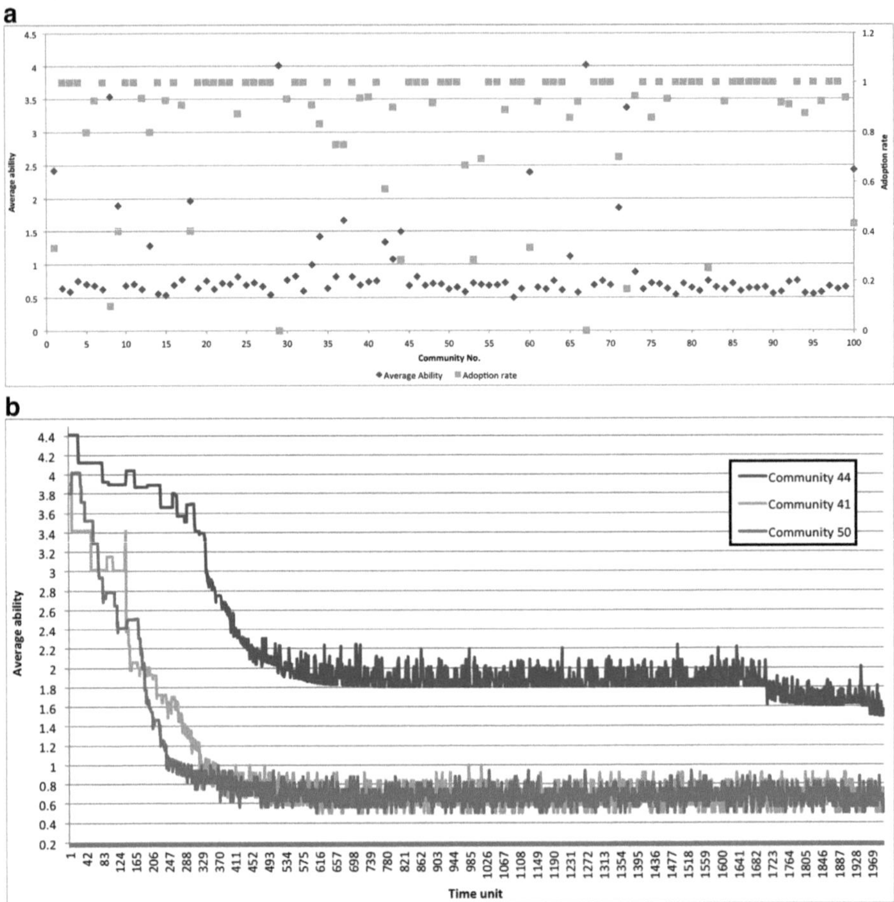

Fig. 6.5 Average ability of each community and the corresponding adoption rate. (**a**) Adoption rate and average ability, (**b**) Average ability trend

community (percentage of preferential groups in the community) 1 (50 %), 8 (60 %), 9 (40 %), 18 (40 %), 29 (67 %), 44 (55 %), 53 (85 %), 60 (33 %), 67 (83 %), 72 (50 %), 82 (50 %), and 100 (25 %), the adoption rate is below 50 %. Especially in the case when preferential groups dominate the community population (over 50 %), the adoption rate will be relatively harder and slower to increase. In addition, we could see that for those communities with lower adoption rate, the average ability of using E-government is relatively low as well. If we take a closer look into the average ability of community 41 (33 %), 44 (55 %) and 50 (25 %) as in Fig 6.5b, we could see that for communities with more ordinary groups (community 41 and 50), the average ability will be improved faster than the one with less ordinary social groups (community 44).

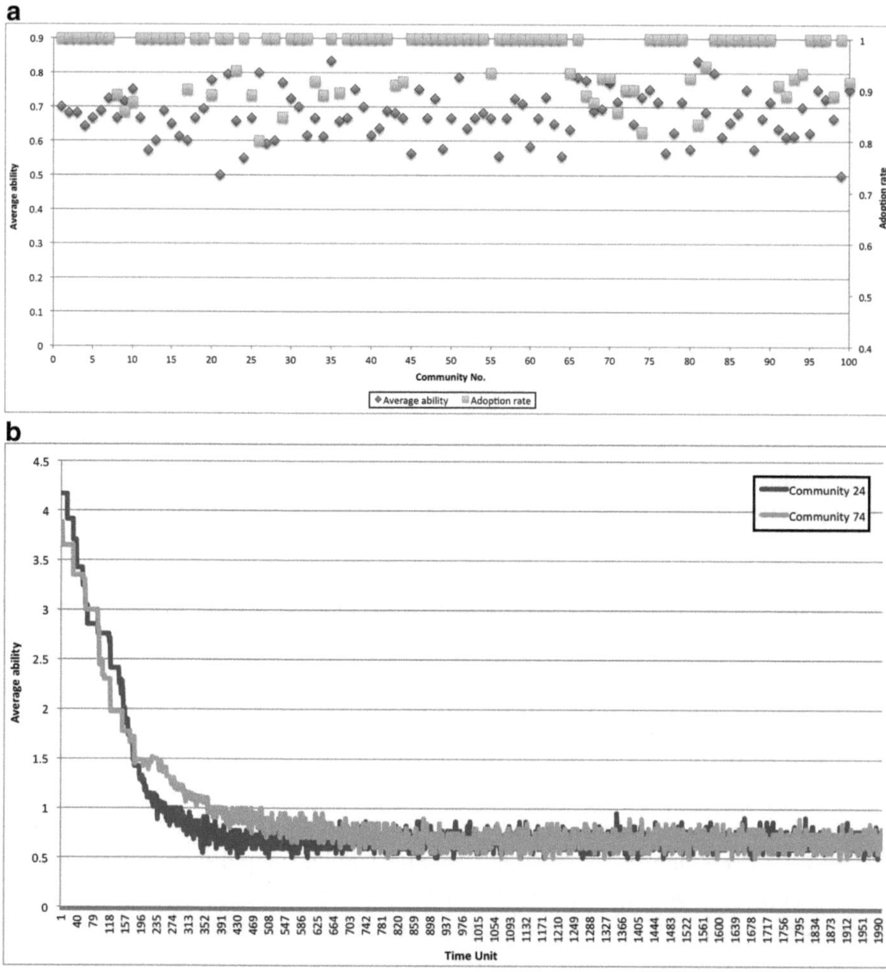

Fig. 6.6 Average ability of each community and the corresponding adoption rate. (**a**) Adoption rate and average ability, (**b**) Average ability trend

Similarly we could check other scenarios. In Fig. 6.6 when the learning group strategy is carried out frequently (per 30 time units) on closed community, the adoption rate for pure ordinary group (community 1–50) and preferential group (community 51–100) at final iteration are quite evenly distributed as shown in Fig 6.6a, and the gap between these two groups is trivial. Furthermore, the average ability between communities with different property, such as community 24 (adoption rate 100 %) and 74 (adoption rate 80 %), will not be obviously distinguishable, as shown in Fig. 6.6b.

3.4 Verification and Validation

For verification, we run the simulation for 10 and 20 times respectively and calculate the average. The result shows that there is no significant difference between the two cases, which indicates that 10 times' run is enough to get a relatively accurate average of the result. For validation, we could get a similar pattern to the one generated by Deguchi's analytical social learning dynamic and support commitment model in both macro level and community level (Deguchi 2004). In Deguchi's model, players will choose between *A* option that is desirable and *B* option that is currently prevailing, and supporting commitment and educational effect are also considered. In our work, E-government could be considered as the *A* option while traditional counter is as *B* option, inverse of utility value of choosing E-government and traditional counter can be treated as the according payoff. Community-based learning could be treated as supporting commitment while public promotion is kind of educational effect to spread correct knowledge of E-government. Without any supporting policy, if the utility value of choosing E-government is smaller, the probability of choosing E-government will converge to almost 100 % after certain time unit and keep stable (*Ordinary group* case), while if it is the opposite case, then the probability of choosing E-government will remain relatively low (*Preferential group* case).

4 Conclusion

In this work, we construct an agent-based model to capture the dynamic process and involved interactions of citizens' channel choice of public services, and to understand the underlying learning mechanisms. Community-based social learning is considered in this model, both in closed community and open community. Based on this model, different strategies which aim at improving E-government adoption rate, such as public propaganda and organizing learning programs are examined in terms of adoption rate and cost-effectiveness. From the result we could observe that in open community, adoption rate of E-government for citizens from preferential group is better compared with the one in closed community. Organizing learning group could be a better strategy compared with others, especially the one organized particularly for preferential groups in closed community. In open community, the cost-effectiveness of strategies is less distinguishable from each other. In addition, we perform the micro-level analysis to provide more profound insight into the community-level dynamics that lead to the macro-level adoption phenomenon. With our best knowledge, this is the first work of understanding the channel choice of public services with community-based social learning by using agent-based simulation. Although the parameters in this work are fixed due to being lack of empirical data and the simulation result interpretation is restricted to the parameter setting, it could still provide some insight for the policy makers. In future works, more experiments could be carried out with different parameter setting to examine the influences. The value of parameters of this model could also be calibrated to fit into a particular situation and thus the result could be validated with empirical data collected from the real world in future.

References

Ahn HJ (2010) Evaluating customer aid functions of online stores with agent-based models of customer behavior and evolution strategy. Inform Sci 180(9):1555–1570

Census and Statistics Department (2009) Hong Kong Thematic Household Survey No. 43. http://www.censtatd.gov.hk/products_and_services/products/publications/statistical_report/social_data/index_cd_B1130243_dt_detail.jsp

Deguchi H (2004) Economics as an agent-based complex system – toward agent-based social systems sciences. Springer, Tokyo, Japan

Gilbert GN (2008) Agent-based models, Quantitative applications in the social sciences. Sage, Los Angeles

Gil-Garcia JR, Luna-Reyes LF (2003) Towards a definition of electronic government: a comparative review. In: Vilas AM (ed) Techno-legal aspects of the information society and new economy: an overview. Formatex, Badajoz

Gouscos D, Kalikakis M, Legal M, Papadopoulou S (2007) A general model of performance and quality for one-stop e-government service offerings. Gov Inf Q 24(4):860–885

Gunasekaran A, Ngai EW (2008) Adoption of e-procurement in Hong Kong: an empirical research. Int J Prod Econ 113(1):159–175

Hossain MD, Moon J, Kim JK, Choe YC (2011) Impacts of organizational assimilation of e-government systems on business value creation: a structuration theory approach. Electron Commer Res Appl 10(5):576–594

Lave J, Wenger E (1991) Situated learning: legitimate peripheral participation. Cambridge University Press, New York

Lean OK, Zailani S, Ramayah T, Fernando Y (2009) Factors influencing intention to use e-government services among citizens in Malaysia. Int J Inf Manag 29(6):458–475

Maruping LM, Venkatesh V, Agarwal R (2009) A control theory perspective on agile methodology use and changing user requirements. Inf Syst Res 20(3):377–399

Reddick CG, Turner M (2012) Channel choice and public service delivery in Canada: comparing e-government to traditional service delivery. Gov Inf Q 29(1):1–11

Schaupp LC, Carter L, McBride ME (2010) E-file adoption: a study of U.S. taxpayers' intentions. Comput Hum Behav 26(4):636–644

Sebie MA, Irani Z (2005) Technical and organisational challenges facing transactional e-government systems: an empirical study. Electron Gov 2:247–276

Sunitiyoso Y, Matsumoto S (2009) Modelling a social dilemma of mode choice based on commuters' expectations and social learning. Eur J Oper Res 193(3):904–914

Venkatesh V, Chan FK, Thong JY (2012) Designing e-government services: key service attributes and citizens' preference structures. J Oper Manag 30:116–133

Yucel G, van Daalen CE (2011) Exploratory analysis of the impact of information dynamics on innovation diffusion. Technol Forecast Soc Change 78(2):358–372

Chapter 7
Preliminary Study on a Method for Space Design Analysis Based on Human Behavior Semiosis Using a Multiagent Simulator

Kumiko Kiso and Teruyuki Monnai

Abstract This paper proposes a method for analyzing architectural space design based on human behavior semiosis by using a multiagent simulator as a design aid. Face-to-face interviews with those who visited a campus plaza were conducted as a case study in order to understand the processes behind human behavior, and the space design based on the interview analysis is considered. This study is organized as follows: (1) a human behavior semiosis model is proposed based on C.S. Peirce's concept of semiosis; (2) an analysis of the interview results based on the model of step 1 is proposed; (3) the site is modeled using cells in a multiagent simulator; and (4) based on the analysis of step 2, the modeled site is evaluated according to the human behavior semiosis performed by the multiagent simulator in step 3.

Keywords Multiagent simulation • Human behavior • Semiosis • Design aid

1 Introduction

The meaning process is a fundamental aspect in human lives, where everything means something to mankind. As far as space design is concerned, humans have been dealing with the meaning of built environments and structures since approximately 70 B.C. (Vitruvius 1960). However, the means of fully designing architectural space based on the meaning process is yet to be understood, and many poorly built environments and structures have been created owing to the lack of an objective method in order to understand the aspects of human meaning regarding architectural space.

K. Kiso (✉)
Graduate School of Engineering, Fukui University, Fukui, Japan
e-mail: kiso@u-fukui.ac.jp

T. Monnai
Department of Architecture, Graduate School of Engineering,
Kyoto University, Kyoto, Japan
e-mail: monnai@archi.kyoto-u.ac.jp

Y. Nakai et al. (eds.), *Agent-Based Approaches in Economic and Social Complex Systems VIII*, Agent-Based Social Systems 13, DOI 10.1007/978-4-431-55236-9_7

Herein, we propose a method to analyze space design based on the meaning process by focusing on the interpretative aspects of human behavior. The meaning process is analyzed from the viewpoint of human behavior, and cellular automata are applied to estimate a space design based on human behavior.

2 Related Research

This study focuses on the computational multiagent modeling of human behavior in a daily situation, for example, when we stop in a park to smoke or relax. In contrast to other research investigating multiagent modeling of human behavior in a daily situation (Antonini et al. 2006; Katsuyama et al. 2005; Dijkstra et al. 2000), this study models human behavior based on Peirce's model of semiosis. The advantage of using Peirce's model as a human behavior model is that it enables us to create a universal model to understand the meaning process of human behavior. Therefore, this research is a first step toward the creation of a general method in order to understand the meaning process of human behavior. There are also various studies involving the computational modeling of Peirce's conception of semiosis that seek, among other things, to create models for artificial intelligence (Gomes et al. 2003, 2005; Pietarinen 2004; Aliseda 2000). Where these previous studies strive to model the human thinking process itself, this study focuses on modeling human behavior as a result of the human thinking process. Therefore, the original contribution of this study is to provide a means of applying Peirce's model to human behavior.

As the first step of the present research, this study analyzes and models the relationship between the point where a person stops within an architectural space and the meanings that are attributable to the architectural space around the stopping point based on Peirce's model of semiosis. Thus, the results of this study help to decide the disposition of the architectural elements based on the meaning process when designing architectural space. This study is developed from the author's previous research (Kiso and Monnai 2013), and the means of applying Peirce's model to the process of human behavior and the derived multiagent model of semiosis are revised in this study.

3 Theoretical Framework

3.1 Modeling of Human Behavior Process as Semiosis

In this study, human behavior is understood from the viewpoint of a meaning process through the concept of semiosis first proposed by Peirce, who was an American semiotician. Semiosis is the process of thinking through signs (CP 2.242) (Peirce 1978). Peirce considered that people think only through signs (Yonemori 1995).

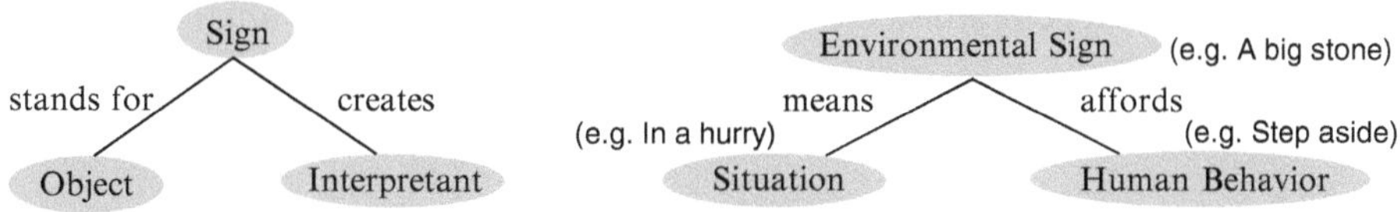

Fig. 7.1 Triadic relation models of semiosis. L: general semiosis; R: human behavior semiosis

For example, when we think of an apple, we never think of the entire apple, but some aspects of the apple, such as "sweet" or "red", and these aspects are defined as signs. According to Peirce, human behavior also involves semiosis on a wider scale (Sezai 1960), wherein human behavior is a response of the human interpretative process of their environment. In other words, human behavior is a representation of the human interpretation of their environment. As described on the left-hand side of Fig. 7.1, Peirce proposed a triadic model by using the concepts of "sign," "object," and "interpretant" in order to classify all aspects of semiosis (CP 8.328) (Peirce 1978). Following his model of semiosis, human behavior is defined in accordance with the right-hand side of Fig. 7.1 in this study as follows: (1) Environmental sign (based on sign (CP 8.332) (Peirce 1978)) is given as a part of the environment that is recognized by a person. (2) Situation (based on object (CP 2.230) (Peirce 1978)) is given as the circumstance or situation of a person that is represented by an environmental sign. (3) Human behavior (based on interpretant (CP 2.303) (Peirce 1978)) is given as human behavior that is a representation of the interpretation of an environmental sign. People follow human behavior through environmental signs. For example, if a big stone stands on a street, one can sit on it or step aside, which represents their interpretation of the stone (Fig. 7.1, right). This process that determines human behavior is considered as semiosis.

3.2 *Modeling of Human Behavior Semiosis by Cellular Automata*

We propose a semiosis model where each person performs each human behavior depending on his interpretation of sign systems. The cellular automaton is modeled as an environmental sign system ($SS_{k,t}(p_{n,t})$) that consists of a set of environmental signs interpreted by each person ($p_{n,t}$) at a time *t*, as given by Eq. (7.1). Each person ($p_{n,t}$) is assigned a set of situations ($SI(p_{n,t})$), as given by Eq. (7.2). Human behavior semiosis is an interpretative process beginning with a situation followed by human behavior $B(p_{n,t})$ based on the interpretation of an environmental sign, as modeled in Eq. (7.3). Human behavior semiosis is thus modeled as a functional process.

$$SS_{k,t}(p_{n,t}) = \{ f_1(p_{n,t}),\ f_2(p_{n,t}),\ f_3(p_{n,t}), \ldots \} \tag{7.1}$$

f is a function that determines the type of sign interpreted by a person.

$$SI\left(p_{n,t}\right) = \left\{g_1\left(p_{n,t}\right), g_2\left(p_{n,t}\right), g_3\left(p_{n,t}\right), \ldots\right\} \quad (7.2)$$

g is a function that determines the type of situation.

$$B\left(p_{n,t}\right) = h\left(SI\left(p_{n,t}\right), \sum_{k=1}^{a} SS_{k,t}\left(p_{n,t}\right)\right) \quad (7.3)$$

h is a function that determines human behavior, and a is the total number of sign systems on–site.

4 Interviews Examining Human Behavior Semiosis

The process determining human behavior was investigated through face-to-face interviews in a campus plaza at Seika University (Kyoto, Japan), where various human behaviors were observed (Fig. 7.2). A total of 109 people onsite were chosen randomly and were interviewed individually. The interviews took place on May 21 through the 24, 2012. Students of the university constituted 95 % of the people interviewed. Interviewers provided questions in order to understand the manner in which people choose the plaza and the types of signs they interpret as follows: (1) The reason for choosing the campus plaza (e.g. the biggest attraction to visit),

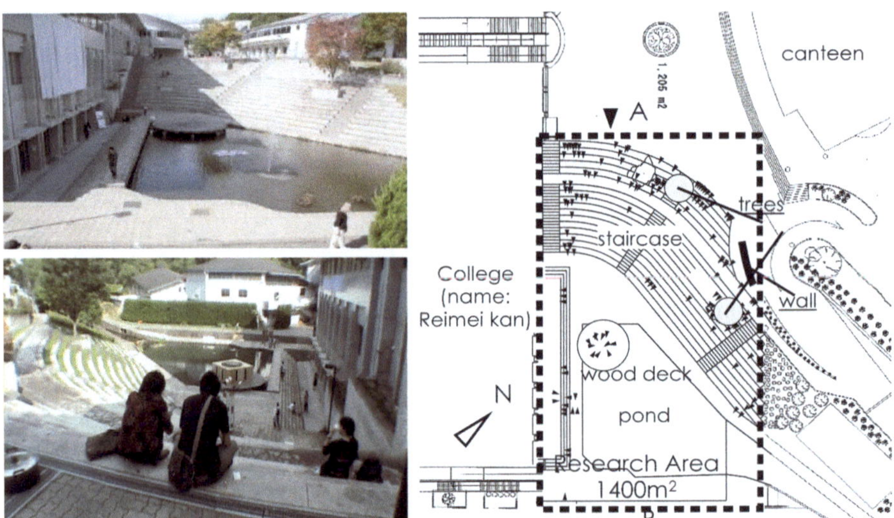

Fig. 7.2 The site where the interviews were conducted. *Left*: a view from *A* (*top*) and a view from *B* (*bottom*); *Right*: map of the research area and the positions of each interviewee seated

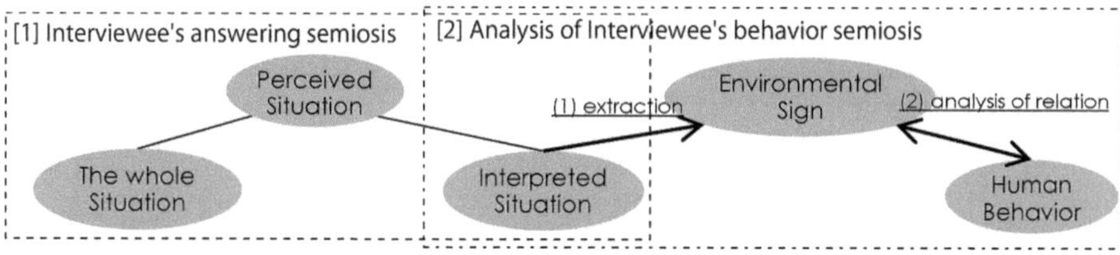

Fig. 7.3 Theoretical framework of the interview and the interview analysis conducted

(2) The place where the interviewee was before coming to the plaza, (3) The place where the interviewee will go after visiting the plaza. The interviews took approximately 5 min for each person (or for each group). Figure 7.3 shows the questionnaire and all the sitting points of the interviewees.

5 Analysis of the Relationships Between Questionnaire Responses and the Sitting Point

5.1 Theoretical Framework of the Interview Analysis

Figure 7.3 illustrates the theoretical framework used for the interview and its analysis. In this framework, we interviewed individuals about their situation, provoking them to think about their situation (we call this the perceived situation in Fig. 7.3). The interviewee then rendered an answer concerning their situation (we call this the interpreted situation in Fig. 7.3). After the interview, the environmental signs are extracted from the interview subject's interpreted situation. Thus, the analysis procedure is given as follows. (1) All the interview proceedings are transcribed. (2) Signs are extracted from the transcription. (3) Variables that express positional relationships between the interview subject's sitting points are proposed relative to the signs extracted in step 2.

5.2 Analysis of Relationships Between the Extracted Signs and Sitting Points Based on Logistic Regression Analysis

Logistic regression analysis is a regression analysis applied to categorical dependent variables that serve as response variables by using a logistic function. This regression analysis was performed to evaluate the general relationship between extracted signs and sitting points. First, explanatory variables that can express each interview subject's sitting point are proposed, as shown in Fig. 7.4 (Kiso and Monnai 2013). Then, logistic regression analysis is subsequently performed with the proposed explanatory variables and the "units" explained below as response variables.

(v1) Number of steps: the number of steps that an interviewee walk up or down

(v2) Distance from a tree: the distance from the nearest tree of 2 trees on the site to each interviewee (interviewee 2 in the right)

(v3) Distance from a pond: the distance from the center of the pond at the site to each interviewee (interviewee 2 in the right)

(v4) Height of steps: 3 types of heights of steps on which interviewees sit (1:flat, 2:around 20 cm, 3: around 40 cm)

(v5) Distance from the passageway A: distance from the passageway A to each interviewee (interviewee 1 in the right)

(v6) Distance from the passageway B: distance from the passageway B to each interviewee (interviewee 1 in the right)

(v7) Height from a bottom: the height from the bottom of the site to each interviewee (Height is 0 at the top, 39 at the bottom)

(v8) Distance from wall C: the distance from wall C to each interviewee (interviewee 2 in the right)

(v9) Distance from previous place: the distance from the site to the place where an interviewee was before the site

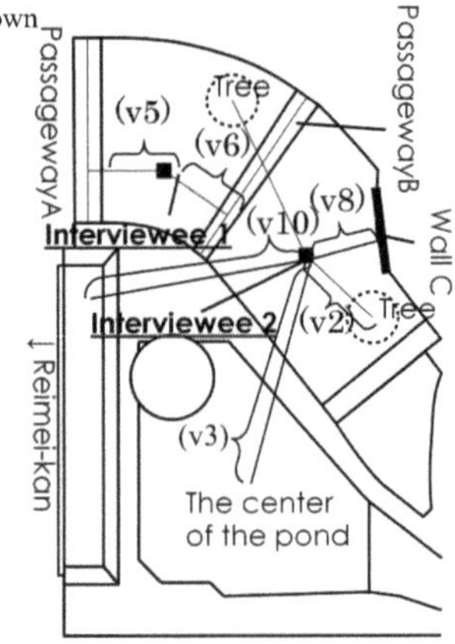

(v10) Distance from Reimei-kan: the distance from Reimei-kan to each interviewee (interviewee 2 in the right)

(v11) Friends: existence of friends with each interviewee (0: sitting with no friend, 1: sitting with friend)

Fig. 7.4 Proposed explanatory variables

The transcription was divided into the smallest "units".[1] For example, when an interviewee states "I came here because this is a beautiful place to sit," the units can be extracted as "this is a beautiful place" and "this is a place to sit". Environmental signs are extracted from these units in order to understand the types of signs recognized by interviewees and determine those signs that are attractions to come to the site and those signs that are not. Table 7.1 shows the units, extracted environmental signs, and indicates the impact of the signs, whether positive or negative.[2]

Table 7.2 shows the results of the regression analysis. The main inferences drawn from the results are as follows. (1) Interviewees whose responses contain the unit "eat lunch" tend to sit with wall C at their back, and this indicates that the wall is chosen instinctively as a place to sit and eat lunch. (2) Interviewees whose responses

[1]Transcription is divided into units as follows: (1) All transcriptions are resolved into words. (2) Jaccard indexes as an indicator of the co-occurrence of every word pair of step 1 is calculated; when A stands for a frequency of a word "A" and B stands for a frequency of a word "B," the index of the word pair "A" and "B" is $(j\ (A, B)) = |A \cap B| / |A \cup B|$. (3) Some words are connected as a unit based on the indexes obtained in step 2. 4) The function words whose indexes are less than 0.23 are not analyzed in the study.

[2]"Units" and "environmental signs" are extracted as follows: (1) When the "unit" is a verb or a verb phrase, a place to do what the verb expresses or a circumstance that the verb expresses is extracted as a sign. (2) When the "unit" is a noun phrase or a noun, the noun is extracted as a sign. (3) When the "unit" is an adjective or an adverb, the circumstance, atmosphere, or place that the adjective or adverb modifies is extracted as a sign. (4) If an extracted sign leads to an interviewee coming to the plaza or to an interviewee choosing a sitting point, the sign impact is positive. If not, the impact is negative.

contain the unit "friends" tend to come from a distance, indicating that people come to the site in order to meet their friends. From this result and that shown in Table 7.1, "friend" is an attractive sign bringing a positive meaning to the site. (3) Interviewees whose responses contain the unit "crowded canteen" tend to sit with their friends in the upper part of the site near the canteen, indicating that they come out of the canteen with their friends because there is no place to sit, and they sit around the upper part of the site nearby. From this result and that of Table 7.1, "canteen" is a sign that brings negative meaning to the plaza but also induces people to come to the site. (4) Interviewees whose responses contain the unit "event, live," or "view" tend to walk on the stairs, indicating that they engage in a significant amount of walking to find a place where they can watch a concert or have a good view.

Table 7.1 Units, extracted signs, and the positive/negative impact of signs

Reason for choosing a plaza					
Unit of Situation	Extracted Sign	Pos./Neg.	Unit of Situation	Extracted Sign	Pos./Neg.
verb			noun		
eat lunch	place to eat lunch	P	favorite place	favorite place	P
relax	place to relax	P	large place	large place	P
wait for something	place to wait for something	P	not many people	circumstance where there is not many people	P
kill time	place to kill time	P	people	people	P/N
come to talk from somewhere	place to come to talk from somewhere	P	friends	friends	P
feel good	place to feel good	P	wind	wind	P
sit on	place to sit on	P	water, pond	water, pond	P
have a time, have nothing to do	circumstance where an interviewee have a time	P	staircase	staircase	P/N
like (this plaza)	favorite plaza	P	view	view	P
adjective, adverb			sound of water	sound of water	P
open-air	open-air place	P	sound (not of water)	sound (not of water)	P/N
silent	silent atmosphere	P	plaza	plaza	P/N
open	open atmosphere	P	good temperature	good temperature	P
good	good atmosphere	P	good weather	good weather	P
calm	calm atmosphere	P	event, concert	event, live	P
peaceful	peaceful atmosphere	P	Reimei-kan (the name of a building)	Reimei-kan (the name of a building)	P/N

(continued)

Table 7.1 (continued)

Reason for choosing a plaza					
Unit of Situation	Extracted Sign	Pos./Neg.	Unit of Situation	Extracted Sign	Pos./Neg.
(somewhere is) indoor	indoor place	N	classroom	classroom	P
(somewhere is) cramped	cramped place	N	noon	noon	P
(I'm) alone	circumstance where an interviewee is alone	P	canteen	canteen	P/N
			crowded canteen	crowded canteen	N
			(I have a) class	circumstance where an interviewee have a class	P
			recess	recess	P

Reason for choosing a sitting point					
Unit of Situation	Extracted Sign	Pos./Neg.	Unit of Situation	Extracted Sign	Pos./Neg.
verb			noun		
sit immediately from somewhere	place to sit quickly from somewhere	P	favorite place	favorite place	P
go up and down	place to go up and down	N	canteen	canteen	P/N
people always walk there	place where people always walk	N	shade	shade	P
like (this point to sit)	favorite place	P	event, concert	event, live	P
adjective, adverb			people	people	P/N
vacant	vacant	P	tree	tree	P
relaxing	relaxing	P	sun	sun	P
near (from somewhere)	a place near from somewhere	P	foot of the stairs	foot of the stairs	N
bothersome to move	a place bothersome to move	N	water, pond	water, pond	P
			friends	friends	P
			somebody's eye	somebody's eye	N
			(don't like) the center	the center	N
			the side	the side	P
			good temperature	good temperature	P
			good weather	good weather	P

Table 7.2 Result of logistic regression analysis by SPSS

Group A (v1, v4, v7, v9, v11)

Units	P/N	Variable	B (Regression Coefficient)	Sig.	Exp(B)	95% C.I. for exp(B) Lower	95% C.I. for exp(B) Upper	Sig. for Regression Eq.
people	P/N	Height from a bottom	−0.052	0.034	0.949	0.904	0.996	0.019
friends	P	Dis. from another place	0.326	0.006	1.386	1.096	1.751	0.007
event, concert	P/N	Number of steps	0.088	0.014	1.092	1.018	1.172	0.015
crowded canteen	N	Friends	1.311	0.032	3.709	1.117	12.317	0.000
		Height from a bottom	−0.101	0.008	0.904	0.839	0.975	0.000
canteen	P/N	Height from a bottom	−0.095	0.009	0.909	0.847	0.977	0.040
view	P	Number of steps	0.099	0.029	1.104	1.010	1.207	0.044
vacant	P	Height from a bottom	−0.325	0.017	0.723	0.553	0.944	0.001

Group B (v5, v6, v8)

Units	P/N	Variable	B (Regression Coefficient)	Sig.	Exp(B)	95% C.I. for exp(B) Lower	95% C.I. for exp(B) Upper	Sig. for Regression Eq.
eat lunch	P	Dis. from wall C	−0.040	0.025	0.960	0.927	0.995	0.030
noon	P	Dis. from passageway A	−0.039	0.049	0.962	0.925	1.000	0.040
		Dis. from passageway B	0.048	0.021	1.049	1.007	1.093	0.040
Reimei-kan	P	Dis. from wall C	0.085	0.049	1.089	1.000	1.185	0.019
Bothersome to move	N	Dis. from passageway B	−0.099	0.027	0.905	0.829	0.989	0.045

Group C (v2)

Units	P/N	Variable	B (Regression Coefficient)	Sig.	Exp(B)	95% C.I. for exp(B) Lower	95% C.I. for exp(B) Upper	Sig. for Regression Eq.
staircase	P	tree	0.045	0.023	1.046	1.006	1.088	0.029
Reimei-kan	P	tree	0.045	0.033	1.046	1.003	1.089	0.042
canteen	P/N	tree	−0.047	0.032	0.954	0.914	0.996	0.013
(I have a) class	P	tree	0.027	0.049	1.027	1.000	1.055	0.050
tree	P	tree	−0.164	0.001	0.849	0.770	0.936	0.000
people	P/N	tree	−0.066	0.010	0.936	0.890	0.984	0.002

Group D (v3, v10)

Units	P/N	Variable	B (Regression Coefficient)	Sig.	Exp(B)	95% C.I. for exp(B) Lower	95% C.I. for exp(B) Upper	Sig. for Regression Eq.
kill a time	P	Dis. from a pond	0.057	0.026	1.059	1.007	1.113	0.037
people	P/N	Dis. from a pond	0.049	0.001	1.051	1.020	1.083	0.002
friends	P	Dis. from a pond	0.056	0.040	1.058	1.003	1.116	0.045
Reimei-kan	P	Dis. from Reimei-kan	−0.106	0.035	0.899	0.815	0.992	0.008
canteen	P/N	Dis. from Reimei-kan	0.048	0.033	1.049	1.004	1.096	0.008
go up and down	N	Dis. from a pond	0.141	0.014	1.152	1.030	1.289	0.001
people	P/N	Dis. from Reimei-kan	0.060	0.013	1.062	1.013	1.113	0.006
foot of the stairs	N	Dis. from a pond	0.081	0.008	1.085	1.021	1.152	0.001
		Dis. from Reimei-kan	0.102	0.043	1.108	1.003	1.223	0.001
vacant	P	Dis. from a pond	0.122	0.014	1.130	1.025	1.246	0.002
near (from somewhere)	P/N	Dis. from Reimei-kan	0.064	0.006	1.067	1.019	1.117	0.002
bothersome to move	N	Dis. from a pond	0.084	0.033	1.087	1.007	1.174	0.007
		Dis. from Reimei-kan	0.144	0.048	1.155	1.001	1.333	0.007

This calculation is conducted by using SPSS statistics by IBM. For avoiding the collinearity problem, explanatory variables are categorized into groups A–D. Non-colored rows are the results reflecting a reason for choosing the plaza, and colored rows are those for choosing the sitting points. Significant variables are those with p values less than 0.05 (e.g., for the unit "friends," "Dis. from another place," and "Dis. from a pond" are significant variables according to groups A and D)

6 Modeling and Simulations of Human Behavior Semiosis

6.1 Modeling of Human Behavior Semiosis by Cellular Automata

6.1.1 Modeling of Environmental Sign Systems

Environmental sign systems are modeled by cellular automata as follows.

1. The site is simplified to a regular grid of cells (a grid cell: 25 cm $\times$ 25 cm; the modeled site: 68 cells $\times$ 108 cells) based on its floor plan (Figs. 7.2 and 7.5).
2. Each grid cell is an environmental sign system, as modeled in Sect. 3.2.
3. A set of environmental signs are arranged in the model of the sign system of step 2, as explained in Sect. 3.2. The environmental signs interpreted by person ($p_{n,t}$) are defined as $SS_{k,t}(p_{n,t})$ by the six functions shown in Fig. 7.5.

6.1.2 Modeling a Person

A person is modeled as an agent wherein each agent has a given situation. These situations are a set of functions, as explained in Sect. 3.2. A situation is defined by the five functions shown in Fig. 7.6. Only the significant units in Sect. 5 are set as the situations shown in Table 7.3, and the view area is defined following the concept of Hall's proxemics (Hall 1963).

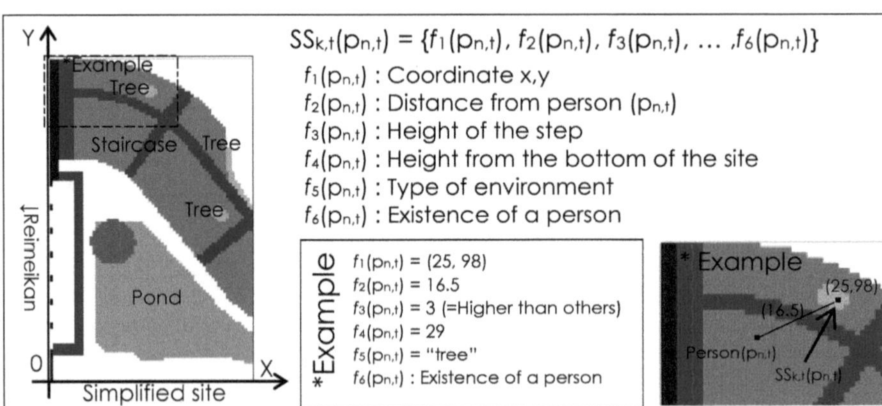

Fig. 7.5 Modeling of environmental sign systems

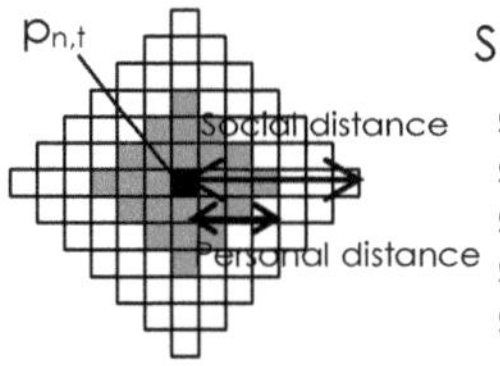

$$SI(p_{n,t}) = \{g_1(p_{n,t}), g_2(p_{n,t}), g_3(p_{n,t}), g_4(p_{n,t}), g_5(p_{n,t})\}$$

$g_1(p_{n,t})$: ID number
$g_2(p_{n,t})$: Coordinate x,y
$g_3(p_{n,t})$: "Unit"
$g_4(p_{n,t})$: Destination to stay
$g_5(p_{n,t})$: View area (social distance and personal distance)

Fig. 7.6 Modeling of a person

Table 7.3 Main significant units that are set according to the results of Sect. 5

(a) "Eat lunch": Interviewees whose responses contain this unit want to stop near wall C. All the distances to the cells within each agent's view from their present location when searching each stop point are calculated, and one of these cells whose distance is shorter than the average distance is selected as their stop point.
(b) "Kill time" or "go up and down": Interviewees whose responses contain this unit want to stop far from the center of the pond. Similar to "(a) eat lunch," one of the cells whose distance is nearer than the average distance within the interview subject's view is selected as their stop point.
(c) "Tree": Interviewees whose responses contain this unit want to stop near one of the 2 trees within their view. Similar to "(a) eat lunch," one of the cells whose distance is nearer than the average distance within the interview subject's view is selected as their stop point.
(d) "Crowded canteen": Interviewees whose responses contain this unit start around the canteen and want to stop at one of the cells whose height from the bottom is higher than the average.
(e) "Concert" or "event": Interviewees whose responses contain this unit can read all environmental signs regardless of their social distance in the site in order to search their favorite point where they think they can see the concert or event well.

6.1.3 Dissatisfaction Score

To determine the number of agents that cannot occupy their favorite points and the points at which they cannot stop, a dissatisfaction score is defined. If another agent is already present at an agent's favorite point, the agent is unable to stop at his/her favorite point and changes his/her destination. In such cases, a point is added to the dissatisfaction score. This score helps to consider the disposition of architectural elements that enable as many people as possible to stop where they like to stop.

6.1.4 Modeling of Human Behavior Semiosis

In this study, only the following simple semiosis is modeled and simulated.

1. Agents enter into the plaza.
2. Each agent starts to read the environmental sign systems within a defined social distance (20 cells[3]) and selects each favorite stop point as the destination depending on the situation.
3. Each agent starts to move to the favorite stop point and stops there.
4. If there is already another agent within the personal distance[3] from the selected stop point, the agent restarts the search and selects another stop point randomly and stops there; then, a point is added to the dissatisfaction score.

6.2 *Simulations of Human Behavior Semiosis by Cellular Automata*

6.2.1 Simulation Procedure

To evaluate conflicts among agents for occupying favorite places, simulations are performed.[4,5] One cycle of simulations consists of the following. (1) One agent is created every five steps in the site. Each agent has only one unit. (2) In total, 100 agents are created. (3) The number of occasions when an agent cannot stop at his/her favorite place is counted. This number is called the dissatisfaction score, as explained in Sect. 6.1.3. (4) When the discrete time reaches 100 steps, the simulation is stopped.

In total, one or two types of units are given to 100 agents per cycle of simulation and three simulation cycles are performed for every combination of units. Figure 7.7 illustrates a simulation cycle of an agent.

6.2.2 Results of Simulations

Tables 7.4 and 7.5 show the results of the simulations.The dissatisfaction score is high in all simulations of agents with the unit "crowded canteen," where sufficient space is not available for people coming from the canteen. The dissatisfaction score is also high in all simulations for the combination of units "crowded canteen" and "eat lunch." The agents whose unit is "eat lunch" stop near wall C, which is near

[3]Social distance and personal distance are tentatively defined in this study.

[4]Artisoc by Kozo Keikaku Engneering, Inc., is used as the simulator.

[5]The aim of the simulation is to evaluate the mechanism of the relationship between the meaning process and human behavior; therefore, the complete recreation of human behavior on the site is not a goal of this study.

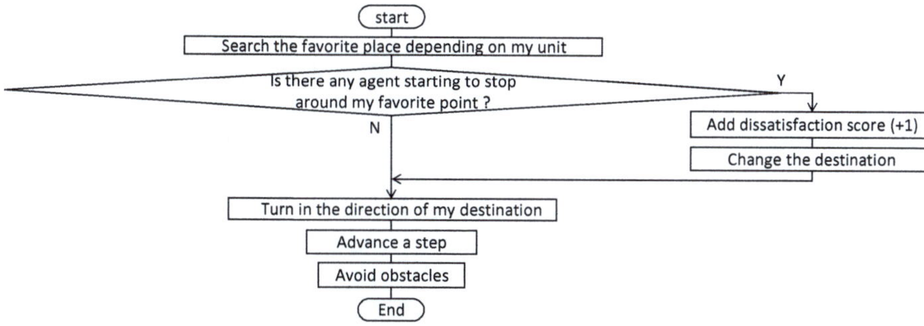

Fig. 7.7 The simulation flow of 1 step for each agent

Table 7.4 Mapping of Agents and the Points at which Dissatisfaction Scores are Added

Combination of Units	Eat lunch	People	Event, Concert	Tree	Tree	Staircase	Staircase	Crowded Canteen
	Crowded Canteen	Crowded Canteen	Event, Concert	Tree	Staircase	Staircase	Crowded Canteen	Bothersome to move
Disposition of persons	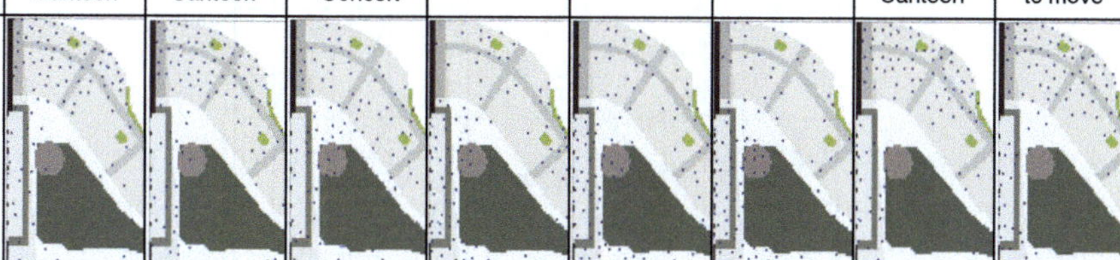							
Dissatisfaction Score	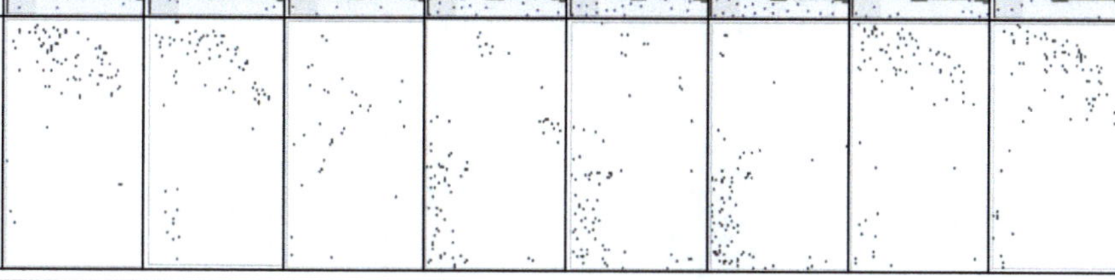							

the canteen. This explains that when people come to eat at the plaza, the area near the canteen tends to be crowded with people. These results appear to correlate with the interview results, where the unit "crowded canteen" has a negative impact on interview subjects. According to these results, in a sense, this section of the plaza is a part of the canteen. Therefore, it is important to provide space for people coming from the overcrowded canteen while redesigning the plaza. On the other hand, the dissatisfaction score is low in all simulations of agents with the unit "event" or the unit "concert"; these agents accept every type of situation.

Table 7.5 Dissatisfaction scores for each pair of units

	Eat Lunch	Kill time	People	Tree	Staircase	Vacant	Foot of the stairs	Near	Noon	Canteen	Crowded Canteen	Reimei-kan	Event, Concert	Bothersome to move
Eat Lunch	58	61	54	65	57	59	62	58	57	60	74	60	47	60
Kill time		69	62	66	58	66	63	65	57	62	66	53	44	63
People			61	69	62	74	62	64	62	62	75	61	42	65
Tree				72	75	66	58	59	62	61	69	61	47	65
Staircase					79	54	60	58	68	60	75	54	47	63
Vacant						60	52	64	52	53	79	59	43	58
Foot of the stairs							61	56	59	54	80	51	43	68
Near								65	58	64	64	57	49	62
Noon									59	62	75	55	51	67
Canteen										69	79	59	43	65
Crowded Canteen											E	80	65	72
Reimei-kan												65	43	64
Event, Concert													34	53
Bothersome to move														74

7 Conclusion

This research, while still in progress, demonstrates a computational method for understanding and estimating space design based on human behavior semiosis. Here, we have proposed a theoretical framework of human behavior semiosis through interviews and proposed functional cellular automaton models of human behavior semiosis. By using the proposed models, we can estimate the space design based on human behavior semiosis through interviews related to human behavior situations. Based on the proposed models and theoretical framework, a cellular automaton model is constructed. This is a preliminary model for applying a computational approach toward understanding the meaning processes people use for an architectural space. By using this approach to simulate the meaning process in an architectural space and a as means to estimate the benefits and disadvantages of a space, we can consider the manner in which we can design architectural spaces that can accommodate several types of human situations. Thus, this research provides a general framework for deriving a space design method based on human behavior semiosis.

References

Aliseda A (2000) Abduction as epistemic change: a Peircean model in artificial intelligence, abduction and induction. Appl Log Ser 18:45–58

Antonini G et al (2006) Discrete choice models of pedestrian walking behavior. Transp Res B Methodol 40(8):667–687, Elsevier

Dijkstra J et al (2000) A multiagent cellular automata system for visualising simulated pedestrian activity, theory and practical issues on Cellular Automata. In: Proceedings of the 4th international conference on cellular automata for research and industry. Springer, London, pp 29–36

Gomes A et al (2003) On a computational model of the Peircean semiosis. In: Proceedings of the international conference on integration of knowledge intensive multi-agent systems KIMAS'03. IEEE Press, Boston, pp 703–708

Gomes A et al (2005) Meaningful agents: a semiotic approach. In: Proceedings of the international conference on integration of knowledge intensive multi-agent systems KIMAS'05. IEEE Press, Waltham, pp 399–404

Hall ET (1963) A system for the notation of proxemic behavior. Am Anthropol N Ser 65(5):1003–1026

Katsuyama M et al (2005) Simulation of appreciation behaviors in a museum by multi-agent systems. In: Proceedings of the conference on computational engineering and science, vol 7(1). The Japan Society for Computational Engineering and Science, Tokyo, pp 57–60

Kiso K, Monnai T (2013) Modeling and simulations of human behavior semiosis based on protocol analysis -Study on semiosis of human behavior afforded by architecture and urban space (Part 3). J Archit Plann Environ Eng Trans AIJ 78(687):1003–1012, Architectural Institute of Japan

Peirce CS (1978) Collected papers of C.S. Peirce. The Belknap Press, *CP x,y: CP = Collected Papers of Charles Sanders Peirce, x = Volume, y = Paragraph

Pietarinen AV (2004) Multiagent systems and game theory-A Peircean manifesto. Int J Gen Syst 33(4):395–414, Taylor & Francis

Sezai Y (1960) Formation of Pragmatism and modern semiotics In: Studies in humanities and sciences of Nihon University, vol 2. Tokyo, pp 1–18 [publication in Japanese]
Vitruvius MP (1960) The ten books on architecture, Book 1, Chapter 1, Paragraph 3, translated by Morris Hicky Morgan (first published by Harvard University Press in 1914). Dover, New York, p 5
Yonemori Y (1995) Peirce's semiotics. Keiso Shobo, Tokyo [Publication in Japanese]

Chapter 8
Simulation Analysis of Vaccination Subsidy with ABM Approach

Jiao Xue, Manabu Ichikawa, and Hiroshi Deguchi

Abstract Vaccination subsidy is one of the major types of public health services. In order to evaluate the efficiency of the subsidy, this research carries out an Agent-Based Simulation approach. By leading strategies with different levels of subsidy into the social system and simulating the spread of influenza infection on a layout based on the daily life of every agent, the research constructs an immunization model depending on decision making of each agent. As a result, the model suggests that vaccination subsidy tend to take a positive role and gives decision support to assess the relative impact of public health services for influenza control.

Keywords Vaccination subsidy for seasonal influenza • Agent-based model • Decision making in immunization

1 Introduction

Vaccination is the most effective method of preventing and ameliorating morbidity from infectious disease. Immunization programs often organize subsidies and public relations in order to obtain high vaccination uptake rates and coverage. One example (Ohkusa 2010) of the great impact of vaccination subsidy is the control of varicella. From May 1st 2007 to March 31st 2008, Mitoyo and Kanonji cities in Kagawa prefecture began a varicella vaccination subsidy for residents under 5 years old. According to the subsidy, vaccination copayment would be cut by 4,500 yen (US$46.75) per dose. As a result, subsidy vaccination coverage at 1 year old rose from 8.0 to 17.2 % in Mitoyo and from 13.0 to 28.9 % in Kanonji.

J. Xue (✉)
Department of Computational Intelligence and Systems Science, Tokyo Institute of Technology, Tokyo, Japan
e-mail: xue11@cs.dis.titech.ac.jp

M. Ichikawa • H. Deguchi
Department of Computational Intelligence and Systems Science, Tokyo Institute of Technology, Yokohama, Kanagawa, Japan
e-mail: ichikawa@dis.titech.ac.jp; deguchi@dis.titech.ac.jp

Y. Nakai et al. (eds.), *Agent-Based Approaches in Economic and Social Complex Systems VIII*, Agent-Based Social Systems 13, DOI 10.1007/978-4-431-55236-9_8

In most of areas in the world, residents are not obligated to accept seasonal influenza vaccination. Some places have enforced a subsidy of influenza vaccination for special group of people.

Although a number of vaccine policies had met with success in increasing the supply and demand for vaccines, unbalanced supply and demand on vaccination market led to massive waste especially in recent years. For example, waste of 16.6 million doses in the value of 21.4 billion yen (US$223 million) was claimed in 2010 (Apital). To solve such problem, vaccination subsidy strives to provide income support to a group of susceptible population and contributes to the improvement of vaccination coverage by enhancing their immunization awareness. In this research, we suppose to prove available vaccine subsidy gives rise to increase in immunization rates, and then analyze the changes in willingness towards immunization of individual resulting from effectiveness of the subsidy.

2 Previous Studies and Association with This Research

In this research, we focus on risk and prevention transmission of seasonal influenza by increasing vaccination coverage and aim to simulate the application of influenza vaccination subsidy into reality and explain the change in immunization awareness.

2.1 Infectious Transmission Model Based on Virtual City System with ABM

We use existing precedent studies, which reflect the spread of influenza with ABM as a reference. In the previous research, Ichikawa and Deguchi (2010) constructed a virtual city model, which is a base tool for simulating social phenomena that occur in a city. A constructed virtual city system should include data for reflecting the individual properties, such as age, sex, household, etc. of each individual. Such data can be achieved from Geographic Information System (GIS) and E-STAT. To make virtual city model available in universal use, the spread of pandemic influenza virus as a social phenomenon was reflected in the virtual city by Kanatani et al. (2008) by implementing the pathological transition model in a virtual city, which was a computer representation of a real city in Japan.

These previous research provided us an available tool to simulate the infectious disease in a virtual city area. Though they also formulate a series of vaccination scenarios through programming aiming to find a proper way for disease control, immunization system and vaccination action of individual level is still awaiting solution. To improve this part, we consider constructing an immunization model as the internal of infection transmission system model to simulate the vaccination phenomenon.

2.2 Health Belief Model

As an agent-based model, we purpose to simulate the immunization behavior in the whole social system model and reflect the immunization psychology in an individual level. Here we consider Health Belief Model (HBM) (Becker 1974), which is one of social cognition models for explaining health behavior change and psychological model. It has been used for studying and promoting the uptake of health services.

Applying to the immunization case, HBM would involve an individuals' opinion about a certain disease and the behavior they encompass to the disease. In other words, individual's behavior to the fact, that he believes he will not get infectious and vaccination is just a waste of money, would likely lead to his contracting the disease.

Although HBM focus on the survey of the relationship among infectious risk, vaccination intention and lost evaluation expression in individual level, it cannot elucidate the connection of each factor in concrete terms. To conquer such weakness, here we improve this model by building up a mathematic description to deal with the connection of each vaccination awareness factor in concrete terms depending on decision-tree analysis and record the change of vaccination awareness in the social system by giving such parameters to each agent.

3 Model Detail

In this research, we deeply explore the part of vaccination and expand the immunization part from precedent studies. Since vaccination belongs to the transmission part, we build up an immunization model and add it into the virtual city system. The image of the model as a whole is shown in Fig. 8.1.

Considering every agent can decide an issue democratically, we design a series of actions and interactions of autonomous agents to reflect the transmission of disease in the population. In the immunization model, by classifying the main factors associated with immunization awareness into three categories in connection with immunization decision-making, we evaluate vaccination awareness of individual through considering initial attitude towards vaccination, risk cognition, and subjective norms in a comprehensive manner. Since vaccination subsidy plays an important role in affecting risk cognition of individual to different extents.

To verify our settings that are implementing the model with fidelity, we implement the immunization model into an existing virtual city system as a case study, and then design a series of scenarios by changing the subsidy. From this simulation result, we aim to suggest that vaccination subsidy is an effective infectious control policy in public health services field, and analyze the relationship between subsidy and its effect on vaccination decision-making. In this section, we will explain the model into detail.

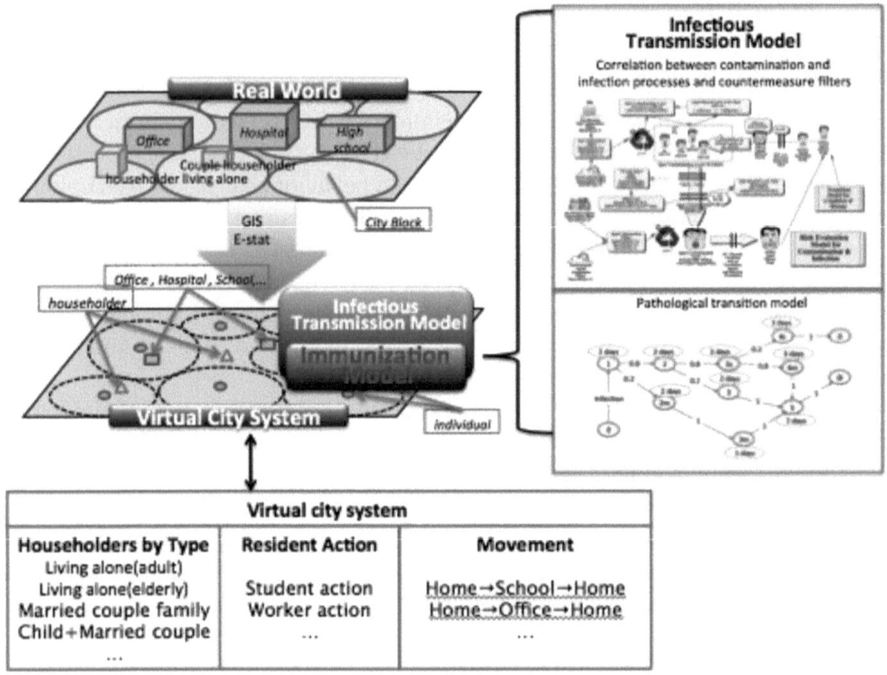

Fig. 8.1 The model structure as a whole

3.1 Influencing Factors of Immunization Awareness

Immunization awareness reflects the psychology of consciousness towards vaccination and controls inoculation action. They were a series of questionnaires trying to make an investigation into the deep reason of vaccination psychology. For example, according to the questionnaire (Japanese Immunization Awareness Investigation by Banyu Pharmaceutical Co. Ltd.) about the degree of recognition towards immunization, about 70 % respondents pointed out that the barrier of immunization was the high immunization fee. They also claimed that the subsidy was essential in the disease control. We classify several main factors associated with immunization awareness from questionnaires into three categories in connection with immunization decision-making.

1. ***The initial attitude toward vaccination:*** For the group of [immunization advocates], their attitudes toward vaccination cannot be altered by the financial pressure or affection risk from outside. Decision of such people is fixed at the beginning.
2. ***Financial cost of vaccine:*** The perceived financial costs of vaccination are directly influenced by a vaccination consumer's reimbursement regime. Since vaccination subsidy plays an important role in affecting risk cognition of

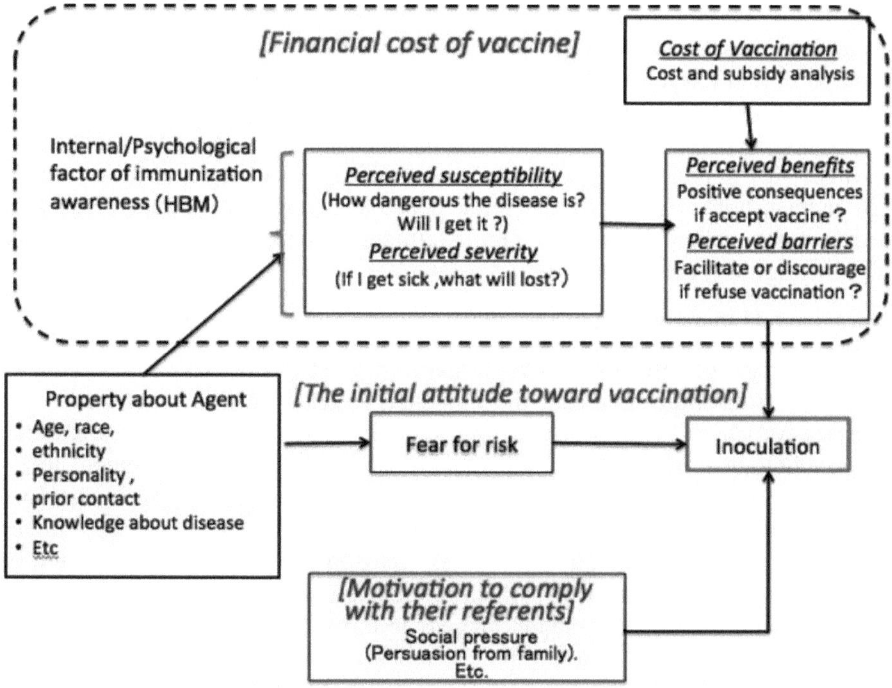

Fig. 8.2 Structure of immunization awareness

individual to different extents, the reason about [high cost of immunization] will be the point of inspection focus.

3. ***Motivation to comply with their referents:*** People are likely to be influenced by others' suggestion. Such phenomenon is called Subjective Norms in psychology.

Combining the three categories, we construct a fundamental structure to reflect the immunization awareness of each individual. Here we consider [The initial attitude toward vaccination] only associated with socio-demographic variables, which include age, health status, gender, profession, etc. Besides, in part of [Financial cost of vaccine], we try to investigate relationships between psychological variables towards financial cost and socio-demographic variables and vaccination intentions. Here we use conceptual frameworks: Health Belief Model (HBM) (Becker 1974); and underlying correlation studies. Finally as an exterior factor, [Motivation to comply with their referents] is also taken into consideration to some extent. The whole structure of the process of evaluating the immunization awareness is shown in Fig. 8.2.

Occasion1. [The initial attitude toward vaccination]

According to Fig. 8.2, at the initial step, each agent holds the initial fear towards immunization risk. Here we set a parameter to evaluate initial attitude towards vaccine and add it into the property of agent. Depending on this parameter, all agents' initial attitudes toward vaccine are divided in three kinds: [Positive], [Stubborn] and [Normal]. [Positive] choose immunization with no doubt. On the contrary, [Stubborn] reject immunization at all. Overall, only group of [Normal] are willing to accept the exterior influence from vaccination subsidy.

Since such initial attitudes are hard to be found the direct connection with the age, or household income, (we also found people with high salary refuse vaccination because of somehow aversion) the initial attitude is decided by probability, which we set the ratio at the beginning.

Occasion2. [Financial cost of vaccine]

In this part we refer to the classic psychological model HBM to construct a fundamental structure to reflect the influence of financial cost in immunization process. As I have mentioned it before, though HBM is a good tool to research the psychological model to explain vaccination behavior, it cannot elucidate the connection of each factor in concrete terms. To conquer such weakness, here we improve this model by building up a mathematic description to deal with the connection of each vaccination awareness factor in concrete terms depending on decision-tree (Fig. 8.3) analysis, which is used to risk assessment. By simulating the immunization decision-making process in a psychology level, we predict the effect of [Financial cost of vaccine] in our model.

The parameter in the decision tree is decided by the property of each agent and varied with the process of agent's movement. The involved parameter is shown as Tables 8.1 and 8.2.

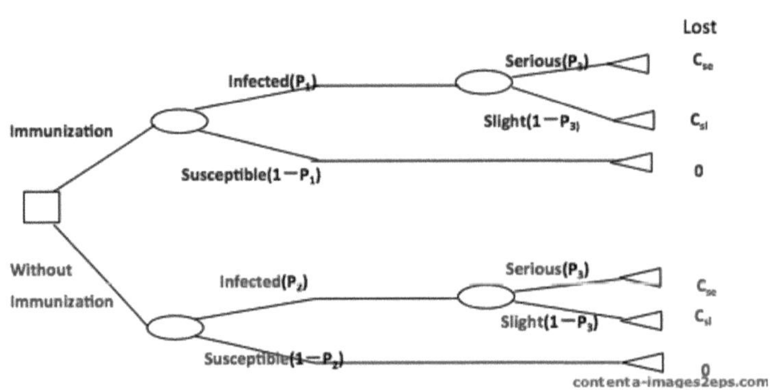

Fig. 8.3 Decision tree

Table 8.1 Parameters relating to "perceived susceptibility"

P1	Infection rate with immunization
P2	Infection rate without immunization
P3	Serious ill rate with immunization
1−P3	Slight ill rate with immunization

Table 8.2 Parameter relating to "perceived severity"

C_{se}	The risk and economic loss of seriously illness
C_{sl}	The risk and economic loss of slight illness

To calculate the parameters, let's review the existing precedent studies. Here P1 = P1[i](k,t), which is infection rate of Agent[i] at Spot[k] at time[t], if Agent[i] is susceptible. At the same time[t], there are another agents have been sick. For each agent, his P1 have direct relationship with sick agent number.

Considering infected agent in different disease stages results in different virus excretion scale, for example, infectious capacity in [morbidity] is less than in [infectious], we define *AES[i]* (Kanatani et al. 2008) (excretion scale of *Agent[i]*, the value depend on the disease condition of *[i]*). We also suppose that *Spot[k]* was polluted by the infected patient at *time[t]*. The pollution degree, which we called *SCL[k]* (Kanatani et al. 2008) (spot contamination level):

$$SCL\,[k]\,(t) = \frac{\sum_{i\ is\ infected\ agent\ in\ spot\ k} AES\,[i]}{Agent\ numbers\ in\ spot\ k}$$

Since *Spot[k]* has been polluted, the contamination level can give rise to the disease risk. Let infection rate without immunization is *P1* = *R*SCL[k](t)*, Here R is individual infection rate, which presents the probability of one infected agent transmitting the virus to another individual in 1 h.

Besides, considering the effectiveness of vaccination is not equal to 100 % in reality, we cannot guarantee all agents will prevent to infecting the disease if they inoculate. According to the result of immunology (Morbidity and Mortality Weekly Report (MMWR) 2007) in 2007, seasonal influenza infection rate of adult could be decreased by 70–90 %. For the elderly, (beyond 65 years old), numbers of patients could be decreased by 30–70 %. Especially, for the elderly who was staying in a social facility, the effectiveness of influenza was lower to 30–40 %. In this research, we take a random number K referring to the result of immunology, which reflect the objective efficiency of seasonal influenza vaccine into the model. Then we define: *P2* = *P1*K*. Value of P3 refers to the investigation report (IASR) from MHLW in 3th August 2011 13th December 2011.

Besides, the value of C_{se} and C_{sl} record the risk and economic loss of illness. As is known to all, getting sick will bring us numbers of trouble beyond the medical fees, economic loss should include all the risk and loss the patient will encounter such as the absence of job because of sickness. Especially, since the old over 65 year-old have a high risk to get another sickness accompany with influenza, the economic loss is considered to be the highest. To reduce the potential of loss, the vaccination subsidy for old play an essential role in immunization policy.

According to the decision tree, we calculate the loss expectation with vaccination and loss expectation without vaccination and finally, acquire expected payment of immunization. The equation is summarized as following:

- Loss expectation with vaccination: $E(vac) = P1P3C_{se} + P1(1 - P3)C_{sl}$
- Loss expectation without vaccination: $E(vac) = P2P3C_{se} + P2(1 - P3)C_{sl}$
- Expected payment of immunization: $C(pay) = E(nov) - E(vac)$.

Since we have achieved expected payment of immunization, the next step, we will use this value to evaluate [Perceived Barriers] and [Perceived Benefits]. Here we would like to introduce the price of vaccine C(vac) as a new parameter into the model. If the price is higher than expected payment of immunization, If $C(pay) > C(vac)$. Agent may care about the price obstacles in the way of adopting immunization and abandon to accept vaccine. In this case, price obstacles are the judgment of [Perceived Barriers]. On the contrary, if the price is lower than the potential economic loss, Immunization is absolutely a brilliant chance to prevent the loss of the money, which is the power of [Perceived Benefits]. Especially, [Cost of Vaccination] control the immunization awareness by adjusting the price of vaccine. To meet up with the efficiency of vaccination subsidy, here we let the subvention is C(sub). If $C(pay) > C(vac) - C(sub)$, Agent will accept vaccination. $C(sub) = C(vac)$ means vaccination is free.

Occasion3. [Motivation to comply with their referents]

[Motivation to comply with their referents] phenomenon can be explained as Subjective Norms, which is a psychological proper name refers to a combination of perceived expectations from relevant individuals or groups along with intentions to comply with these expectations. In other words, if referents in agent's social environment are vaccinated or recommend the vaccination, agent's behavioral intentions are likely to be influenced.

Here we introduce a threshold model. Each agent hold a threshold value (from 0 to 1) randomly at the initial step. If the ratio of inoculated agents, who are around the target agent, is higher than threshold value. The mind of target agent will be changed to choose inoculation.

3.2 *Flowchart of Decision Making Process*

For [Normal] agent, the decision making process is reflected as the Fig. 8.4.

4 Model Validation

To verify our model that incorporates implementation fidelity, we develop a certification plan, in which we imitate the real world for designing a hypothetical city and apply the immunization module into the Oshima Virtual City Model, which has been constructed by Ichikawa (Ichikawa and Deguchi 2010). The population is shown as Table 8.3. According to the statistic data, the numbers of elderly

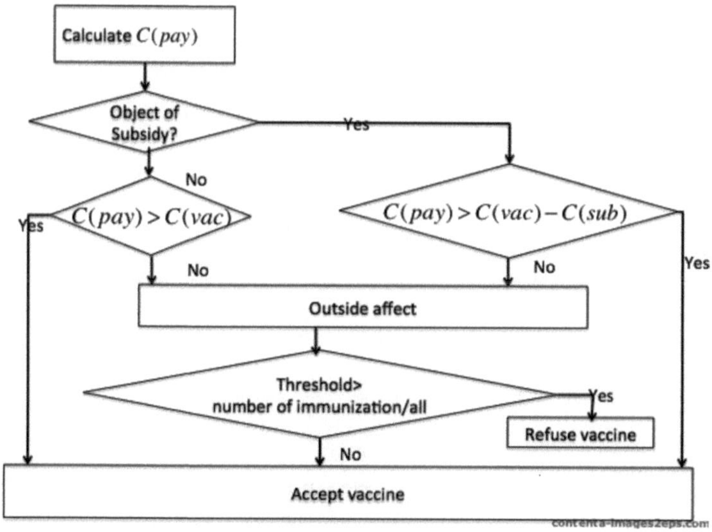

Fig. 8.4 Flowchart of decision making process

Table 8.3 Fundamental setting of the virtual city: population composition

Age bracket	Number
1–9	1,440
20–64	4,970
65	2,553

in this area hold a huge ratio. Since Oshima is enforcing the elderly subsidy in immunization system, the subsidy will take an important role with aging society with fewer children in the future.

We implement the same subsidy into the model, which provides the cheaper influenza vaccination for residents over 65 years old, and then calculate the effectiveness of existing vaccination subsidy with ABM approach. We also assume a series of condition including some extreme cases, which are so ideal that cannot be realized in the reality. Here we design four kinds of cases: (probability of [Positive] is 5 %, [Stubborn] is 18.5 %)

- ***Scenario 1***: No subsidy. Vaccine price is normal (3,600 yen)
- ***Scenario 2***: Subsidy for Child (primary school student and child in kindergarten). Vaccine price is changed from 3,600 yen to 1,000 yen with subsidy
- ***Scenario 3***: Subsidy for elderly (beyond 65 years old). Vaccination price is changed from 3,600 yen to 1,000 yen with subsidy
- ***Scenario 4***: Price = 0. All the residents enjoy free vaccine.

We simulate the 4 scenarios in the virtual city 10 times and calculate average infected number at every time step so that the efficiency of vaccination can be observed. The change of infection rate is shown as Fig. 8.5.

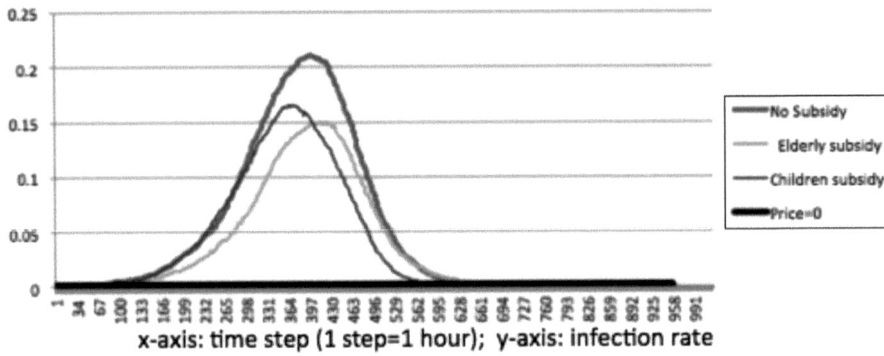

Fig. 8.5 Status of epidemic transmission with different subsidy scenarios

Table 8.4 Immunization rate in different scenarios

Age	1–19	20–64	65
No subsidy	41.59 %	31.21 %	53.97 %
Child subsidy	69.03 %	21.67 %	63.29 %
Elderly subsidy	43.54 %	28.01 %	74.54 %
Price = 0	93.33 %	92.78 %	84.22 %

It is the most obvious that different immunization rate results in infection rate varying in a big way, especially in the extreme scenarios. Comparing the scenario 1 with others, since there is no subsidy in this area, the epidemic rate is the highest one. On the contrary, the total subsidy of scenario 4 brings out extremely effective infectious control. Besides, subsidies for the different target group of people also have an influence on effect of epidemic disease control. The infection statuses result from the different immunization rate with different scenarios obviously. The immunization rate of each scenario is show as Table 8.4.

For one thing, comparing the scenario 2 and 3 with another scenarios, which carry out the subsidies, the immunization rate of target group raises sharply because of the subsidies. Especially, the immunization rate of the elderly in scenario 3 is about 1.40 times as large as the normal one in scenario 1. Since high immunization rate results in the decrease of infection rate, efficiency of subsidy is shown obviously.

For another, though vaccine is free in scenario 4, inoculation in all residents scale cannot be realized because that [Stubborn] exist to a considerable extent, and the most importantly, minority of agents seldom undertake risk to contact virus. For example, immunization rate of children is much less than the others'. Such results are the same as reality, though government in Japan provide mass influenza vaccination campaign for the children before 1994, the immunization rate could not be diffused to all.

Furthermore, the vaccination rates are likely to be affected with the upward of vaccination rate in another group of people. For instance, though the subsidy for child improves the immunization coverage in a whole, the vaccination rate of the elderly also increases accompanying with the progressive changes. On the contrary, subsidy for the elderly seldom affects the immunization rate of child. That is because the inoculation action decreases the infected risk for surrounding people so that their immunization awareness can be altered to some degree. And also Subject Norms phenomenon promotes the immunization awareness at the same time. All in all, agents in the system interact with each other, which result in efficiency diversity of subsidy.

Finally, referring to the status of epidemic transmission in Fig. 8.5; we conclude that the high immunization rate results in the decrease of infectious. Since the subsidy affects the immunization status, we can also claim that vaccination subsidy is powerful to control the transmission of disease. There is no doubt that the free vaccination cannot be applied into the reality. However, vaccination subsidy is able to govern the infection status infinitely approaching to the ideal case. Reasonable subsidy is available for increase in immunization rate as well as disease control.

5 Immunization Awareness Analysis in Individual Level

To explain the process changing in more detail, we randomly choose one of an agent, and record his action. We also make the process of immunization awareness changing visible. The agent we select has the following properties:

1. A student under 19 years old
2. He cannot enjoy subsidy, vaccination price = 3,600 yen
3. His family structure: Child + Married Couple
4. He is at school from 8:00 to 16:00 everyday
5. There are always 167–216 students in his school Between 8:00 and 16:00.

Change of his [Willing to Pay] is shown as Table 8.5

Before 10/9:00, since the number of [Willing to Pay] of this agent is always lower than 3,600 yen, the agent cannot get vaccination.

Table 8.5 Immunization awareness changing process

Time	Infected students number	Willing to pay
2/08:00	1	6.53 yen
4/08:00	2	8.75 yen
...	...	...
9/09:00	17	2774.24 yen
...	...	...
9/15:00	17	2774.24 yen
...	...	...
10/9:00	3,896.84 yen, vaccinated	

Moreover, according to the result, [Willing to Pay] increase as well as Number of Infected Student. The larger the infected number is, the higher [Willing to Pay] will be. Because, the increase rate of infection can stimulate the sense of impending crisis, so that [Willing to Pay] increase sharply.

6 Conclusion

We provide an agent-based method to deal with the evaluation of immunization awareness. By applying the method to a virtual city, we verify that influenza subsidy vaccination plays an important role in increase of immunization coverage. According to our model, the price of vaccine is of critical significance and operates the inoculation decision-making of people. That subsidy control the cost of vaccine so that adjust the vaccination rate has been proved in our simulation.

In the future, we plan to estimate the economic impact of immunization subsidy. Vaccine is viewed as a special commodity, and government can manage the price and the total number of supply. Considering limited vaccination resource and economic burden, government may do not need to provide the free vaccine for all. But government can control the consumption by enforce the vaccination subsidy. Since setting the vaccination subsidy is a pattern of investment, there is a trade-off relationship between the investment and possible immunization coverage change. Such investment can fulfill the balance with vaccination rate.

Acknowledgments My deepest gratitude goes foremost to foundation for the FOST (Fusion Of Science and Technology), thanks for their financial support.

References

Becker MH (1974) The health belief model and personal health behavior. Slack, Thorofare

Hideki Tanuma, Hiroshi Deguchi, Tetsuo Shimizu (2005) SOARS: spot oriented agent role simulator design and implementation (Springer Tokyo, 2005). In: Agent-based simulation: from modeling methodologies to real-world applications, vol 1, pp 1–15

Ichikawa M, Deguchi H (2010) Virtual city environment with life spaces for urban simulation, Joint agent workshop and symposium, October 2010. Proceedings of JAWS2010

Infectious Agents Surveillance Report (IASR) Infectious Disease Surveillance Center. 2011/2012, vol 32, pp 314–316

Japanese Immunization Awareness Investigation by Banyu Pharmaceutical co.ltd (2010) http://www.msd.co.jp/newsroom/banyu-archive/pdf/product/product_news_0520.pdf

Kanatani Y, Deguchi H, Saito T (2008) The project analysis and pandemic preparedness program against new type influenza. Oper Res 53(12):667–671

Morbidity and Mortalit Weekly Report (MMWR) (2007) Centers for Disease Control and Prevention (CDC) 56(50):1309–1336

Ohkusa Y (2010) Varicella vaccination policy subsidy evaluation. J Jpn Assoc Infect Dis 84(2):159–164

SOARS Project [Online]. Available: http://www.soars.jp. Accessed 15 Aug 2012

Chapter 9
Trust, Growth, and Inequality: An Agent-Based Model

Shu-Heng Chen and Bin-Tzong Chie

Abstract An agent-based model of the investment game is proposed to study the complex dynamics between trust, growth, and inequality with different underlying technologies. It is found that agents in this economy, through learning to trust and to be trustworthy, are able to coordinate themselves well in networking, which hence facilitates wealth creation. The excessive smoothness in economic growth is, therefore, prevalent in all simulations, and the underlying technologies can only determine the speed of growth and network formation. While the advancement of technology can ameliorate the inequality of wealth distribution, it also lowers the social mobility of the agents.

Keywords Investment game • Network game • Cohesiveness hypothesis • Clique • State-dependent multiplier • Logit distribution • NetLogo

1 Motivation and Literature Review

Recent empirical studies show that social trust is an important determinant of social prosperity and economic growth (Zak and Knack 2001; Beugelsdijk et al. 2004; Berggren et al. 2008; Dearmona and Grier 2009; Algan and Cahuc 2010).[1] In this paper, we build an agent-based model of trust and growth dynamics upon the existing literature on the laboratory experiments of investment games. In this section, we shall first review the origin of the investment game experiments.

[1] For a brief survey, see (Chen et al. 2014).

S.-H. Chen (✉)
AI-ECON Research Center, Department of Economics, National Chengchi University, Taipei, Taiwan
e-mail: chen.shuheng@gmail.com

B.-T. Chie
Department of Industrial Economics, Tamkang University, New Taipei City, Taiwan
e-mail: chie@mail.tku.edu.tw

Y. Nakai et al. (eds.), *Agent-Based Approaches in Economic and Social Complex Systems VIII*, Agent-Based Social Systems 13, DOI 10.1007/978-4-431-55236-9_9

Trust and reciprocity have been studied in experimental economics since Berg et al. (1995) published a paper reporting the results of the now deemed prototypical investment game. In this two-stage game, the two players are endowed with \$10 each. In stage 1 the first mover decides how much money to pass to an anonymous second mover. All money passed is tripled. In stage 2 the second mover decides how much to return to the first mover. In this original experiment, out of the 32 first movers, 30 sent a positive amount; only 2 sent 0. Out of the 28 second movers who received amounts greater than \$1, 12 returned \$0 or \$1, and 12 returned more than the amounts their paired players sent them. So, the results clearly departed from the Nash equilibrium outcome that would be reached by the perfectly rational and selfish players. This experiment has been replicated many times since then, and the results are, from a qualitative point of view, quite robust. It is now widely accepted that trust and reciprocity are fundamental aspects of human social behavior.

The rest of the paper is organized as follows. Section 2 gives the main body of the paper, i.e., the agent-based modeling of the investment game. To do that, we first extend the original two-person one-role-playing model into a multi-person two-role-playing model (Sect. 2.1). We then introduce the essence of the model, i.e., the *network cohesiveness hypothesis* and, by that, we modify the original constant multiplier as a state-dependent multiplier. The second part of the model deals with agents' behavior (Sect. 2.2). In this model, the agents' decisions involve networking, portfolio, and kickbacks. Following a discrete stochastic choice model (Luce 1959; McFadden 1974, 1990), the agents base all these three aspects of decisions on trust. Section 3 shows the simulation results, and is followed by the conclusion (Sect. 4).

2 Network-Based Investment Game

The original version of the investment game has three essences: two persons, the role (either trustor or trustee) played by each person, and a fixed multiplier. In our extended version, we consider N persons, each taking a dual role, and a state-dependent multiplier.

2.1 *The Model Sketch*

The network-based investment game is a hybridization of the *repeated investment games* and the *network games*. It is outlined as follows. N agents engage in a repeated investment game with T repetitions (T rounds). In each round, each agent has to make a two-stage decision: *networking* and *investment*.

1. (*Partner Selection*) In the first stage, which is called the *network formation stage* or the *partner selection stage*, the subject i ($i = 1, 2, \ldots, N$), acting as a *trustor*, has to decide whom he would like to choose to be his *trustees*, say

j ($j \neq i$). Denote this decision by δ_{ij}.

$$\delta_{ij} = \begin{cases} 1, & \text{if } i \text{ chooses } j, \\ 0, & \text{otherwise.} \end{cases} \tag{9.1}$$

A link between i and j is said to be formed only if either $\delta_{ij} = 1$ or $\delta_{ji} = 1$; that is, all links are *undirected*.

2. Based on the first-stage decisions of all agents, a network topology is determined by a set of links, g,

$$g = \{\overline{ij} : \delta_{ij} = 1 \text{ or } \delta_{ji} = 1, \ 1 \leq i < j \leq N\}. \tag{9.2}$$

The *neighbors* of agent i, denoted by N_i, are defined as follows:

$$N_i = \{j : \delta_{ij} = 1 \text{ or } \delta_{ji} = 1, \ j = 1, 2, \ldots, N \text{ and } j \neq i\}. \tag{9.3}$$

3. In the second stage, a standard investment game is implemented on each pair connected by a link $\overline{ij}$. This will separate agent i's neighbors into two sets: the trustees of i (to whom agent i will send money, $\delta_{ij} = 1$), denoted as $N_{i,S}$ and $N_{i,R}$, respectively. Obviously, $N_i = N_{i,S} \cap N_{i,R}$, but $N_{i,S} \cap N_{i,R}$ may be nonempty.
4. (*Investment*) Then, constrained by his/her endowment or wealth, agent i has to make an investment decision on each link, $k_{i,j}$ ($j \in N_{i,S}$), where he or she plays the role of a trustor ($\delta_{ij} = 1$).

$$\sum_{j \in N_{i,S}} k_{i,j} \leq K_i, \tag{9.4}$$

and send the money. In the meantime, agent i's trustors js ($j \in N_{i,R}$) also make their investment decisions on i and send the money to him. As to the investment decision per se or the determination of $k_{i,j}$, they will be discussed in Sect. 2.2.
5. (*Social Cohesiveness Hypothesis*) The investment on each $k_{i,j}$ will then be associated with a multiplier $\tau_{i,j}$, which depends on the network topology. This leads to the major novelty and key contribution of the paper. The *multiplier*, basically, is related to productivity. The idea is to fully acknowledge the significance of the network size or the network scale effect on productivity. A similar idea has been found in many places in the economic literature, such as the knowledge externality or spillover in endogenous growth theory, the agglomeration effect in economic geography (Fujita and Krugman 2004), and so on.

   In the investment game, all business relations are simply *dyadic*. The dyadic relation is not isolatedly placed; instead, it is embedded within a large network where many other dyadic relations co-exist. We first assume that the *cohesiveness* of this social embeddedness functions as an *infrastructure* which can be productivity-enhancing, and then use the size of the *clique* containing the specific dyadic relation as a measure of the size. A clique is a completely (fully) connected subnetwork of a given network. Let $g^*_{\overline{ij}}$ be the *clique* (the largest fully connected subnetwork) that $\overline{ij}$ or, equivalently, $\overline{ji}$ belongs to:

$$g^*_{\overline{ij}} = \left\{\left(i', j'\right) : \delta_{i'j'} + \delta_{j'i'} \neq 0, \text{ if } \delta_{uv} + \delta_{vu} \neq 0, \ u \in \{i, j\}, v \in \left\{i', j'\right\}\right\} \tag{9.5}$$

The *network cohesiveness* is then defined as the degree of $g^*_{\overline{ij}}$ and we denote it by $N_{\overline{ij}}$.

By Eq. (9.5), we are searching for the maximally fully connected subnetworks within which the business relationship between i and j is embedded. Intuitively. If the business between i and j is run within a well-connected society instead of a fragmentally isolated small group, then we expect a larger scale effect.

6. (*State-Dependent Multiplier*) Consequently, we assume that the multiplier $\tau_{i,j}$ is monotonically increasing in $N_{\overline{ij}}$. We now set the investment multiplier as a linear function of the cohesiveness of the social embeddedness of the partner relation (i, j), i.e.,

$$\tau_{i,j} = 1 + \alpha\left(\frac{N_{\overline{ij}}}{N}\right), \tag{9.6}$$

where α is a constant. Notice that when the cohesiveness comes to its maximum, i.e., $N_{\overline{ij}} = N$, $\tau_{i,j} = 1 + \alpha$. By setting $\alpha = 2$ and removing the scale effect characterized by $N_{\overline{ij}}/N$, we then have the usual setting of having a multiplier of three, frequently used in experimental economics. The production function and the total return received by the trustee is

$$y_{i,j} = \tau_{i,j} k_{i,j} \tag{9.7}$$

By Eq. (9.6), $\tau_{i,j} = \tau_{j,I}$; hence, $y_{j,i} = \tau_{j,i} k_{j,i}$.[2]

7. (*Kickbacks*) Then, as the usual second stage of the investment game, agent i has to make his/her decision on the share of the yield $y_{j,i}$ ($j \in N_{i,R}$) that he would like to return to his trustors j. We denote his/her own reserve by $y^i_{j,i}$ and hence his trustworthiness by $y^j_{j,i}$.

$$y^i_{j,i} + y^j_{j,i} = y_{j,i} \tag{9.8}$$

[2]This function (6) can be made more flexible to accommodate different hypotheses of network productivity; for the details, see (Chen et al. 2014).

In the meantime, he also receives money from his own trustees, $y^i_{i,j}(j \in N_{i,S})$. The details of the decision on kickbacks will be fully developed in Sect. 2.2.

8. This finishes one round of the network-based investment game. An end-result is the net income earned by agent i:

$$K_i\,(t+1) = K_i(t) + \sum_{j \in N_{i,S}} \left(y^i_{i,j}(t) - k_{i,j}(t)\right) + \sum_{j \in N_{i,R}} y^i_{j,i}(t). \tag{9.9}$$

9. We then go back to step (1). Each subject renews the network formation decisions, and they together form a (possibly) new network topology. The investment game, step (3) to (8), is then played within this renewed social network. It will be interesting to study what are the additional links that these subjects add or delete.
10. The cycle from step (1) to (8), as described in (9), will continue until T is achieved.

2.2 *Trust-Based Heuristics*

Section 2.1 provides a general description of the network-based investment game model. However, unlike most studies on the investment game, which involve human-subject experiments, this study is based on agent-based simulation. Hence, we need a separate section to address the behavioral aspects of the model. That is, we need to formulate the possible interesting behavior of artificial agents in this model, which, of course, can be further verified using the lab experiments. Based on the description in Sect. 2.1, there are three major behavioral aspects that need to be addressed, namely, decisions on *trustee selection* (Step 1), *investment and portfolios* (Step 4), and *kickbacks* (Step 7).

2.2.1 Trustee Selection

The initial question is how to characterize an appropriate set of alternatives for agents. We can make no restriction on the set of candidates, i.e., the agent can always consider every one in the society except himself $\{1, 2, \ldots, N\}\backslash\{i\}$; nonetheless, how many trustees can he choose at each run of the game? One obvious setting is as many as he wants. However, in considering all the transactions costs, such as communication, search and computation, it seems reasonable to assume that an incremental process exists for the upper limit of the number of trustees that an agent can choose. This upper limit is primarily restricted by the cost affordability of the agent. Here, without making these costs explicit, we indirectly assume that the affordability depends on the wealth of the agent, i.e., K_i. Hence, in a technical way, we assume that the additional number of trustees (links) is available if the wealth increases up to a certain threshold. For example, an agent's links may increase if he has positive growth of wealth, and vice versa.

$$l_{\max}(t) = \begin{cases} l_{\max}(t-1) + 1, \text{ if } \dot{K}_i(t) > 0, \text{ unless } l_{\max}(t-1) = N-1 \\ l_{\max}(t-1) - 1, \text{ if } \dot{K}_i(t) \le 0, \text{ unless } l_{\max}(t-1) = l_{\min} \end{cases} \tag{9.10}$$

where

$$\dot{K}_i(t) = \ln \frac{K_i(t)}{K_i(t-1)} \tag{9.11}$$

Note that Eq. (9.10) serves only as a beginning for many possible variants, but the idea is essentially the same: each agent starts with a minimum number of links, say, $l_{\min} = 1$, and gradually increases the number of links associated with his good investment performance, and vice versa. One can certainly consider different measures of investment performance, but we shall leave this issue for further study. The rule (10) leaves two possibilities for the agent to change at each point in time: either adding one link (if he has not come to the maximum) or deleting one link (if he has not come to the minimum). For the former case, he will choose one from those who were not his trustees in the last period, i.e., the set $\mathbf{S} - N_{i,S}(t-1)$; for the latter case, he will choose one from his last-period trustees, i.e., the set $N_{i,S}(t-1)$. Let us assume that for both cases, his main concern for this one-step change is *performance-based* or *trust-based*. We call this the *trust-based selection mechanism*, which basically says that the agent tends to add the most trustworthy agent and delete the least trustworthy agent. To do so, let us define the *effective rate* of return of the investment from agent i to j, measured in terms of its kickbacks, as

$$\kappa_{i,j}(t-1) = \begin{cases} \frac{y^i_{i,j}(t-1)}{k_{i,j}(t-1)}, & \text{if } k_{i,j}(t-1) > 0 \\ 0, & \text{if } k_{i,j}(t-1) = 0. \end{cases} \tag{9.12}$$

Then the frequently used logit distribution can be used to substantiate the trust-based selection mechanism as follows.

$$\text{Prob}\left(j \middle| j \in (\mathbf{S} - N_{i,S}(t-1))\right) = \frac{\exp\left(\lambda_1 k_{j,i}(t-1)\right)}{\sum_{j \in \mathbf{S} - N_{i,S}(t-1)} \exp\left(\lambda_1 k_{j,i}(t-1)\right)} \tag{9.13}$$

$$\text{Prob}\left(j \middle| j \in N_{i,S}(t-1)\right) = 1 - \frac{\exp\left(\lambda_1 \kappa_{j,i}(t-1)\right)}{\sum_{j \in \mathbf{S} - N_{i,S}(t-1)} \exp\left(\lambda_1 \kappa_{j,i}(t-1)\right)} \tag{9.14}$$

Equation (9.13) above applies to the situation where agent i can add links, whereas Eq. (9.14) applies to the situation where agent i needs to delete a link. By Eq. (9.13), agent i tends to favor more those agents who have trusted in him and invested in him, i.e., $j \in N_{i,R}(t-1)(k_{j,i}(t-1) > 0)$, than those who did not $j \notin N_{i,R}(t-1)(k_{j,i}(t-1) = 0)$. By Eq. (9.14), agent i will most likely cut off the investment to the agent who offers him the least favorable return rate, i.e., the lowest κ.

2.2.2 Investment and Portfolios

Once the new set of trustees ($N_{i,S}(t)$) is formed, the trustor has to decide the investment portfolio applied to them, i.e., how to distribute the total wealth, $K_i(t)$ over $N_{i,S}(t) \cup \{i\}$. We assume again that this decision will be *trust-based*. The idea is that agent i tends to invest a higher proportion of his wealth in those who look more promising or trustworthy, and less to the contrary. Technically, very similar to the decision on the trustee deletion (Eq. 9.14), let us assume that agent i will base his portfolio decision on the effective rate of return $\kappa_{i,j}(t-1)$. Those who reciprocated agent i handsomely in the previous period will be assigned a larger fund and vice versa. Then a trust-based portfolio manifested by the logit distribution is as follows:

$$w_{i,j}(t) = \frac{\exp\left(\lambda_2 \kappa_{i,j}(t-1)\right)}{\sum_{j \in N_{i,S}(t) \cup \{i\}} \exp\left(\lambda_2 \kappa_{i,j}(t-1)\right)}, \quad \forall j, j \in N_{i,S}(t) \cup \{i\} \tag{9.15}$$

where $w_{i,j}(t)$ is the proportion of the wealth to be invested in agent j; consequently,

$$k_{i,j}(t) = w_{i,j}(t) K_i(t). \tag{9.16}$$

Two remarks need to be made here. First, part of Eq. (9.15) is self-investment, i.e., $w_{i,i}(t)$.

$$w_{i,i}(t) = \frac{\exp\left(\lambda_2 \kappa_{i,i}(t-1)\right)}{\sum_{j \in N_{i,S}(t) \cup \{i\}} \exp\left(\lambda_2 \kappa_{i,j}(t-1)\right)} \tag{9.17}$$

Like the typical investment game, agent i can certainly hoard a proportion of the wealth for himself; however, based on the rule of the investment game, this capital will have no productivity and its effective rate of return is always 1, $\kappa_{i,i}(t) = 1, \forall t$. Therefore, by Eq. (9.15), hoarding becomes more favorable when an agent suffers general losses on his investment, namely, $\kappa_{i,j}(t-1) < 1$ for most j. Of course, when that happens, the social trustworthiness observed by agent i is lower and thus he may take a more cautionary step in external investment.

Second, for the new trustee ($j \notin N_{i,S}(t-1)$), $\kappa_{i,j}(t-1)$ is not available. We shall then assume that it is $\kappa_{i,0}$, which can be taken as a parameter of agent i's general trust in the case of *strangers*. The culture or the personality which tends to have little trust for strangers, being afraid that they will take all the money away, has a lower κ_0 or zero, and serves as the extreme. The culture or the personality which tends to be more friendly toward strangers has a relatively higher κ_0. The introduction of this parameter then leaves us room to examine how this initial trust may impact the later network formation.

2.2.3 Kickbacks

Finally, we consider the decision related to kickbacks. When investing in others, agent i also plays the role of a trustee and receives money from others $k_{j,i}(j \in N_{i,R})$. In the end, the total revenues generated by these investments are

$$Y_i(t) = \sum_{j \in N_{i,R}(t)} y_{j,i}(t) = \sum_{j \in N_{i,R}(t)} \tau_{j,i}(t) k_{j,i}(t) \tag{9.18}$$

Let us assume that the total fund available to be distributed over agent i himself and all of his trustors is simply this sum, $Y_i(t)$. That is, agent i will not make an additional contribution from his *private* wealth to this distribution.[3] Furthermore, we assume that the decision regarding kickbacks is also *trust-based*. We assume that agent i tends to reciprocate more to those who *seem* to have a higher degree of trust in him and less to those who *seem* to have less. This subjective judgement is determined by the received size of investment, $k_{j,i}(t)$.[4] Hence, a straightforward application of the logit model leads to the proportions of kickbacks allocated to each trustor of agent i.

$$\omega_{i,j}(t) = \frac{\exp\left(\lambda_3 k_{i,j}(t)\right)}{\sum_{j \in N_{i,R}(t) \cup \{i\}} \exp\left(\lambda_3 k_{i,j}(t)\right)}, \forall j, j \in N_{i,R}(t) \cup \{i\}, \tag{9.19}$$

where $\omega_{i,j}(t)$ is the proportion of $Y_i(t)$ that will be returned to agent j as kickbacks. Hence,

$$y^j_{j,i}(t) = \omega_{i,j}(t) Y_i(t). \tag{9.20}$$

---

[3]For either altruistic reasons or other strategic reasons, violations of this assumption are possible, but in this paper we shall refrain from the more thoughtful design.

[4]Here, we use the term "seeming" or "subjective", because agent i cannot have a direct observation of agent j's portfolio,

$$\left\{w_{j,l}(t)\right\}_{l \in N_{j,S}(t) \cup \{j\}},$$

to estimate his proportion in agent j's portfolio. For example, $k_{j,i}(t)$ can be large in absolute size, but relatively small in terms of its weight in the portfolio. In this case, agent j may not trust agent i as much as may be apparent.

Note that part of Eq. (9.19) is the reserve that agent i keeps for himself. In fact,

$$\omega_{i,i}(t) = \frac{\exp\left(\lambda_3 k_{i,i}(t)\right)}{\sum_{j \in N_{i,R}(t) \cup \{i\}} \exp\left(\lambda_3 k_{i,j}(t)\right)}. \tag{9.21}$$

By Eq. (9.16) and (9.17), the self-investment is

$$k_{i,i}(t) = w_{i,i}(t) K_i(t), \tag{9.22}$$

and the “retained earnings” are

$$\sum_{j \in N_{i,R}(t)} y^i_{j,i}(t) = \omega_{i,i}(t) Y_i(t). \tag{9.23}$$

Then the behavioral interpretation of Eq. (9.21) is that an agent who has a large hoarding size, kept as “retained earnings” for himself, tends to be more selfish. These people are, therefore, less social and less cooperative. The parameter which dictates this behavior is κ_0, as introduced in Sect. 2.2.2.

3 Simulation

The above agent-based model of the investment game is written using *NetLogo*, version 5.0.5, developed by one of our co-authors, Bin-Tzong Chie. The model code can be found at http://www.openabm.org/model/3915/.

3.1 Simulation Goals

To run the model, we first decide the main goal of our simulations, i.e., what we would like to know. In this paper, the simulation goal is as follows:

1. First, regarding *wealth creation*, we want to know whether agents are able to self-coordinate to fully explore the network productivity by attaining the largest possible clique and hence becoming the most productive economy. If such self-coordination is possible, how fast can it happen? If not, how far is it away from the ideal state? Specifically, we denote the full multiplier $1 + \alpha$ by τ^* and the realized τ time t by τ_t. Then the convergence behavior of τ_t toward τ^* becomes what interest us.
2. Second, we are interested in knowing the effect on wealth distribution when a society is becoming richer. Will the rich get richer and the poor get poorer during the development process?

Table 9.1 Tableau of control parameters

Parameter	Interpretation	Value
N	Number of agents	100
$K(0)$	Initial capital	1.00
α	Multiplier	0.2, 0.5, 0.8, 1.1
$l_{\min}$	Initial linkage number	1
λ_1	Trustee selection	0.04
λ_2	Portfolio	0.04
λ_3	Kickbacks	0.04
κ_0	Initial trust for strangers	2
T	Number of iterations	100

3.2 Parameter Settings

There are two kinds of parameters to be set before running the model: one is related to technology, i.e., α, and the other is related to behavior, i.e., the decision heuristics (stochastic choice). In this paper, we mainly focus on the former, and consider four different values of it, i.e., $\alpha = 0.2$, 0.5, 0.8, and 1.1. For the role of the behavioral parameters, such as κ_0 and λ, the interested reader is referred to (Chen et al. 2014). The parameter setting is summarized in Table 9.1. We run 30 trials for each set of parameters (mainly, different values of α), and the result presented below is based on the summary statistics of these 30 trials.

3.3 Simulation Results

Our simulation with a network of 100 agents shows:

1. The development of social capital depends on the involved technology. A higher α, as expected, leads to a well-connected society, rich in social capital (Fig. 9.1, left panel; also see Table 9.2, the row "Social Capital").
2. The development of social capital further helps the growth of wealth of individuals, and they are coupled together (Fig. 9.1, right panel; Table 9.2, the row "Physical Capital").
3. Wealth distribution measured by the Gini index declines with α. Figure 9.2 shows the shape of Lorenz curves with respect to different α (also shown in Table 9.2, the row "Gini Index"). The figures indicate that the richer the society is, the more equal the distribution is. Despite the more equal wealth distribution, the social status of agents, however, becomes less mobile in a richer society. To see this, we develop a rank statistic for each individual by first tracing his rank in terms of his physical and social capital throughout his life span. Figure 9.3 provides one example of an individual's rank over the time course. In fact, the plot of the time course of this chosen individual shows the high mobility of his social status:

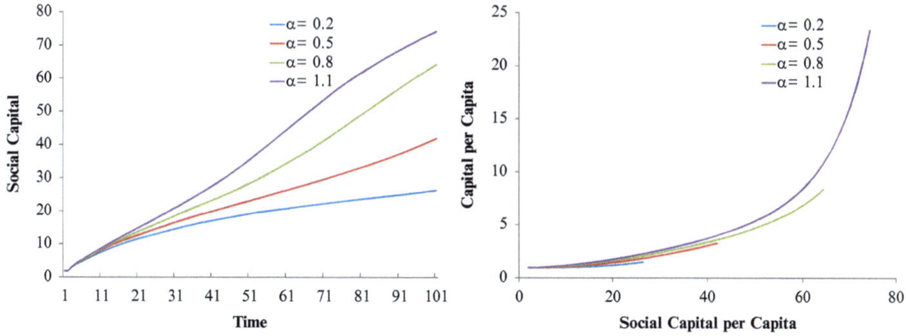

Fig. 9.1 Technology and the growth of social capital and physical capital. The *left panel* shows the growth of social capital under the different technology levels characterized by the parameter α, whereas the right panel shows the relationship between social capital per capita and physical capital per capita over time, with respect to different values of α. Physical capital is defined as the asset that the agent has, i.e., K_i; social capital is defined as the number of connections that the agent has, i.e., the cardinality of N_i or simply $\#(N_i)$

Table 9.2 Summary statistics

α	0.2	0.5	0.8	1.1
κ	91.49	96.98	102.26	104.25
	(1.34)	(1.41)	(0.81)	(0.38)
Physical capital (K)	1.55	3.3	8.27	23.56
	(0.01)	(0.07)	(0.37)	(2.02)
Maximum clique	3.82	4.42	5.26	5.83
	(0.08)	(0.17)	(0.34)	(0.45)
Gini index	0.34	0.32	0.19	0.11
	(0.01)	(0.01)	(0.01)	(0.01)
Social capital	27.71	43.56	65.37	75.52
	(0.67)	(1.34)	(1.40)	(0.91)
cc	0.33	0.48	0.66	0.75
	(0.01)	(0.02)	(0.01)	(0.01)
apl	1.74	1.58	1.36	1.25
	(0.01)	(0.01)	(0.01)	(0.01)

The summary statistics show the corresponding indicators of the termination period ($T = 100$), averaged over 30 runs and inside the parentheses are the respective standard deviations. If the indicator itself is a kind of average, then the average is taken over all 100 agents. Hence, from the top to the bottom, κ is the average gross return on investment (average taken over 100 agents); K, the average physical capital; maximum clique, the extent of the largest fully connected network; *Gini index*, an inequality measure defined as the area above the Lorenz curve but below the 45° line; *social capital*, the average number of connections; *cc*, the average cluster coefficient; *apl*, the average path length

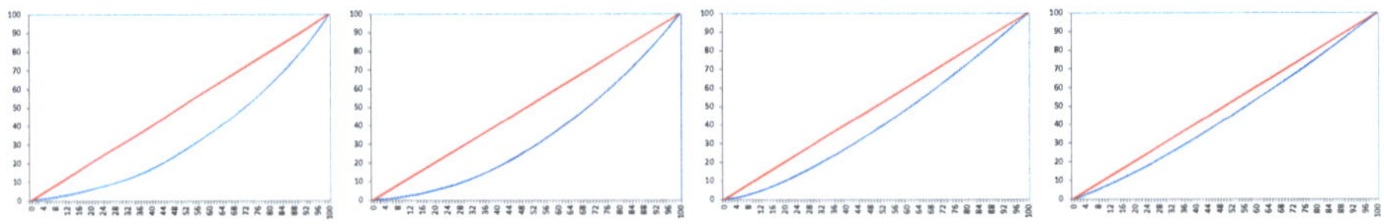

Fig. 9.2 Lorenz curve. From *left to right*, the four Lorenz curves correspond to the case of α being equal to 0.2 (*leftmost*), 0.5 (*middle left*), 0.8 (*middle right*), and 1.1 (*right most*)

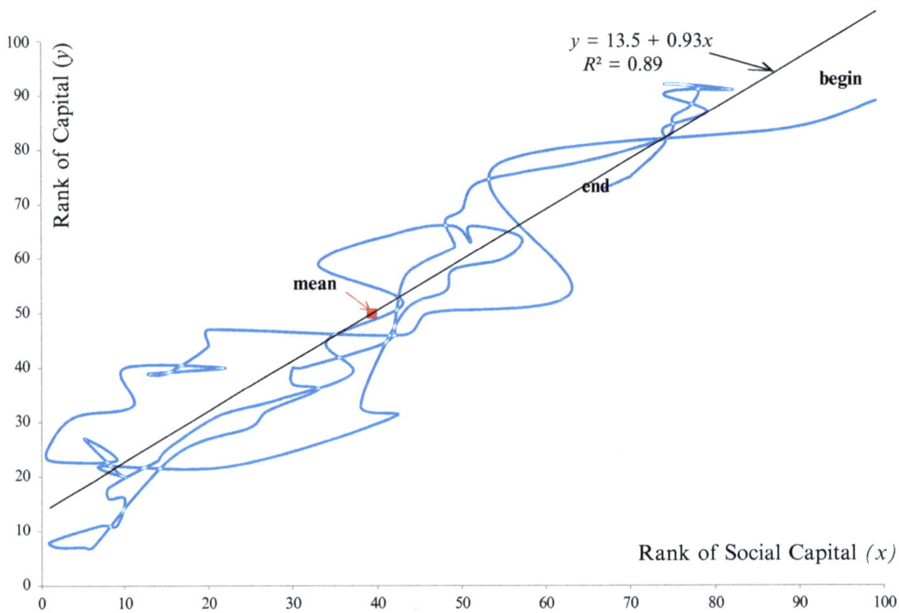

Fig. 9.3 Social mobility: a representative individual, the ranks of his capital and social capital over the entire time course

he was at the top, then slipped down to the bottom, then came back, but slipped down again to another bottom, and finally came back all the way to the top.

We then take the average of the ranks over each individual's life span. Figure 9.4 demonstrates the rank distribution of both social capital and physical capital under the different values of α. If the high-status agents remain high, and vice versa, then we may expect the distribution to be closer to a uniform distribution ranging from 1 to 100, but obviously this is not the case. The social status mobility is much higher as compared to the one represented by the uniform distribution. However, in the richest society ($\alpha = 1.1$), we start seeing that some richest agents can remain in that position permanently, a phenomenon which does not exist for the less rich society (a society with smaller value of α). In addition, the medium of the rank distribution begins to fall further below 50 when α becomes larger.

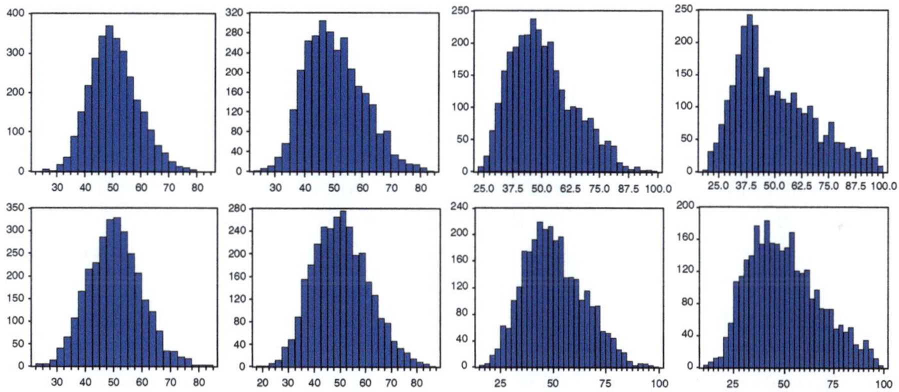

Fig. 9.4 Rank statistics: capital and social capital. The rank distribution of the capital (*upper panel*) and the rank distribution of the social capital (*lower panel*). From the left to the right is the distribution corresponding to $\alpha = 0.2$, 0.5, 0.8, and 1.1, respectively

4. Although the clique size increases with α, possibly due to our rather conservative range of α, all societies have a rather primitive structure with only a small clique being formed (Table 9.2, the row "Maximum Clique"). However, the trend of both the cluster coefficient and the average path length is quite evident (Table 9.2, the rows "cc" and "apl"). Hence, a longer running time may be required before we see the formation of a large clique.
5. Finally, it is interesting to notice that the investment return is negative for most agents when α is relatively small. An average κ of less than 100 % indicates that agents did not even get their fair shares back (Table 9.2, the row "κ"). With this negative investment return, two questions arise. First, how could people generally get richer and richer? Second, why did they still invest? The answer to the first question is that they got rich by receiving investment from others through the productivity-related multiplier. The result show that even though the investment return can be negative, so long as people mutually trust each other and invest in each other, the agglomeration effect can dominate the deficiencies in kickbacks. Here, trust is built not only upon returns, but also upon the investment reciprocity. *This is essentially the unique feature of this network-based economy, showing how trust alone can beef up the economy*. Nonetheless, this strong, mutual investment is mainly a result of Eq. (9.10), which says that agents tend to find new partners (add links) as long as they are not financially constrained. Because of this *extroversive* personality, agents will always invest even though the received return is negative. Hence, in future work, some modifications and relaxations should be considered for the society with a mixture of extroversive and introversive agents. It would be also useful to conduct economic experiments to see whether there is any difference between extroversive and introversive people in their networking behavior.

4 Conclusions and Further Work

In this paper, we setup a baseline version of an agent-based model of multi-person investment games, which serves as the canonical theoretical model to provide a plausible trust mechanism in wealth creation and distribution. Under the chosen behavioral heuristics and parameters, we can generate a smooth growth pattern and the wealth distribution along the growth line. Altogether, they not only show how the underlying technology characterized by α can matter for the speed of the accumulation of both physical capital and social capital, but also show that they can impact wealth distribution, both in terms of the Gini index and social mobility. Despite its simplicity, this baseline model provides us with an avenue into more realistic explorations of the complex intertwining relationship between trust and growth.

Acknowledgment The authors are grateful to the two anonymous referees for their comments and suggestions. The NSC grant NSC 101-2410-H-004-010-MY2 is also gratefully acknowledged. The remaining errors are solely the responsibility of the authors.

References

Algan Y, Cahuc P (2010) Inherited trust and growth. Am Econ Rev 100(5):2060–2092
Berg J, Dickhaut J, McCabe K (1995) Trust, reciprocity, and social history. Games Econ Behav 10:122–142
Berggren N, Elinder M, Jordahl H (2008) Trust and growth: a shaky relationship. Empir Econ 35(2):251–274
Beugelsdijk S, de Groot H, van Schaik A (2004) Trust and economic growth: a robustness analysis. Oxf Econ Pap 56:118–134
Chen S-H, Chie B-T, Zhang T (2014) Network-based trust games: an agent-based model. Journal of Artificial Societies and Social Simulation. Forthcoming
Dearmona J, Grier K (2009) Trust and development. J Econ Behav Organ 71:210–220
Fujita M, Krugman P (2004) The new economic geography: past, present and the future. Pap Reg Sci 83:139–164
Luce D (1959) Individual choice behavior: a theoretical analysis. Wiley, New York
McFadden D (1974) Conditional logit analysis of qualitative choice behavior. In: Zarembka P (ed) Frontiers of econometrics. Academic, New York
McFadden D (1990) Economic choices. Am Econ Rev 91(3):351–378
Zak P, Knack S (2001) Trust and growth. Econ J 111:295–321

Part III
Management and Business

Chapter 10
Exploring Optimal Wage Incentive System Using ABS

Isamu Okada and Ichiro Takahashi

Abstract Players are motivated by social norms and morale to exert extra efforts in a work place with high morale. However, we often observe that the initially high performance of an organization gradually declines. In order to seek for an optimal wage incentive system, we have constructed an agent-based model with a small group of heterogeneous or homogeneous workers. The model has the following features: players' behavior is subject to random shocks; inertia effect is introduced; and players are rewarded on the basis of their performances. The virtual experiment demonstrates that an organization, consisting of homogenous players, is more viable against the erosion than that with heterogeneous players, and that an organization with homogenous players is far more vulnerable to the erosion than that with heterogeneous players when subject to random shocks. Interestingly, an organization with heterogeneous agents can enjoy high morale among players that allows them to maintain high performance. We also show that the reward incentive is remarkably effective in any organization and it is particularly powerful in homogenous organizations. We have compared the two personnel rating systems: one based upon the level of performance relative to other workers' contemporaneous ones and the other upon her own past performance. In inducing higher performance of the workers, the latter system excels the former for the heterogeneous organization, whereas the former system will outperform for the homogeneous one.

Keywords Morale • Wage • Organizational structure • Agent-based simulation

1 Introduction

Since it is definitely important for managers of firms to seek an optimal wage incentive system, many researchers have been trying to analyze the system. Companies continue to place greater emphasis on the role of teams and work groups in an

---

I. Okada (✉) • I. Takahashi
Department of Business Administration, Soka University, Hachioji, Tokyo, Japan
e-mail: okada@soka.ac.jp

Y. Nakai et al. (eds.), *Agent-Based Approaches in Economic and Social Complex Systems VIII*, Agent-Based Social Systems 13, DOI 10.1007/978-4-431-55236-9_10

effort to design highly participative workplace (Ross et al. 1992) and to encourage employees to become mutually accountable (Heneman and Hippel 1995; Colquitt et al. 2002). The continued popularity of work teams urges corporate managers to motivate employees working in group settings to improve group-level performance by appropriately compensating them. To support this trend, pay to employees tends to be linked with performance of the team. This attempt is successful over all (Scott et al. 2002). Employee morale influences both quantity and quality of work, thus having a significant impact on business performance. Based on the results of 2.5 million employee surveys taken since 1994, Sirota et al. (2006) observed that many of our clients have been notable for their long-term success. They share one thing: the morale of their workers, as measured in our surveys, is much higher than most other companies. Hence, it is crucially essential for all socio-economic organizations to keep employee morale high.

Why does the norm or morale in a socioeconomic organization gradually decline over time? Constructing a multi-player version of prisoner's dilemma game Kandori (2003) provides an ingenious explanation. In his model, players are motivated by psychological factors such as norms and morale in such a way that each player suffers from negative psychological cost if his or her effort level falls short of the accepted one. The strength of the psychological cost depends on how closely players uphold the norms and the standard. Workers tend to be lazy if their colleagues do not work hard. The players' performance is subject to perpetual random shocks. By mathematically deriving the set of long-run stochastically stable states, Kandori (2003) shows that "a gradual erosion of morale and norms results through the interplay of material incentives and psychological factors, under perpetual random shocks."

By constructing an agent based model with players of heterogeneity in ability and psychological tendency, this paper attempts to examine when norms and morale are sustained and when they are subject to gradual erosion. We shall also show how effectively one can prevent their erosion. We generalize Kandori's model in several directions: (1) somewhat unnatural random shocks are replaced by standard ones; (2) the players are heterogeneous in ability and psychological attributes; (3) they are inclined to take the same actions as those in the previous period, which is referred as an inertia effect; (4) reward and punishment are differentiated depending on the ranking of players' performance.

Our agent based simulation shows that penalizing the least productive workers help an organization maintain high level of morale. We also demonstrate that segmentalizing an organization into small homogeneous groups enhances binding power of morale, which results in high performance of the organization.

2 Model

Under competitive conditions, workers are paid the value of their marginal products. If monitoring the productivity is not costly, one may think that the optimal wage should be based on individual performance (Katz 1986). Player i achieves performance x_i according to $x_i = e_i + u_i$ where $e_i \in \{0, 1, 2, \cdots, L\}$ denotes the level of effort and u_i is a random component (white noise) drawn out of a discrete version of uniform distribution over $\{\pm M, \pm (M-1), \cdots, 0\}$. For future reference, we call M the size of cognitive error. Player i's payoff is given by

$$u_i = \sum_{j=1}^{N} x_j (t) - c\left(e_j (t)\right) - k (t) \left[m (t) - x_j (t)\right]_+$$

where $c(\cdot)$ is the cost function of effort, $m(t) = \text{median}\{x_1(t-1), x_2(t-1), \cdots, x_N(t-1)\}$ represents a norm among workers. $[x]_+$ denotes $\max\{0, x\}$. We specify the cost function as follows: $c(e_i) = \alpha e_i + {e_i}^2/L + \beta(e_i(t) - e_i(t-1))^2$ where $\alpha > 0$. Parameter α represents the ability of each player and Parameter β represents one's inertia effect which gives some "stickiness" to the effort level the players choose. $k(t)$ is defined as $k(t) = K\left(\sum_{j=1}^{N}\left[m(t) - x_j(t-1)\right]_+\right)$ where $K(\cdot)$ is a non-negative decreasing function. We specify that $K(Z) = k_0(Z - k_1)^p$, where $k_o = L(N-1)/2$, and $k_1 = \gamma/{k_1}^p$. Parameter γ represents the strength of a player's psychological tendency with which she abides by the social norm. Warm-glow giving is an economic concept developed by Andreoni (1990) that attempts to explain impure altruism. Instead of being motivated solely by an interest in the welfare of the recipients of their largesse, "warm-glow givers" also receive utility from the act of giving itself and thus have an egoistic motivation for donating. This egoistic motivation may come from the boost to their self-esteem that they get from thinking of themselves as selfless and socially responsible, and/or from other people's recognition of their philanthropy. Moreover, Dorfman and Stephan (1984) showed experimentally that organizational performance increases if the group cohesiveness and their binding power are strong.

Consider N-player tournaments in which the rules of the game specify a fixed price of W_r dollars to the winners and a penalty of W_p dollars to the losers. Based on the performance profile, the winners of the contest are determined by the largest x. Specifically, top ε% performers get extra W_r dollars while the bottom ε% performers must pay W_p dollars as a penalty.

We consider two types of personnel rating systems whose assessment determines the amount of reward or penalty: Group and Individual Rating Systems. Under the Group Rating System (GRS), top ε_t % performers get extra W dollars whereas the bottom ε_b% workers must pay penalty of W dollars. Let Y_i^G denote this (possibly negative) prize that Worker i receives. Formerly, order workers' performances according to their sizes such that $x_{(1)} \leq x_{(2)} \leq \cdots \leq x_{(N)}$. Then, for a given GRS $(W, \varepsilon_t, \varepsilon_b)$,

$$Y_i^G\left(\mathbf{x}(t)\,\middle|\,W,\ \varepsilon_t, \varepsilon_b\right) = \begin{cases} W & \text{if } x_i \geq x_{\left(\left[N\left(1-\frac{\varepsilon_t}{100}\right)+1\right]\right)} \\ -W & \text{if } x_i \leq x_{\left(\left[N\frac{\varepsilon_b}{100}\right]\right)} \\ 0 & \text{otherwise.} \end{cases}$$

where [ ] denotes Gauss' symbol.

Under the Individual Rating System (IRS), an individual worker is compared with her past performance. She gets extra W dollars if her performance improves by more than or equal to one unit from the last period while she must pay the same amount as penalty if it worsens by D units or more.

With IRS (W, D),

$$Y_i^I\left(x(t), x_i(t-1)\middle|D\right) = \begin{cases} W & \text{if } x_i(t) \geq x_i(t-1)+1 \\ -W & \text{if } x_i(t) \leq x_i(t-1)-D \\ 0 & \text{otherwise.} \end{cases}$$

We assume that each worker expects the other workers to select the same levels of effort as their observed performances. Moreover, the workers contemplate only the present payoff to each choice, and not the expected stream of future payoffs. These assumptions together with $E[x_i(t)]=e_i(t)$ simplifies the maximization problem of Worker i's expected payoff:

$$\max_{e_i(t)}\left(\sum_{j\neq i} x_j(t-1) + e_i(t) - c(e_i(t)) - k(t)\left[m(t)-e_i(t)\right]_+ + Y(t)\right),$$

where Y (t) is either $E[Y_i^G|e_i(t)]$ or $E[Y_i^I|e_i(t)]$.

3 Simulation

The parameter values are set as follows: Periods of simulation = 100, Maximum level of 3 of effort = 0.8 L, and the power associated with K (·), (p) = 32.

We assume that each attribute of (α, β, γ) consists of three types of agents. Thus, there are altogether $3 \times 3 \times 3 = 27$ different types of agents. The parameters are set as shown in Table 10.1.

There are two kinds of societies: a heterogeneous one and a homogeneous one. We further assume that in a heterogeneous society, there is only one player of each type, implying that the organization consists of 27 heterogeneous agents. This choice of number is made from two reasons: interaction among workers seems to be important when the size of organization is relatively small; and the median value of effort can easily be computed if the number of players in the group is

Table 10.1 Cost of effort and psychological preferences

Ability	α	Inertia	β	Cohesion	γ
High	1/3	Strong	1/L	Strong	1.0
Medium	1/2	Medium	0.5/L	Medium	0.75
Low	2/3	Weak	0	Weak	0.5

odd. In order to create a homogeneous society, consider first a homogeneous group consisting of 27 agents of the same type. Next, generate 27 homogeneous groups which cover all types of agents. We will conduct a simulation for each of these homogeneous groups. Then, we will take an average of the 27 simulations. For expositional convenience, we use the term, a homogeneous society, to refer to this normalized society.

We generate 30 simulations for each combination of experimental parameter values, each run beginning with a different random seed. Data we shall observe in evaluating the performance of organizations would be the median of efforts. The average payoff to the agents seems to be more desirable in evaluating the performance of the organization. However, these two indicators move almost parallel so that we will ignore the average payoff.

4 Result

First, we will observe basic performance of the model. Then we discuss the heterogeneous case. For each of the two rating systems, GRS and IRS, we attempt to design the best policy. Finally, we will examine workers' performance for the homogeneous organization when the same best policies are applied.

4.1 *Basic Performance*

First, we verify the influence of costs of effort and psychological preferences in Table 10.1 on organizational performance. Table 10.2 shows the effects of median efforts on workers ability (α). As expected, the lower the cost (the higher the ability) is, the more the level of median efforts is. Moreover, the cognitive error decreases performance drastically and the extra wage incentives (bonus and penalty) increases one slightly. On the other hand, the median efforts do not depend on workers inertia (β) and their cohesion (γ).

Table 10.2 Equilibrium levels of median efforts

	$(w_r, w_p) = (0, 0)$		$(w_r, w_p) = (0.1, 0.1)$		$(w_r, w_p) = (0.5, 0.5)$	
Workers ability	M = 0.0	M = 0.02 L	M = 0.0	M = 0.02 L	M = 0.0	M = 0.02 L
High	70	34	70	39	70	59
Medium	63	25	65	30	70	50
Low	54	17	56	22	60	42

Note: All the simulations are set with same types of workers with (β, γ) = (medium, medium). Workers ability (α) also corresponds to each other, and the values of it are shown in the table

Table 10.3 Equilibrium levels of median efforts in the heterogeneous society

	W = 0.0	W = 0.1	W = 0.5
M = 0.0	31.2	32.9	46.0
M = 0.02 L	34.0	38.0	37.0
M = 0.05 L	32.0(*)	34.0(*)	36.0(*)

Note: (*) means that the value is unstable

Table 10.4 Equilibrium levels of median efforts in the homogeneous society

	W = 0.0	W = 0.1	W = 0.5
M = 0.0	60.6	61.9	63.2
M = 0.02 L	25.2	30.2	50.2
M = 0.05 L	26.2	26.4	31.2

Table 10.5 The effect of wage incentives on equilibrium levels of median effort

	A homogeneous society		A heterogeneous society	
(w_r, w_p)	M = 0.0	M = 0.02 L	M = 0.0	M = 0.02 L
(0.0,0.0)	60.6	25.2	31.2	34.0
(0.5,0.0)	60.8	50.9	31.0	35.0
(0.0,0.5)	60.6	61.5	36.0	34.4
(0.5,0.5)	63.2	50.2	46.0	37.0

Second, we observe the performances of the heterogeneous and homogeneous societies defined in the previous section. Table 10.3 shows the relationship between wage incentives and cognitive error in a heterogeneous society. Table 10.4 shows the same relationship for a homogeneous society. Table 10.5 shows the median effort of four different societies, i.e., two homogeneous societies with M = 0.0 and M = 0.02 L, and two heterogeneous societies with M = 0.0 and M = 0.02 L for four different incentive pairs, i.e., (W_r,W_p) = (0.0,0.0), (0.5,0.0), (0.0,0.5), (0.5,0.5). While the performances depend on the cognitive error drastically in the homogeneous society (Table 10.4), they depend on the cognitive error hardly in the heterogeneous society (Table 10.3). Especially, a strong wage incentive system (W = 0.5) have big effects on the performance under the mild cognitive error (M = 0.02 L) in the homogeneous society. Table 10.5 suggests that a punishment system is effective than a reward system, but we need more discussions.

4.2 *Heterogeneous Organization*

To examine either carrot or stick is more effective in inducing higher level of performance, consider GRS with W = 0.5. Figure 10.1 shows the trendof average performance of each category of workers with different incentive schemes. The parameter values $(\varepsilon_t, \varepsilon_b)$ are (0,0), (10,10), (10,0) and (0,10) in Fig. 10.1a through d respectively. As seen in Fig. 10.1b, the oscillation occurs when both reward and punishment incentives are installed, with significantly higher performance on average than the case with neither incentive (Fig. 10.1a). Without the penalty

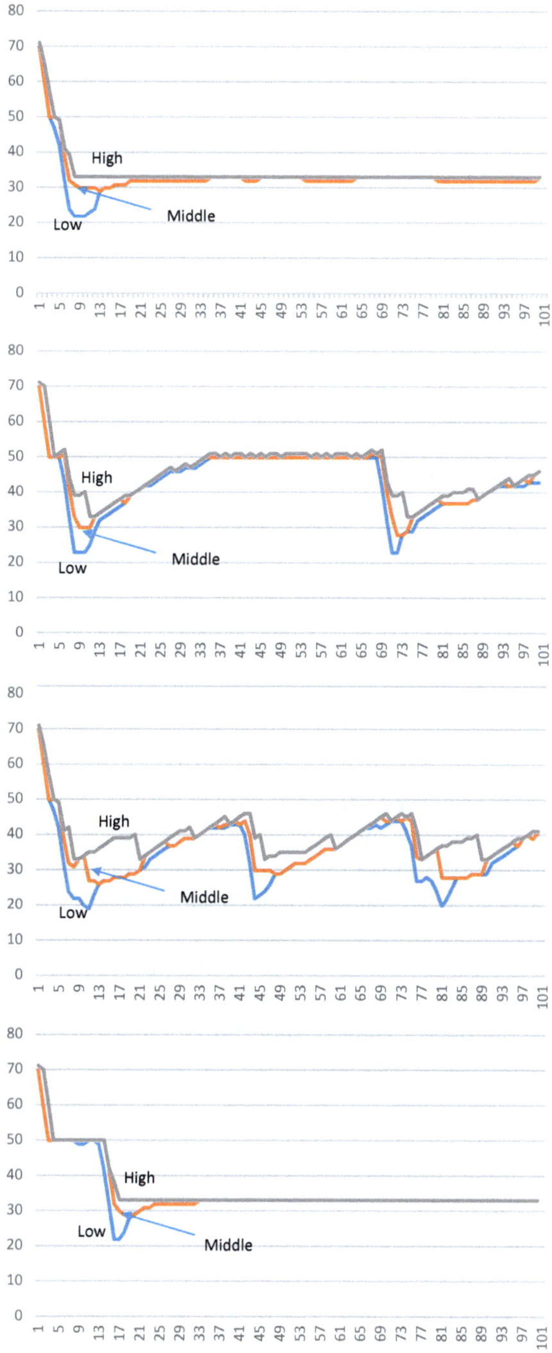

Fig. 10.1 Average performance of each category of workers in a case with (ε_t, ε_b) = **a** (0,0), **b** (10,10), **c** (10,0), **d** (0,10)

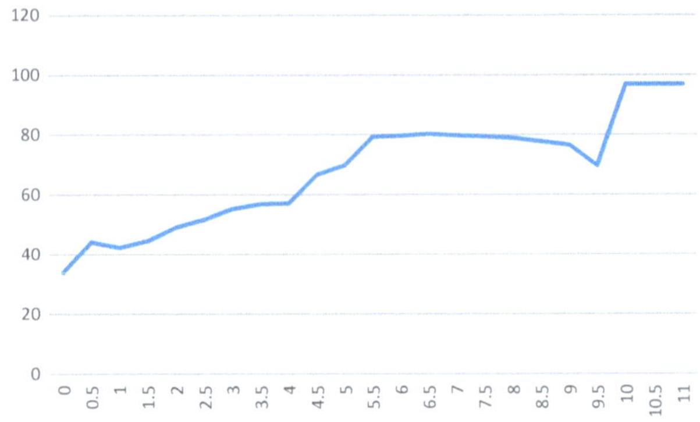

Fig. 10.2 Effort level with different size of W when $(\varepsilon_t, \varepsilon_b) = (10,10)$

incentive (Fig. 10.1c), the binding power is weak because low ability workers have less incentive to move upward. The trend of performance shows similar oscillating dynamics but the level itself is significantly reduced. As shown in Fig. 10.1d, without reward payment the trend does not oscillate because there is no strong upward movement driven by the top performers.

Thus, it appears to be important for an organization to reward the best workers to give upward momentum. To make full use of the binding power it is also essential to punish the least efficient workers. To sum up, in order to raise the general level of performance, the incentives for both high and low performing workers need to be installed, as in the case of Fig. 10.1b.

A natural question then arises: what would be the optimal level of incentives? To answer this question, we vary the amount of W while keeping $(\varepsilon_t , \varepsilon_b)$=(10,10). Figure 10.2 shows that as the size of W increases the oscillation becomes intensified with larger amplitude although the average performance keeps rising. If we interpret the cost of effort as the magnitude of stress a worker undergoes, the sharp declines in effort level may imply depression or burnout syndrome. Another problem of a large size of incentive in GRS is that it can make the workplace excessively competitive so that it will damage cooperative culture of the organization. Can we avoid these problems by adopting IRS?

First, note that each of these schemes gives quite strong incentive for workers of all types to raise their productivity. Figure 10.3-x depicts the average performance of each category of workers when (W,D)=(0.5, 2x-1). When $D = 1$ and $D \geq 5$, the performance trends oscillate. The mechanism working in $D = 1$ case is similar as in GRS with both reward and penalty. When $D = 5$ or larger, workers are not afraid of being punished so that the same mechanism works as in no penalty scheme of GRS, inducing the low level of performance.

With $D = 3$, there is virtually no oscillation and the average performance during the simulation period is as high as 48.34, which is even higher than 44.22 under GRS (Fig. 10.1b). All the type of workers are not exposed to the risk of punishment caused by adversary random shocks. This implies that there is no excessive upward

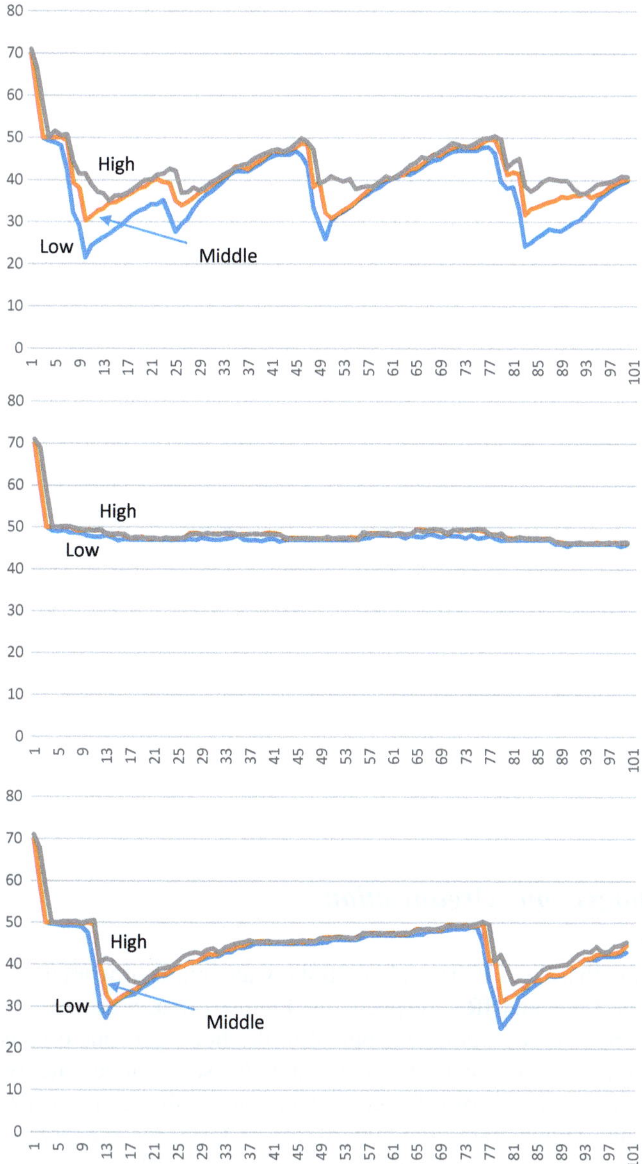

Fig. 10.3 Average performance of each category of workers when (W,D) = **a** (0.5,1), **b** (0.5,3), **c** (0.5,5)

momentum, which suppresses the oscillation. But reducing effort intentionally can trigger punishment when subject to negative random shock. D = 3 (Fig. 10.3b) is the adequate allowance in reference to the size of uncertainty M = 2.

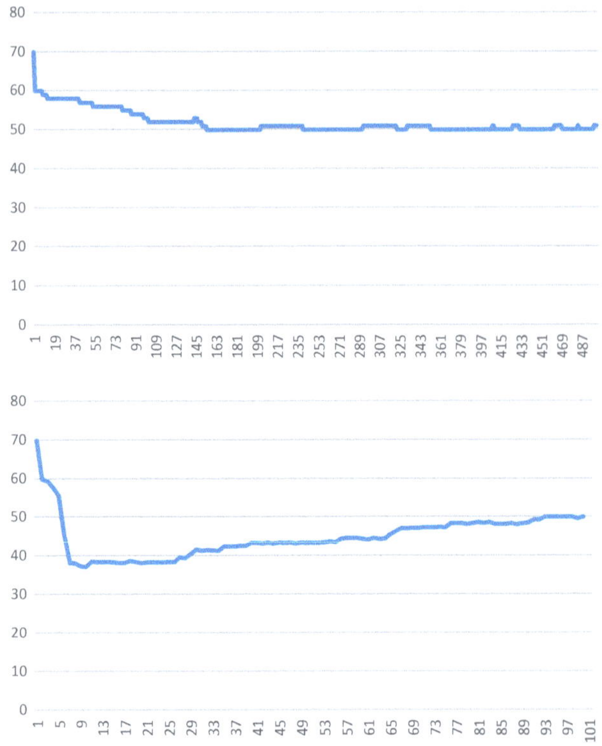

Fig. 10.4 Average performance of homogeneous workers in a case with $(\varepsilon_t, \varepsilon_b)$ = **a** (10,10), **b** (0.5,3)

4.3 Homogeneous Organization

We have found that Figs. 10.1b and 10.3b show the trends of workers' performance under the best GRS and IRS, respectively. Figure 10.4a, b are the corresponding trends with the same two policies applied to the homogeneous organization. The saturated levels of average performance are the same under the two systems, however, the performance of GRS consistently stays above that of IRS until they converge. This demonstrates the superiority of GRS for the organization with homogeneous workers, contrasting the superiority of IRS for the heterogeneous organization. Which of the two personnel rating system is desirable given that a manager of a firm can choose whether its organization is homogeneous or heterogeneous? Comparing Figs. 10.3b and 10.4a, GRS for the homogeneous organization induces higher performances than IRS for the heterogeneous one.

5 Discussion

In order to examine the efficacy of wage incentives to prevent morale erosion, we have modeled an artificial organization which consists of agents having various psychological preferences. We have found that an agent based simulation is useful in revealing the mechanisms working behind complex socioeconomic systems.

The following insights were obtained: (1) the erosion of morale demonstrated by Kandori (2003) was reproduced by our agent based model, (2) by segmentalizing an organization into small homogeneous groups comprised of members with similar productive ability and psychological preferences, wage incentives can enhance the cohesiveness of morale sharply enough to cancel out the negative effect of perturbation, resulting in high performance of the organization, and (3) in the above organization where norms and morale effectively bind members, demerit system like punishment on bad performing players is more instrumental than merit system, (4) even though cognitive errors increase or decrease the variance of distribution of workers' performances equally likely, binding power which has once been reinforced may exhibit irreversibility in a highly diversified organization.

Wage incentive encourages employees to perform to their potential by tying pay directly to performance. On the other hand, it has a variety of disadvantages. This paper shed light on another advantage of wage incentive: it will encourage employees to work harder through sustained morale by penalizing less productive workers financially. The analysis implied that, by punishing only small fraction of the least productive workers, one can effectively prevent morale erosion while minimizing the disadvantage of pay system with wage incentives.

Productive effort of a worker has positive externality so that the workers under consideration are tempted to be free riders. By conducting virtual simulations of an agent-based model with heterogeneous and homogeneous workers, we have examined various wage incentive systems.

They show that the interaction of the binding power and workers' incentive to get reward or evade punishment generates interesting dynamics of their efforts. The two personnel rating systems are compared: one based upon the level of performance relative to other workers' performances and the other upon her own past performance. Our simulation shows that, in inducing higher performance of the workers, the latter system excels the former for the heterogeneous organization, whereas the former system will outperform for the homogeneous one.

For future extension, myopic expectation and behavior should be replaced with more sophisticated workers capable of learning.

Acknowledgments This capture was partially supported by Kakenhi 22510160, 22530284, and 26330387. We also thank the reviewers for their comments.

References

Andreoni J (1990) Impure altruism and donations to public goods: a theory of warm-glow giving. Econ J 100(401):464–477
Colquitt JA, Noe RA, Jackson CL (2002) Justice in teams: antecedents and consequences of procedural justice climate. Pers Psychol 55(1):83–109
Dorfman PW, Stephan WG (1984) The effects of group performance on cognitions, satisfaction, and behavior: a process model. J Manag 10(2):173–192
Heneman RL, Hippel CV (1995) Balancing group and individual rewards: rewarding individual contributions to the team. Compens Benefits Rev 27(4):63–68
Kandori M (2003) The erosion and sustainability of norms and morale. Jpn Econ Rev 54:29–48
Katz LF (1986) Efficiency wage theories: a partial evaluation. In: Fischer S (ed) NBER macroeconomics annual 1986, vol 1. MIT Press, Cambridge, MA, pp 235–290
Ross TL, Hatcher L, Collins D (1992) Why employees support (and oppose) gainsharing plans. Compens Benefits Manag 8:17–27
Scott KD, Floyd J, Benson PG, Bishop JW (2002) The impact of the Scanlon plan on retail store performance. WorldatWork 11(3):18–27
Sirota D, Mischkind LA, Meltzer IM (2006) Why your employees are losing motivation. Harv Manag 11(1).http://hbswk.hbs.edu/archive/5289.html

Chapter 11
Does Stock Market Contribute to the Growth of Company? An Agent-Based Simulation of Industrial Model in Which Stock Markets and Product Markets Exist

Hao Lee

Abstract In this Study, we design a multi agent system within various agents such as enterprise agents, investor agents, and customer agents in our model. Enterprise agents using stock as collateral for loans from banks, they use these resources to execute business activities such as purchase and production, and sell products to consumers to gain profit, part of profit will become dividends to investors.

We design a simple model of enterprises' financial statements. Not only technical analysis but also fundamental analysis will be implemented as measures of investments in our model. We will clear up influence of trading strategies of investor agents in the artificial market to business managements in our agent based model.

As the results, measures of investments of investors in a stock market influence on business activities in our rational assumptions. Totally, the environments exert healthy influence on business activities are trend strategy dominating markets and random strategy dominating markets. The key point is a stable stock price or a good predictability of stock price.

Keywords Financial statements • Measure of investment • Agent-based simulation

1 Introduction

Artificial market research is an important category of social simulation studies. For example, U-Mart, a virtual market as a common test bed aiming at RoboCup in Economics is a pioneering project in Japan. U-Mart researchers design virtual markets and simulation to carry out understanding of follow subjects. First one is

---

H. Lee (✉)
Department of Informatics, Graduate School of Integrated Science and Technology, Shizuoka University, Hamamatsu, Japan
e-mail: lee@inf.shizuoka.ac.jp

Y. Nakai et al. (eds.), *Agent-Based Approaches in Economic and Social Complex Systems VIII*, Agent-Based Social Systems 13, DOI 10.1007/978-4-431-55236-9_11

the behavior of human in trading activities. Second one is behavior of the emerging market, and institutional devices to control them. Third one is evolution, learning, collective intelligence through developing trading programs.

Application of evolutionary algorithm in an artificial market, learning artificial intelligence agents as market makers, artificial exchanges market and artificial stock market studies are not only performed in Japan. In United Stated, some researchers in Santa Fe Institute use an artificial market to calculate theoretical value of stock by interests rate and dividend (Arthur et al. 1996). In Taiwan, some researchers in AIECON research center use genetic programming to analyze stock price and verify efficiency of trading strategies (Chen and Yeh 1996).

Generally, these studies focus on follow subjects. First, find out efficient trading strategies to predict stock price correctly and analyze trading activities of human trader. Second, to design a market mechanism that against market crash by speculative or panic traders, or to design an efficient prices determine algorithms in an inactive market. Third, artificial intelligence studies such as evolutionary system, adaptation learning and more.

However, most researchers are interested in trading activities INSIDE a Stock Market and not going to research OUTSIDE a Stock Market, such as the value of enterprise. In various studies, researchers focus on technical analysis and trace movements of stock prices. However, researches of fundamental analysis in an artificial market are much lesser.

In this Study, we design a multi agent system within various agents. Not only stock markets but also product markets are constructed in our model. We focus on not only stock market itself but also how trade activities influence business activities of enterprises.

There are three kinds of agents and two types of markets in our model. First kind of agents is enterprise agent that is learning agent. Rest two kinds of agents are not learning agents, they are investor agents that use various measures of investment to evaluate enterprises and customer agents that adjust their budget dynamically and purchase goods from enterprise agents.

Two types of markets are stock market and product market. The basic dynamics of enterprise is as follows. Enterprise agents using stock as collateral for loans from banks, they use these resources to execute business activities such as purchase and production, and sell products to consumers to gain profit, part of profit will become dividends to investors.

Normally, stakeholders such as shareholders, business manager, staffs and more, are supposedly to be looking for long-term growth of an enterprise. However, shareholders who carry weight not always pursue for long-term growth of enterprise and some of them care more about short-term profit of themselves. Shareholder's measures of investment influence to stock market hugely, and the stock market influence business environments. Therefore, shareholder's measures of investments influence business managements of enterprises indirectly. Generally, these measures are designed for shareholders but not for long-term growth of enterprises.

In this study, we design a model of enterprises' financial statements. Not only technical analysis but also fundamental analysis will be implement as measures of investments in our model. We will clear up influence of trading strategies of investor agents in the artificial market to business managements in our agent based model.

2 Model

We assume that enterprise agents are tea factory because the structure of business is simple. One material, one piece of equipment, and one product are elements in a tea industry. An enterprise agent use tea leaves as material, employ production/sales/management staffs as labors, purchase tea machine as production equipment, and gain profit by producing and selling tea. There are several types of enterprise agents depending on management indicator they emphasize, such as profit oriented, share oriented, and stock price oriented.

Consumers in our model are simple autonomous agents. Material markets, equipment markets, labor markets and financial markets are assumed as the perfect competitive market. Material price, equipment price, labor cost, and interest rate is fixed.

In our previous research (Lee 2008), we did not contribute a stock market and enterprises are asked to satisfy only one measure of investment for one investor. In this study, we contribute a stock market that there are various investors in it. We introduce five types of measures, such as PBR (price book-value ratio) and PER (price earning ratio) in fundamental analysis, trend strategy and RSI (relative strength index) in technical analysis, and random strategy for comparison.

2.1 Units

Units in this model are as follows.

- Currency: 1 million yen
- Tea (product), tea leaves (material): 1 ton
- Tea machine (equipment): 1 unit
- Labor: 1 person

2.2 Assumption of Business Model

The enterprise model and business process will be described in following sections. Business activities and the influences to accounting systems in previous study (Lee 2008) are based on manufacturer model in virtual economy that designed for national economic accounting (Deguchi 2000). We improve the models of previous study for this paper.

Table 11.1 P/L of an enterprise agent

Sales	75
Sales of goods	75
Cost of sales	36
Cost of goods sold	36
Gross margin	39
Sales administrative expense	10
Administrative expense	8
Sales expense	6
Operating profit	25
Non-operating income and cost	0
Interest payment	5
Current profit	20
Tax payment	10
Corporate tax	10
Net profit	10

Table 11.2 B/S of an enterprise agent

debit		credit	
Property	0	Liability	0
Equipment	0	Bank loan	0
Current assets	200		
Cash	200	Equity	200
Material	0	Capital	200
Product	0	Internal reserve	0
Assets	200	Liabilities and equity	200

2.2.1 Financial Statements

In this study, enterprise model is designed as a minimum set of Profit & Loss statement and Balance Sheets for various accounting calculations. Table 11.1 is an example of P/L and Table 11.2 is an example of B/S.

2.2.2 Financing

Enterprise agents are able to borrow from bank but can not increase or decrease capital for financing in this model. Maximum bank loan amount is calculated by stock price of an enterprise. Capital and percentage of profit for dividend are assumed as fixed.

- Enterprise borrows money from bank. Enterprises pay interest at end of term. Interest rate is fixed to 10 % in this model.
- Maximum bank loan amount is calculated by multiplying stock price and coefficient s. In this study, s = 1.

- Enterprises must return the bank loan at beginning stage on next term. If an enterprise dose not has enough cash, it must borrow again.
- If an enterprise cannot return the bank loan or cannot pay interest, it will go bankrupt.

2.2.3 Production

Material, equipment and labor are needed for production in this model.

1. Material
   (a) Two units of material are needed for one unit of product.
2. Equipment
   (a) One unit of equipment is possible to produce five or more units of product in a term.
3. Labor
   (a) To operate one unit of equipment, four units of labor are needed. If there are more than four units of labor work for a tea machine, more products will be produced. Function of production is a diminishing return model. We introduce such a model to increase variations of ratio between personnel expenses and depreciation expense in profit and loss statements.

In expression (11.1), QL_t denotes production per equipment in term i, floor is cutoff function, e denotes base e of natural logarithm, LP_t denotes labor per equipment in term i.

$$QL_t = floor\left(5\frac{2}{1 + 20e^{-2.5*LPt}}\right) \tag{11.1}$$

Relationship between LP_t and QL_t is shown as Fig.11.1.

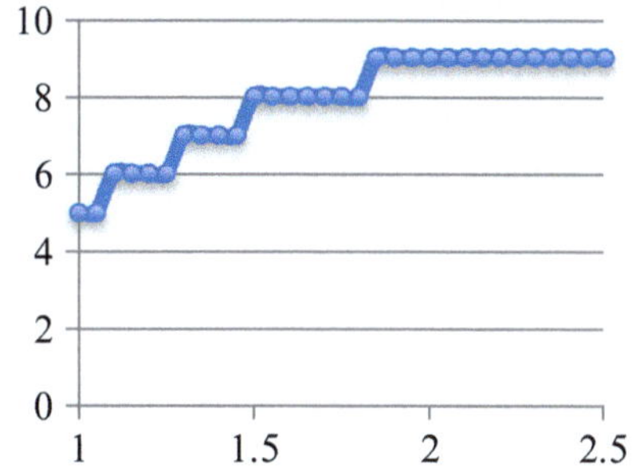

Fig. 11.1 Relationship between labor per equipment and production per equipment

2.2.4 Employment

Three types of labor are needed for business activities in this model.

1. Labor for production
   (a) Labor for production is described in 2.2.3.
2. Labor for sales
   (a) Labor for sales is necessary for product selling. One unit of labor is needed for four units of selling product.
   (b) Labor for sales, the salesmen are possible to increase budget of consumers. The ratio of budget increase is equal as ratio of units of labor per four units of product. For example, if there are two units of labor for four units of product, budget of consumers will be twice, if there are three units of labor for four units of product, budget of consumer will be three times. We introduce such a model to increase variations of price strategies of enterprises to product market.
3. Labor for management.
   (a) Labor for management is needed to manage labors. One unit of labor for management is needed for four units of labor for production or labor for sales. And one unit of labor for upper management is needed for four units of labor for lower management. We introduce such a model to increase variations of personnel expenses in profit and loss statements.

2.2.5 Depreciation

Enterprises use straight-line depreciation in this model. Depreciation period is five terms. Residual value is zero. Depreciation amount is 20 % of equipment price.

2.3 Macro Parameters

Business activities are influenced by fixed macro parameters that are given externally. These parameters are verified in our gaming simulation model (Lee 2010).

- Corporate tax:50 %
- Bank interest:10 %
- Standard wage (cost of labor):2 money unit
- Tea machine price (price of production equipment):100 money unit
- Tea leaves price (price of material):1 money unit

2.4 Cost Accounting

Actual cost accounting is adopted in this model as expression (11.2). PC_t denotes production cost per product in term t, M_t denotes material cost in term t, W_t denotes labor cost of production, D_t denotes depreciation cost in term t, Q_t denotes Quantity of production in term t.

$$PC_t = \frac{M_t + W_t + D_t}{Q_t} \tag{11.2}$$

Average product cost is calculated by weighted average as expression (11.3). C_t denotes average product cost in term t, S_{t-1} denotes product stock quantity in term $t-1$.

$$C_t = \frac{PC_t Q_t + C_{t-1} S_{t-1}}{Q_t + S_{t-1}} \tag{11.3}$$

2.5 Products Market

In previous study (Lee 2008), products market is described as a general demand function. In this study, product market is constructed by numbers of agents.

An initial number of consumer agents is 100, and be increased 10 % every term. To construct a decent market and industry, we design a consumer-increasing model in this study. We did not adopt a random growth model because it will cause a difficulty to compare simulation results.

Initial budget of consumers is 30 money units. Purchase activities of agents are as follows:

1. Consumers choose an enterprise randomly.
2. Consumers compare their budget and price offered by enterprise; they will purchase the goods if price is lower than their budget. Budget will be raised depends on number of enterprise's salesmen.
3. If consumers do not purchase a product, they have five more chance to match another product.
4. Budget in next term is calculated as expression (11.3).

$$B_{m,i+1} = B_{m,i} + (T_{m,i} - 3) \tag{11.4}$$

$B_{m,i}$ denotes consumer m's budget in term i, $T_{m,i}$ denotes how many matches needed for consumer m to purchase a product in term i. If matching time is three, budget will no be changed. If matching time lesser than 3, budget will be decreased, if matching time greater than 3, budget will be increased.

Table 11.3 Ranking table of enterprises

	Enterprise A	Enterprise B	Enterprise C
Investor 1	1(+4 pts)	2(+2 pts)	3(+1 pts)
Investor 2	1(+4 pts)	3(+1 pts)	2(+2 pts)
Investor 3	1(+4 pts)	2(+2 pts)	3(+1 pts)
Investor 4	2(+2 pts)	1(+3 pts)	3(+1 pts)

Table 11.4 Stock prices of enterprises

	Enterprise A	Enterprise B	Enterprise C
Stock Price	14(=4 + 4 + 4 + 2)	9(=2 + 1 + 2 + 3)	5(=1 + 2 + 1 + 1)

2.6 *Stock Market*

In this study, profit or loss of investors is not as important as profit or loss of enterprises. Instead to contribute a rich trading model in stock market such as U-Mart, we create a very simple price algorithm to describe a stock market.

Each investor uses its measure of investment to evaluate all enterprises and make a ranking table. An enterprise on top rank receives four evaluation points, an enterprise on second rank receives two evaluation points and an enterprise on rank n receives $4/n^2$ evaluation points. Stock price of an enterprise is simply total evaluation points from all investors.

For example, if there are three enterprise agents such as A, B and C and the investors' ranking table is summarized as Table 11.3. Stock price of each enterprise will be calculated as Table 11.4.

3 Simulation Model

We adopt SOARS (Spot Oriented Agent Role Simulator[1]), a simple and multifunctional simulator for social simulation as our simulation engine in this study because exchange-algebra module that is very helpful to construct financial statements is supported by SOARS.

3.1 *Model Validation by Gaming Simulation*

To verify our model and parameters, we designed and performed a gaming simulation in previous study (Lee, 2010). Gaming simulation is a good method to

[1] http://www.soars.jp/

Table 11.5 Decision making items

Financing	Bank loan ratio
Purchasing	Machine purchase ratio
Employing	Labor for production ratio
	Labor for selling ratio
Selling	Product price

Table 11.6 Omitted decision items

Depreciation	Method	Straight-line method
Capital	Dividend ratio	50 %
	Capital increase	N/A.
	Capital decrease	N/A.
Purchasing	Material purchasing	Calculated by using number of product this term.
Production	Number of product	Calculated by labor of production and number of machine.

verify parameters in a model and the model itself (Lee and Deguchi 2005; Lee and Deguchi 2006).

3.2 *Decision Making*

If there are too many decisions to be made by a learning artificial intelligence in an agent-based simulation, learning process will be complicated and hard to be well tuned. Therefore, enterprise agents in our model simply make five decisions such as Table 11.5. Other omitted decision items will be calculated by rules in Table 11.6.

3.3 *Exchange Algebra*

Exchange algebra that is possible to describe financial statements easily is embedded in SOARS. We implement all accounting transaction in this model by using exchange algebra. List of exchange algebra is summarized in Table 11.7.

3.4 *Rule Design of Reinforcement Learning*

Rules of reinforcement learning are designed as Tables 11.8 and 11.9. Twenty-five rules will be created randomly for one condition set. In our model, over 1,200 rules will be created for each enterprise agent after the pre-learning process.

Table 11.10 is an example of created rules.

Table 11.7 List of exchange algebra

Exchange algebra	Transaction
BS	Balance sheet
PL	Profit and loss statement
Employ	Cash, personal expenses
Price adjust	Price adjust loss or profit, balance of goods
Interest payment	Cash, financing cost
Material purchasing	Cash, material
Tax payment	Cash, corporate tax
Machine purchasing	Cash, equipment
Depreciation	Depreciation, equipment
Financing	Cash, liabilities
Production	Goods, material, personal expenses, value added
Selling	Goods, cash
Selling and management cost appropriation	Personal expenses, selling and management cost
Dividend payment	Cash, internal reserve
Settlement: added value transfer	Value added, internal reserve
Settlement: price adjust transfer	Price adjust profit/lost, internal reserve
Settlement: interest payment transfer	Financing cost, internal reserve

Table 11.8 Condition part of a rule

Criteria	Formulation	Range
Cash c in B/S	$min\left(9, floor\left(\sqrt{c}/10\right)\right)$	0~9
Product stock d	$min\left(9, floor\left(\sqrt{d}/2\right)\right)$	0~9
Number of machine m	$min\left(9, floor\left(\sqrt{m}/2\right)\right)$	0~9

Table 11.9 Action part of a rule

Decisions	Range	Formulation
Bank loan f_t in term t	A_f 0~4	$f_t = f_{t-1} * A_f * 0.25$
Machine purchase b_t in term t	A_b 0~2	$b_t = M_{t-1} * A_b * 0.1 M_{t-1}$ denotes number of machines last term
Ratio of labor for production pl_t in term t	A_{lp} 0~2	$pl_t = pl_{t-1} + pl_{t-1} * \left(A_{lp} - 1\right) * 0.2$
Ratio of labor for selling sl_t in term t	A_{ls} 0~2	$sl_t = sl_{t-1} + sl_{t-1} * (A_{ls} - 1) * 0.2$
Product price p_t in term t	A_p 0~2	$p_t = p_{t-1} + p_{t-1} * \left(A_p - 1\right) * 0.2$

Table 11.10 An example of reinforcement learning rules

Condition	Action	Weight
5,0,1	0, 2, 1, 0, 1	269.3
5,0,1	4, 2, 0, 0, 2	5.5
5,0,1	1, 1, 1, 0, 2	755.9
5,0,1	1, 2, 1, 0, 2	157.8
5,0,1	1, 0, 0, 0, 0	89.3
5,0,1	1, 1, 2, 0, 2	433.1
5,0,1	2, 0, 2, 1, 1	364.7
5,0,1	2, 2, 0, 0, 0	50.6
5,0,1	3, 2, 0, 0, 1	41.6
5,0,1	4, 1, 0, 1, 1	0.0

Enterprise agents calculate evaluation of rules as Table 11.11 depending by their oriented type. After evaluation process, enterprise agents calculate weights of rules by their evaluation

Table 11.11 Evaluation for reinforcement learning

Enterprise type	Evaluation
Profit oriented	Difference between net profit and average net profit in industry
Market share oriented	Difference between sales and average sales in industry
Stock price oriented	Difference between stock price and average stock price in industry.

Weight of rules is calculated by logistic function as expression (11.4). W_t denotes weight in term t, V_t denotes evaluation in term t. However, $W_t = 0$ if an enterprise went bankrupt

Enterprise agents calculate evaluation of rules as Table 11.11 depending by their oriented type. After evaluation process, enterprise agents calculate weights of rules by their evaluation.

Weight of rules is calculated by logistic function as expression (11.4). W_t denotes weight in term t, V_t denotes evaluation in term t. However, $W_t = 0$ if an enterprise went bankrupt.

$$W_t = \frac{20}{1 + 5e^{-0.02 * Vt}} \tag{11.5}$$

In our model, past actions influence current evaluation, weight will be calculated for recent four terms.

3.5 *Measure of Investments*

Investor agents rank enterprises by their measures of investments shown in Table 11.12.

Table 11.12 Measure of investments

Type	Measure
PBR	Ascending order by [stock price/total assets]
PER	Ascending order by [stock price/net profit]
RSI	Same as RSIStrategy in u-mart
Trend	Same as TrendStrategy in u-mart
Random	Random walk function in SOARS

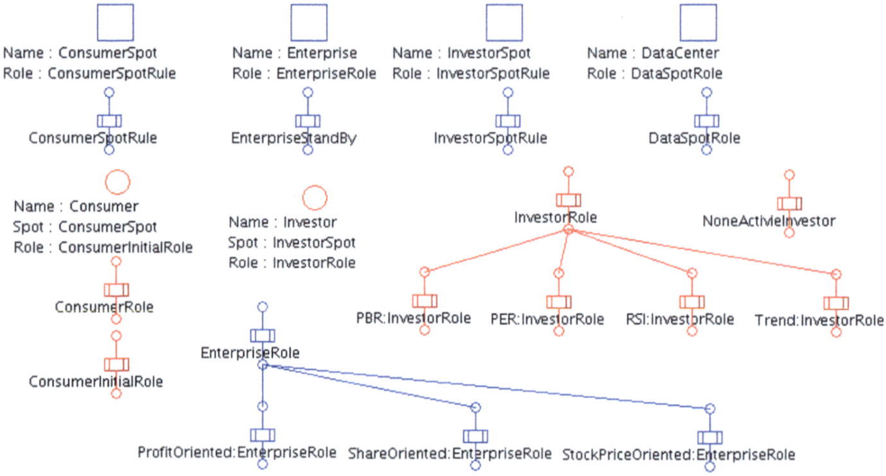

Fig. 11.2 Agents and roles

3.6 SOARS Script

There are 22 SOARS objects and 16 stages in our model. We construct agent model as Fig.11.2 and stage model as Table 11.13. There are enterprise spot, data spot, investor spot, consumer spot and those roles, five kinds of investor agents, consumer agents and those roles in Fig. 11.2.

4 Simulation Design and Simulation Results

There are 1 terms in 1 simulation round; we assume 1 term as 1 year. Investors act every month and consumers act every 2-month. In other words, investors act 12 times, and consumers act 6 times in a term. We perform ten round for each environment and collect data latter.

Table 11.13 Stages in SOARS

Initial
Investment
Decision make
Financing
Purchasing
Machine calculation
Employment
Production
Depreciation
Selling
Cash flow calculation
PL calculation
BS calculation
Bankrupt judgment
Evaluation and learning
End of term

Table 11.14 Profit and loss statement

Enterprise type		Profit oriented	Share oriented	Stock price oriented
Gross margin	AVG	1,389.7	1,135.3	759.7
	STDEV	1,389.7	1,135.3	759.7
Operating profit	AVG	1,278.3	1,044.1	690.7
	STDEV	1,389.7	1,135.3	759.7
Current profit	AVG	1,182.8	938	609.1
	STDEV	732.5	624.6	450
Net profit	AVG	591.2	468.8	304.3
	STDEV	366.2	312.2	224.9

4.1 Basic Set

In our basic set of simulation, there is 1 agent for each type of enterprise, 30 agents for each type of investors and 100 consumers. Number of enterprise agents and investor agents are fixed, but number of consumer agents increases 10 % in each term. There will be 240 consumers on final term.

Simulation results are summarized in Tables 11.14, 11.15 and 11.16.

In Table 11.14, 11.15, and 11.16, relationship between B/S, P/L, and stock price is strongly positive. Correlation coefficient between B/S and P/L is calculated and summarized in Table 11.17. In P/L, all correlation coefficient between gross margins, operating profit, current profit, and net profit are more than 0.99. In B/S, correlation coefficient between cash and internal reserve is 0.74. However, correlation coefficient between cash and the bank loan, internal reverse, and bank loan are −0.37 and −0.29. In Table 11.17, correlation coefficient between stock prices, net profit, cash and internal reverse are weakly positive.

Table 11.15 Balance Sheet(partial)

Enterprise type		Profit oriented	Share oriented	Stock price oriented
Cash	AVG	6,163.2	5,017	3,544.2
	STDEV	3,157	3,527.9	2,830.3
Internal reserve	AVG	6,698.7	6,113.3	5,386.2
	STDEV	2,750.5	2,882.3	2,581.2
Bank loan	AVG	113.3	115.5	136.3
	STDEV	47.7	89.1	65.1

Table 11.16 Stock price

Enterprise type	Profit oriented	Share oriented	Stock price oriented
AVG	377.5	355.1	317.4
STDEV	79.3	68.6	65.1

Table 11.17 Correlation coefficient between profit, stock price and B/S

	Profit	Cash	Retained earnings	Bank loan
Stock price	0.43	0.41	0.42	−0.08
Profit	–	0.66	0.53	−0.24

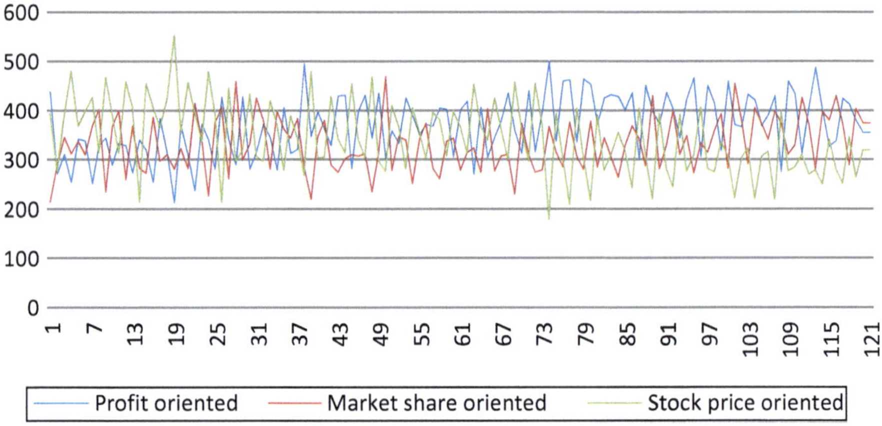

Fig. 11.3 An example of full-time stock price series

Based on previous relationship analysis, we focus on net profit in P/L, internal reverse and stock price to analyze our simulation results in 4.2. Figures 11.3 and 11.4 is examples of stock price series. Stock price series for investors is shown in Fig. 11.3 and stock price series for enterprise is shown in Fig. 11.4.

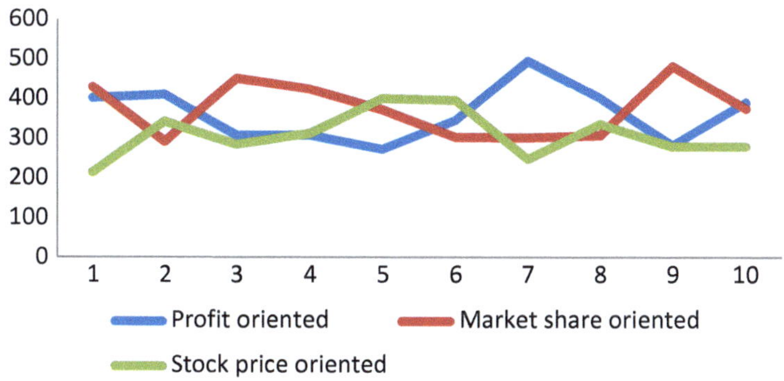

Fig. 11.4 An example of stock price series in 10 term

Table 11.18 Net profit

Investor		Enterprise			
		Profit oriented	Share oriented	Stock price oriented	Total
Basic set	AVG	591.2	468.8	304.3	454.8
	STDEV	366.2	312.2	224.9	305.9
PBR dominating	AVG	485.9	427.6	555.4	489.6
	STDEV	274.5	241.2	178.2	222.1
PER dominating	AVG	395.5	544.1	576.1	505.2
	STDEV	239.3	602.2	364.3	402.3
RSI dominating	AVG	546.5	597.7	0	381.4
	STDEV	253.3	259.2	0	335.3
Trend dominating	AVG	717.1	626.7	597.4	647.1
	STDEV	383.9	427.6	396.8	373.9
Random dominating	AVG	747.4	635.2	327.8	570.1
	STDEV	303.4	325.2	616.7	441.6

4.2 *Advanced Set: When Ratio of Investors Are Not Equal*

In this session, we assume a case that specific type of investor dominates the stock market. There are 30 investors of each type in basic set, and it will be changed that 90 investors of specific type and 15 investors of other types. For example, there will be 90 PBR investors, 15 PER investors, 15 RSI investors, 15 Trend investors, and 15 Random investors in a PBR dominating market. Simulation results are summarized in Tables 11.18, 11.19 and 11.20.

In Table 11.18, all types of enterprise make good profits in a stock market that dominated by trend strategy. Performance of enterprise agents in random strategy dominating market, and fundamental analysis dominating market is also good.

Profit oriented enterprise agents are rather profitable in stock markets other than a PER dominating stock market. Net profit is used in calculation of PER, and

Table 11.19 Internal reverse

Investor		Enterprise			
		Profit oriented	Share oriented	Stock price oriented	Total
Basic set	AVG	6,698.7	6,113.3	5,386.2	6,066.1
	STDEV	2,750.5	2,882.3	2,581.2	2,700.4
PBR dominating	AVG	7,126	8,401.5	8,696.8	8,074.8
	STDEV	2,494.9	2,917.8	4,205.9	3,098.3
PER dominating	AVG	5,637	5,742.1	5,669.6	5,682.9
	STDEV	2,251.7	4,213.1	2,604.8	2,885.9
RSI dominating	AVG	6,805.6	7,965.3	2,120.2	5,630.4
	STDEV	2,363.9	3,407.7	615.1	3,395.3
Trend dominating	AVG	6,831.7	5,766.3	7,162.2	6,586.7
	STDEV	1,479.7	2,453.8	3,464.3	2,459.7
Random dominating	AVG	8,670.8	7,681.7	4,832.1	7,061.5
	STDEV	2,016.2	2,352.6	7,818.5	4,756.4

Table 11.20 Stock price

Investor		Enterprise			
		Profit oriented	Share oriented	Stock price oriented	Total
Basic set	AVG	377.5	355.1	317.4	350
	STDEV	79.3	68.6	65.1	73.2
PBR dominating	AVG	314	394.4	341.6	350
	STDEV	112.3	118.6	125.5	114.4
PER dominating	AVG	281	355	414	350
	STDEV	92.9	119.5	112.7	114.3
RSI dominating	AVG	315	446	289	350
	STDEV	114.1	99.1	99.3	118.6
Trend dominating	AVG	357.1	304.4	388.5	350
	STDEV	109.6	127.5	87.2	106.5
Random dominating	AVG	370	346.7	333.3	350
	STDEV	26.5	19.6	26.2	27.1

we expect that profit oriented agents are advantageous in a PER dominated stock market, but the results are opposite.

The share oriented enterprise agents are profitable in all stock markets.

Stock price oriented enterprise agents are profitable in PBR/PER dominating markets. However, the performance of stock price oriented agents in technical analysis dominating market is totally bad. Particularly, price oriented agents cannot make any profit in in a RSI dominating market. We run our simulation again in a RSI dominating market; the result is not as bad as previous simulation, but still not good.

What is the reason that profit oriented agents are not profitable in a PER dominating market? The stock price is mainly evaluated by PER method in that market, and it will be a goal of stock price oriented enterprise agents. Their action guideline, PER, is calculated by stock price and net profit. So they can take care about the balance of these two indexes indirectly. Therefore, PER dominating market is a good environment for stock price oriented agents. Profit oriented enterprise agents only focus on net profit, therefore, their performance is not good and their positions are taken by as stock price oriented enterprise agents in a PER dominating market.

In Table 11.19, the best performance of internal reverse is in a PBR dominating market. Performance of enterprise agents in a random strategy dominating market and trend strategy dominating market is above average, and others are below average.

In a random strategy dominating market, the stock prices are much stable than other markets, it cause a stable loan amount in our assumption. Performance of profit oriented enterprise agents, and share oriented enterprise is totally good. Performance of stock price oriented enterprise agents is good in a PBR dominating market and a trend strategy dominating market; however, their performance is not good in a random strategy dominating market and a RSI dominating market.

In our stock price calculation mechanism, if there are 150 investors and three enterprises in an industry, average stock price is fixed at 350 in our model. An investor is possible to vote one or two or four points to enterprises. There are 150 investors so total points are $(1+2+4)*150=1{,}050$ points. And there are three enterprises, $1{,}050/3=350$ point, and 350 is average of stock price in our model. Therefore, average stock price in Table 11.20 is 350 for all environments. Standard deviation of stock price in random dominating market is lowest in our simulation results, and it is quite large in other environments.

Either PBR strategy and PER strategy is looking for undervalued stocks. If investors of these types interested a specific undervalued stock, stock prices will be higher and not undervalued anymore. So, stock price will not be stable in the markets that dominated by PBR strategy and PER strategy.

Profit oriented enterprise agents that have good performance in net profit and internal reverse, are not evaluated in a PBR dominating market and a PER dominating market and stock prices are low. However, a low but a stable evaluation might be a reason of the enterprise's good achievement, because stability of business environment is important in our model.

5 Conclusions

In this study, we focus on the influence of measure of investment to business activities by constructing an enterprise model with minimum financial statements and we verify the results of agent-based simulation. Our model is a little more complex than The KISS principle by Axelrod (Axelrod 1997) but fundamental analysis cannot be done with a simpler model.

As the results, measures of investments of investors in a stock market influence on business activities in our rational assumptions. Totally, the environments exert healthy influence on business activities are trend strategy dominating markets and random strategy dominating markets. The key point is a stable stock price or a good predictability of stock price. It is hard to manage a business if the stock price moves up and down dynamically.

We construct an accounting system by exchange-algebra in SOARS, and it works well in our study. By using double entry in exchange-algebra, it is almost impossible to make mistakes in accounting transaction operation.

However, we do not use FALCON Seeds; a helpful subsystem of SOARS to do transfer operations in accounting. As a result, scripts for transfer operations are quite complex in our SOARS model. If we use transfer operations in FAL-CON Seeds, it is possible to describe a more complex value chain system other than a simple tea factory.

The problem of this study is that standard deviation in most results is strikingly high in our simulations. We will increase rounds of our simulation and try to gather more persuasive data in the future.

Also, we will increase the variations of investor agents and enterprise agents and analyze the how ratio of these agents influence stock price and an achievement of an enterprise.

Acknowledgment This work was supported by JSPS Grant-in-Aid for Young Scientists (B) Grant Number 23730390.

References

Arthur W, Holland J et al (1996) Asset pricing under endogenous expectations in an artificial stock market. In: Arthur WB et al (eds) The economy as an evolving complex systems II. Addison-Welsley Publishing, Reading, pp 15–44

Axelrod R (1997) The complexity of cooperation. Princeton University Press, Princeton

Chen S-H, Yeh C-H (1996) Genetic programming and the efficient market hypothesis. In: Koza JR, Goldberg DE, Fogel DB (eds) Genetic programming: proceedings of the 1st annual conference. The MIT Press, Cambridge, pp 45–53

Deguchi H (2000) Economics as complex system, towards economics of autonomous agents group science. JUSE Press, Ltd., Tokyo

Lee H (2008) Relationship between measure of investors and continuous growth of company limited – a simulation analysis by virtual market. In: Proceedings of the evolutionary economics, vol 12 (in Japanese), Kagoshima

Lee H (2010) Scenario based business game for enterprise strategy learning. In: Proceedings of the Japan association of simulation and gaming national conference autumn (in Japanese), Chiba

Lee H, Deguchi H (2005) The agent-based simulation and gaming simulation of firm's strategy in high-tech industry. J Jpn Assoc Simul Gaming 15(1):1–12 (in Japanese)

Lee H, Deguchi H (2006) The gaming of firm strategy in high-tech industry: human agents and artificial intelligence agents intermingled in a simulation model. In: Agent-based modeling meets gaming simulation. Springer, New York, pp 31–38

Chapter 12
A Formal Test of Behavioral Heterogeneity: The Case of a Structural Stochastic Volatility Model

Tae-Seok Jang

Abstract In this chapter, we examine the empirical relationship between return volatility and behavioral heterogeneity in a structural stochastic volatility model. First, we study the empirical performance of the model with two trading mechanisms via moment-based estimation from S&P 500. Second, we compare the empirical performance of both specifications. In particular, a simulated test distribution is used to evaluate the significant difference between the two models. The result of the formal test shows that the model incorporating herding fits the data better than the model incorporating wealth, but that they are not significantly different at the 5 % level.

Keywords Behavioral heterogeneity • Formal test • Herding • Structural stochastic volatility • Wealth

1 Introduction

The term "behavioral heterogeneity" has been widely used to describe a variety of trading strategies in agent-based models (ABMs) of asset pricing. For example, asset pricing models have been extended to include simple behavioral rules in the expectation formation process and allow for their feedback effects on group dynamics; see Brock and Hommes (1997, 1998). Indeed, a bottom-up approach in ABMs assumes one-to-one mapping between price movements and traders' behavior, and we can consider dynamics under endogenous group formation as resulting directly from economic interactions; see Gaunersdorfer (2000), Gaunersdorfer and Hommes (2007), Chiarella and He (2002), De Grauwe and Grimaldi (2006), and others. These artificial economies can then be used to describe group behavior in the real world where market interactions in a micro-founded model develop adjustment

T.-S. Jang (✉)
Department of Economics, BK21Plus, Seoul National University, 599 Gwanak-ro, Gwanak-gu, Seoul 151-742, Republic of Korea
e-mail: taeseok.jang@gmail.com

Y. Nakai et al. (eds.), *Agent-Based Approaches in Economic and Social Complex Systems VIII*, Agent-Based Social Systems 13, DOI 10.1007/978-4-431-55236-9_12

mechanisms in the face of excess demand and supply. In particular, ABMs predict that the empirical regularities observed in financial data involve interconnections between market turbulence and economic behavior. Hence, the empirical application of ABMs to the real world often aims to examine the effects of changes in group behavior on price movement.

In most cases, however, group behavior feeds back on macroscopic variables (or market prices), for which we cannot easily find an analytical solution using ABMs. Because of analytical intractability, for example, model parameters are often calibrated, and so the exact mapping between the model and real data remains unknown.[1] In addition, analytical moment conditions cannot be derived for these particular complex models so we need to approximate them based on simulations; see also Gilli and Winker (2003). In other words, the biggest challenges when undertaking the empirical analysis of ABMs is to find any significant relation of the model to the summary of the data generating process, and to overcome the ineffectiveness of simulation-based inference.

In our study, we attempt to bridge these gaps between complex models and the real world. To achieve this, first we study two types of switching rules in a structural stochastic volatility (SSV) model by Franke and Westerhoff (2011, 2012a). The specifications of the SSV models may serve as good examples for testing ABMs, as the notion of behavioral heterogeneity is formalized by switching rules in accordance with the discrete choice theory. Then, we estimate the model parameters using a simulated method of moments, and provide an empirical assessment of trading mechanisms from S&P 500; see also Winker et al. (2007). For that purpose, we use a formal test to evaluate whether investors (i) continue with a profitable strategy based on their own past performance (wealth) or (ii) follow the opinions of successful peer groups (herding). Note that our empirical application rests on the stylized facts of financial markets: the absence of autocorrelations in raw returns, a fat-tailed distribution, volatility clustering, and a long memory.

Though Franke and Westerhoff (2012a) investigate the fit of several variants of SSV and rank the competing models, according to the moment conditions (i.e. the joint moment coverage ratio), they do not formally examine the reliability of the model validation. Thus, in this chapter, we provide formal evidence for the empirical performance of the models, according to Hnatkovska et al. (2012) [HMT hereafter]. And, more generally, the goal of this study is to examine the effects of trading mechanism on price movements, and to formally test the empirical performance of SSV. The main finding of the study is that the model with herding has a better goodness-of-fit to the data than the model with wealth, but that, at the 5 % level, there is no statistically significant difference between the two. Notwithstanding this

[1]For example, Amilon (2008) estimated a modified version of the adaptive belief system (ABS) via a GARCH-type auxiliary model, and found that the model cannot explain long memory effects in high frequency financial data. Similarly, Franke (2010) found that the model dynamics of ABS depends on unrealistic stochastic noise when approximating the real world. See also Longtin (2003) and Fagiolo et al. (2007).

inconclusive result, this study does suggest that simulation-based inference and the formal test can serve as a basis for providing a "correct" specification for the data-generating process.

The chapter proceeds as follows. Section 2 presents the basic properties of SSV and the effects of trading mechanism on price movement. Section 3 explains the estimation methodology and model comparison. The empirical results based on the formal test are discussed in Sect. 4. Finally, Sect. 5 concludes. All relevant details of the study are given in the Appendix.

2 A Structural Stochastic Volatility Model: Herding Versus Wealth

The artificial economy of a structural stochastic volatility (SSV) model is populated by heterogeneous investors. The mean reversion and trend following strategies are adopted by fundamentalists and chartists, respectively. The demand shocks account for variation of the trading rule within each group, as follows:

$$d_t^f = \phi \left(p^* - p_t\right) + \varepsilon_t^f, \qquad \varepsilon_t^f \sim N\left(0, \sigma_f^2\right) \tag{12.1}$$

$$d_t^c = \chi \left(p_t - p_{t-1}\right) + \varepsilon_t^c, \qquad \varepsilon_t^c \sim N\left(0, \sigma_c^2\right) \tag{12.2}$$

where the state variables d_t^f and d_t^c denote the demands of average fundamentalists and chartists. ϕ and χ measure the response to price changes from the fundamentals (p^*) and previous price (p_{t-1}), respectively. The demand shocks are represented as two independent and normally distributed random variables, ε_t^f and ε_t^c, for both groups of investors.

The fundamentalist and chartist investor groups combined make of a total of $2N$ investors; i.e., $n_t^f + n_t^c = 2N$. The majority index of the fundamentalists can be written as follows:

$$x_t := \frac{n_t^f - n_t^c}{2N}. \tag{12.3}$$

Note here that extreme market sentiments are represented by "$x = \pm 1$". For example, the majority index suggests that the markets are driven by the fundamentalists ("+1") or the chartists ("−1").

Now, the price can be aligned with the market demand from the investors. Indeed, the dominance of chartists' and investors' interactions can result in excess demand. The price will rise until the disequilibrium disappears. The adjustment equation for the price at period $t + 1$ can be set up from Eqs. (12.1, 12.2, and 12.3), as follows:

$$p_{t+1} = p_t + \frac{\mu}{2}\left\{(1+x_t)\,\phi\left(p^* - p_t\right) + (1-x_t)\,\chi\left(p_t - p_{t-1}\right) + \varepsilon_t\right\} \quad (12.4)$$

$$\varepsilon_t \sim N\left(0, \sigma_t^2\right), \; \sigma_t^2 = \frac{(1+x_t)^2\sigma_f^2 + (1-x_t)^2\sigma_c^2}{2},$$

where the excess demand is adjusted by a market maker with a constant proportionality factor $\mu > 0$. Note that the total demand shocks can be summarized by two normal random distributions with mean zero and two single variances. Hence, the model predicts that price volatility is driven by market microstructure; the noise term σ_t^2 in Eq. (12.4) changes according to heterogeneous demand shocks. Thus, the current demand is closely associated with the time-varying share of fundamentalists, $(1 + x_t)\,\sigma_f$, and chartists, $(1 - x_t)\,\sigma_c$.[2]

To examine the effects of the trading mechanisms (herding and wealth) on the model, we apply the discrete choice theory to the switching mechanism, to create the endogenous group dynamics within the SSV. The market shares, then, are represented as:

$$n_t^s = \frac{\exp\left(\beta u_{t-1}^s\right)}{\exp\left(\beta u_{t-1}^f\right) + \exp\left(\beta u_{t-1}^c\right)}, \; s = f, c. \quad (12.5)$$

Note that β denotes the intensity of choice. To make Eq. (12.5) more understandable, we express it in terms of the utility advantage of the fundamentalists over the chartists:

$$n_t^f = \frac{1}{1 + \exp\left\{-\beta\left(u_{t-1}^f - u_{t-1}^c\right)\right\}}, \quad (12.6)$$

$$n_t^c = 1 - n_t^f.$$

For the sake of simplicity, we use the attractive index a_{t-1} to denote the utility difference between the groups (i.e. $u_{t-1}^f - u_{t-1}^c$). Note that the past capital gains are based on the pay-off difference between fundamentalists (u^f) and chartists (u^c). From this, we see that the group dynamics of SSV is a direct result of the utility difference observed at time $t-1$. Note that, although a different set of specifications could be chosen to describe the attractive index, for the purpose of this model comparison, we have used the herding and wealth trading strategies.

[2]The relative share of fundamentalists and chartists at group level can be represented by a simple transformation of the majority index; that is, $1 + x_t = \frac{n_t^f}{N}$ and $1 - x_t = \frac{n_t^c}{N}$.

2.1 Discrete Choice from Herding

The model with herding incorporates the mix of the mean reversion and majority index into the attractive index a_t. See Eq. (12.7). The market sentiment is based on the opinion formation process caused by group behavior, and in turn affects the attractive index:

$$a_t\left(x_t, p_t\right) := \alpha_0 + \alpha_x x_t + \alpha_d \left(p_t - p^*\right)^2, \tag{12.7}$$

where α_0 measures the predisposition of traders to the fundamentals. α_x and α_d denote group pressure and the influence of misalignment ($\alpha_{x,}$ $\alpha_d > 0$).

2.2 Discrete Choice from Wealth

The model with wealth shows that the investors can exploit observed differences in profit between the two groups. Thus, any change in capital gains can create endogenous switching dynamics, given that agents with a lower payoff may switch to the trading strategy with a better performance record:

$$\begin{aligned} g_t^s &= \{\exp(p_t) - \exp(p_{t-1})\} \cdot d_{t-2}^s \\ \omega_t^s &= \eta \omega_{t-1}^s + (1-\eta)\, g_t^s \\ a_t\left(x_t, p_t\right) &:= \alpha_\omega \left(\omega_t^f - \omega_t^c\right), \end{aligned} \tag{12.8}$$

where current wealth is a weighted sum of previous wealth (ω_{t-1}) and current profits (g_t). The coefficient η measures agents' memory of previous profit ($0 \leq \eta \leq 1$), while α_ω denotes their speed of switching between pay-off strategies ($\alpha_\omega > 0$).

3 Estimation Method and Model Comparison

This section outlines the estimation method and model comparison. We use the simulated method of moments (SMM) to approximate the analytical moments, since a non-linear specification of the switching mechanism makes the model solution analytically intractable. Then, the behavioral parameters can be estimated by minimizing the distance between the simulated and empirical moments.

To enable a comparison of the models, we consider the objective function for both, as follows:

$$J_I(\theta) = \min_{\theta \in \Theta} \left\{\widehat{m}_T - m^I\left(\theta^I\right)\right\}' \widehat{W} \left\{\widehat{m}_T - m^I\left(\theta^I\right)\right\}, \; I = A,\ B \tag{12.9}$$

where the notation I is used to indicate the specifications for herding (A) and wealth (B). m^I denotes a vector of the model-generated moments, and $\widehat{m}$ is an estimate of true moment m_0. Note that the moment conditions can be approximated by simulations (i.e. $m^I\left(\theta^I\right) = \frac{1}{\psi \cdot T}\sum_{t=1}^{\psi \cdot T} m_t$). To reduce approximation errors the simulation size ψ is set to 100.

The weight matrix $\widehat{W}$ is estimated using the moving block bootstrap method:

$$\Omega_{BB} := Var\left(m^b\right) = \frac{1}{BB}\sum_{b=1}^{BB}\left(m^b - \overline{m}\right)\left(m^b - \overline{m}\right)', \tag{12.10}$$

where m^b is a vector of the bootstrapped sample moments, BB is the number of repetitions in the block bootstrap sampling and $\overline{m}$ is the mean value of the bootstrapped moments. The variance-covariance matrix of moments is based on 1,000 moving block bootstrapped samples. We use the inverse of the matrix for the weight matrix in the objective function; i.e. $\widehat{W} = \widehat{\Omega}_{BB}^{-1}$. The window size of the block length is set to 250 days.[3] The double block bootstrap method generates both the variation when estimating moments and the covariance between them; see Appendix 2.

Under standard regularity conditions, the estimated parameters converge asymptotically to true one in distribution with a normal random vector of mean zero and covariance of Λ_ψ (Lee and Ingram (1991) and Duffie and Singleton (1993)):

$$\Lambda_\psi = \left\{\left(D_\psi\ W\ D'_\psi\right)^{-1}\right\}\ D'_\psi W\ \left(1 + \frac{1}{\psi}\right)\Omega\ W\ D_\psi\left\{\left(D_\psi\ W\ D'_\psi\right)^{-1}\right\}', \tag{12.11}$$

where D_ψ is the simulated partial derivative of the moments. This can be numerically computed at optimum $\left(D_\psi \equiv E\left[\frac{\partial m(\theta)}{\partial \theta}\right]\right)$.

Next, we consider the hypotheses used to compare the goodness-of-fit of the competing models. The null hypothesis H_0 is that the two non-nested models fit the data equally:

$$H_0\ :\ \left\|\sqrt{W}\ \left(\widehat{m}_T - m^A\left(\theta^A\right)\right)\right\| - \left\|\sqrt{W}\ \left(\widehat{m}_T - m^B\left(\theta^B\right)\right)\right\| = 0. \tag{12.12}$$

To test H_0, we define the quasi-likelihood-ratio (QLR) statistic as follows:

[3] In the bootstrap method, we can adapt to a long sample, as the window length might be evidenced by a long range dependence in the data. The performance of double blocks-of-blocks procedures has been compared by Bühlmann (2002), Horowitz et al. (2006), Lee and Lai (2009), and others. In particular, autocorrelations in S&P 500 can be distorted where the window length of more than one year is used; see also Winker and Jeleskovic (2007).

$$\widehat{\text{QLR}} = J^B\left(\widehat{\theta}^B\right) - J^A\left(\widehat{\theta}^A\right). \tag{12.13}$$

The models A and B are evaluated according to the hypothesis testing method of Vuong (1989). We conduct two sequential procedures with the QLR statistic; see Hnatkovska et al. (2011) [HMT-sub henceforth].

The first step of the model comparison is to compute critical values of QLR.[4] The simulated QLR is based on the following χ^2 -type distribution:

$$Z'\widehat{\sum_m}^{1/2} W\left(V^B - V^A\right) W\widehat{\sum_m}^{1/2} Z,\ Z \sim N\left(0, E_{n_m}\right) \tag{12.14}$$

where Σ is a positive definite covariance matrix of the moment estimates, and Z is drawn from the multivariate normal distribution (n_m).

If $\widehat{\text{QLR}}$ exceeds the critical threshold value from a 95 % confidence interval, then the null hypothesis is rejected. Next, the second step is to investigate the uncertainty about the rejection. The suggested test statistic has a standard normal distribution (z):

$$w_0 = 2 \cdot \sqrt{\left(m^B\left(\theta^B\right) - m^A\left(\theta^A\right)\right)' W\left(m^B\left(\theta^B\right) - m^A\left(\theta^A\right)\right)}, \tag{12.15}$$

where we use w_0 to denote the uncertainty about the $\widehat{\text{QLR}}$ estimates of the two models. Accordingly, the null of the equal fits can be rejected when either $\sqrt{T} \cdot \frac{\text{QLR}(\widehat{\theta}^B, \widehat{\theta}^A)}{\widehat{w}_0} > z_{1-0.05/2}$ making A the preferred model, or $\sqrt{T} \cdot \frac{\text{QLR}(\widehat{\theta}^B, \widehat{\theta}^A)}{\widehat{w}_0} < -z_{1-0.05/2}$ making B the preferred one.

4 Empirical Application

This section describes the empirical application's data set and moment conditions. According to the estimation results of the SSV model, we evaluate both models' fit to the data with a formal test.

4.1 Data and Moment Conditions

We explore the relation between the model and the data-generating process, based on a set of stylized facts about financial data. The main focus of our study is the time-dependent behavior exhibited in daily historical data from the S&P 500 index from

[4] Appendix 1 presents intermediate steps for simulating the QLR distribution. Its derivation is based on the mean value expansion of binding function (or moment conditions).

Table 12.1 Empirical and Bootstrapped Moment Estimates from S&P 500

Label		Empirical	Moving BB
m_1	Mean	0.0427	0.0421
m_2	Variance	1.0628	1.0706
m_3	$Corr(r_t, r_{t+1})$	0.0196	0.0191
m_4	$Corr(\|r_t\|, \|r_{t+1}\|)$	0.1825	0.1746
m_5	$Corr(\|r_t\|, \|r_{t+5}\|)$	0.2131	0.2041
m_6	$Corr(\|r_t\|, \|r_{t+10}\|)$	0.1531	0.1455
m_7	$Corr(\|r_t\|, \|r_{t+20}\|)$	0.1264	0.1138
m_8	$Corr(\|r_t\|, \|r_{t+50}\|)$	0.1070	0.0850
m_9	$Corr(\|r_t\|, \|r_{t+100}\|)$	0.0703	0.0406
m_{10}	5–10 % right tail of Hill	3.2722	3.2981
Test		95 %: 19.07	99 %: 25.44

Note: Moving BB means the moving block bootstrapped data
The summary statistics are based on 1,000 repetition of the bootstrap procedure

Jan.02.1980 to Sep.29.2006. The sample size of the returns is 6,750.[5] Table 12.1 presents a summary of the empirical and block bootstrapped moment estimates from the S&P 500 index.

The mean (m_1) and variance (m_2) capture the general shape of the data distribution. The first lag of autocorrelation of raw returns (m_3) is chosen to cope with the empirical fact that returns are not serially correlated; if the 1st lag appears to have no correlation, then the raw returns do not exhibit significant dependence over the subsequent lags. The short- and long-term dependence of returns on volatility can be taken into account when considering the autocorrelations of absolute returns (m_4, m_5, m_6, m_7, m_8, m_9). Finally, the Hill estimator (m_{10}) measures the fat-tailedness of extreme distributions in the data.

Figure 12.1 depicts a kernel density of the objective function, based on 1,000 resampled data sets. It shows that the 95 % and 95 % criteria are 19.07 and 25.44. Model misspecification is indicated by a QLR statistic exceeding the threshold. Thereby, we can evaluate whether the model successfully matches the data along the chosen moment conditions.

4.2 Estimation Results and Formal Test

In this section, we first present the estimation results from the SMM, and discuss the model comparison. Because of identification issues in non-linear switching dynamics, the level parameters, ϕ, χ, and μ, in the price equation are calibrated.

[5]Note that the choice of moments can be based on the relevant research goals. The moments in the study is motivated by Pagan (1996), as well as Winker and Jeleskovic (2006, 2007).

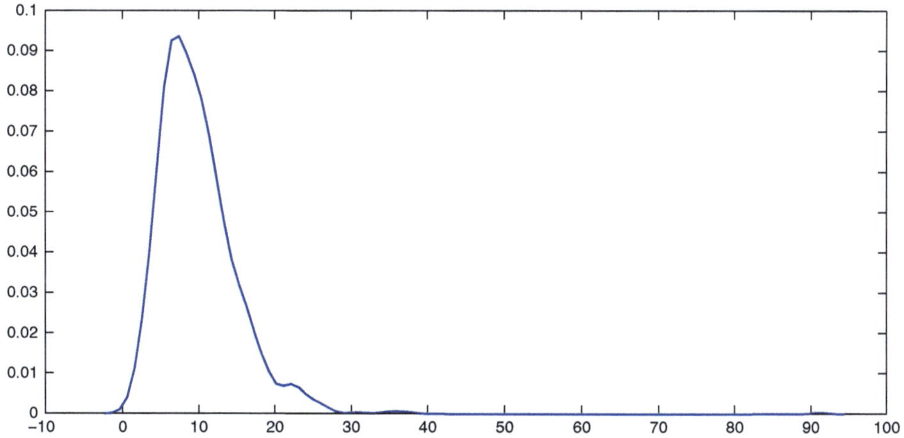

Fig. 12.1 Simulated distribution of objective function

Table 12.2 Parameter Estimates of Herding and Wealth

Label	Herding	Wealth
$\widehat{\alpha}_0$	−0.417 (−0.640 −− 0.195)	–
$\widehat{\alpha}_x$	1.773 (1.280 − 2.267)	–
$\widehat{\alpha}_d$	19.022 (11.128 − 26.916)	–
$\widehat{\alpha}_\omega/100$	–	21.248 (0.0 − 99.129)
$\widehat{\eta}$	–	0.986 (0.981 − 0.992)
$\widehat{\sigma}_f$	0.788 (0.706 − 0.870)	0.684 (0.609 − 0.759)
$\widehat{\sigma}_c$	2.983 (2.414 − 3.551)	1.957 (1.522 − 2.391)
$\widehat{J}(\theta)$	26.11	49.85

Note: The bracket ( ) indicates the 95 % confidence interval of parameter estimates

In particular, the intensity of choice is set to a value such that the model allows for a moderate degree of switching behavior (i.e. $\beta = 1$); see also Manski and McFadden (1981), as well as Goldbaum and Mizrach (2008). For the herding mechanism, the parameters are set to the following values: $(\beta, \phi, \chi, \mu) = (1.0, 0.12, 1.5, 0.01)$. For the wealth mechanism, they are set to the following values: $(\beta, \phi, \chi, \mu) = (1.0, 1.0, 1.0, 0.01)$.[6]

Both models are estimated using the SMM; see Table 12.2. A direct comparison of the different models' estimation results is not meaningful, since the two models are driven by switching processes derived from different attractive indices. However

[6]These level parameters are chosen following Franke and Westerhoff (2012a, b). Admittedly, some changes in those parameters can result in different objective function values. Nonetheless, note that the aim of this study is to show how the formal test can be applied to ABMs, rather than undertake an elaborate estimation of SSV. Jang (2015) explores in more depth the parameter variations of a stochastic agent-based model with respect to particular parameter space.

the estimated values of the demand shocks are important to mention here. For example, the parameter estimation for the herding mechanism suggests that for chartists the influence on demand shock is significantly higher than that of the wealth mechanism ($\widehat{\sigma}_c$: 2.98 (herding) > 1.96 (wealth)), but for fundamentalists it is only marginally so ($\widehat{\sigma}_f$: 0.79 (herding), 0.68 (wealth)). This result shows that in the model with herding, the price movements are mainly driven by the demand shock of the chartists. However, in the model with wealth, the price reacts strongly to changes in the utility difference between investors ($\widehat{\alpha}_\omega$).

Focusing on the above estimation results, we conduct a formal comparison of the two models. According to Vuong (1989), the two models are overlapping if (i) they have common moment conditions and (ii) neither model is nested in the other. Both models are based on the same structure except for the specification of the attractive index.

Also, more generally, the classification for both models can be derived using the following intermediate steps: first, we use $\theta^h = (\widehat{\alpha}_0, \widehat{\alpha}_x, \widehat{\alpha}_d)'$ and $\theta^w = (\eta, \alpha_\omega)'$ to denote the parameter set for the herding and wealth mechanism. In the particular case where $\theta^h = 0$ and $\theta^w = 0$, the models have same moment conditions of $m^A\left(\theta^h\right) = m^B\left(\theta^w\right)$. In other words, the fit of the two models to the true data-generating process is equally accurate. Thus, we can exclude the case of strictly non-nested models. In addition, one model is not nested in another, since each model builds on a different trading mechanism, implying that each model can generate different moment conditions, according to their particular parameter values. Both models, then, can have different moments asymptotically $m^A\left(\theta^h\right) \neq m^B\left(\theta^w\right)$ if $\theta^h \neq 0$ and $\theta^w \neq 0$. Therefore, the models with herding and wealth meet the criteria required to be overlapping.

Following HMT, we use a two step sequential test. First, we compare the minimum values of the objective function, 26.11 for herding and 49.85 for wealth. Subtracting these values we obtain a significant difference of 23.74 ($B - A = 23.74$).

This estimated significant difference between the two objective function values of 23.74, does not exceed the simulated critical value for the model comparison, calculated to be 141.21 at 5 % level using the method in Appendix 2. Because, therefore, we cannot reject the hypothesis that the models fit the data equally, we cannot meaningfully proceed to the second step of thc comparison.

To see the details, we can compare the model-generated and empirical moments. Tables 12.1 and 12.3 show that the fit of both herding and wealth to empirical moments is fairly good. Moreover, the numerical values of the estimated objective function indicate that the model-generated moments are not significantly different from the empirical moments at the 5 % level. The inconclusiveness of the result can be verified by visual inspection; see Figs. 12.2 and 12.3.

The reason behind the inconclusive result is likely to be closely related to a high variation in the financial data samples, particularly the information relating to extreme returns. Overall, the results show that when matching the empirical features of the data, the switching dynamics is robust to the attractiveness index.

Table 12.3 Model-generated Moments: Herding versus Wealth

Label	Herding	Wealth
m_1	0.000	0.000
m_2	1.306	1.351
m_3	0.008	0.007
m_4	0.239	0.241
m_5	0.226	0.215
m_6	0.208	0.198
m_7	0.172	0.166
m_8	0.105	0.104
m_9	0.056	0.049
m_{10}	2.912	3.285

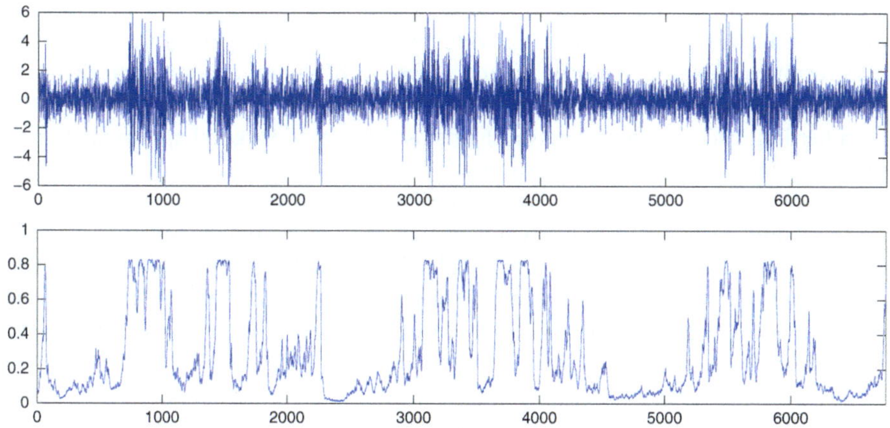

Fig. 12.2 Returns (*upper*) and Fraction of Chartists (*lower*): Herding

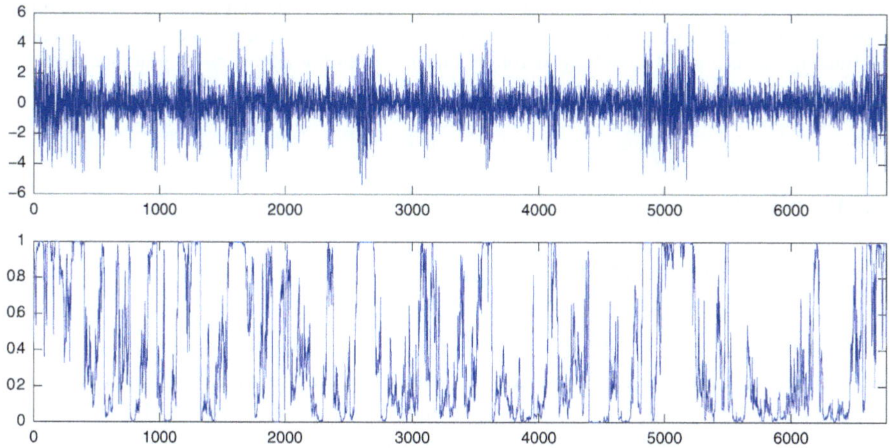

Fig. 12.3 Returns (*upper*) and Fraction of Chartists (*lower*): Wealth

Thus, it can be concluded that the proportion of chartists plays an important part in approximating the stylized facts of financial volatility; a higher proportion of chartists leads to a higher volatility of returns.

5 Conclusion

In this study, we examined the importance of behavioral heterogeneity when describing the stylized facts of financial data. To show this, we evaluated the empirical performance of models with herding and wealth in SSV. We found that the model with herding can provide a better fit to the volatility of financial data than the model with wealth. However, according to a formal test, we cannot reject the null hypothesis that both models provide an equal fit to the data at the 5 % level. The result implies that a formalization of group behavior, according to different switching rules, is not inconsistent with empirical data. Hence, we conclude that both herding and wealth trading mechanisms can provide a good approximation to the data generating process in this study.

It goes without saying that the development of the psychological behavior of traders would be an interesting research agenda as a variety of heuristics can serve as a convenient way to describe the group behavior of heterogeneous agents. However, the micro-level analysis should be undertaken with care as a behavioral rule can give rise to model misspecification in an empirical application context. Because of the uncertainty about the model space, the model comparison method can be applied to find any appropriate approximation of "wrong" models to the real world. More empirical scrutiny of ABMs is necessary.

Acknowledgment A preliminary version of this paper was presented at seminars in the Kiel Institute for the World Economy in Germany, at the 10th Annual Advances in Econometrics Conference at Southern Methodist University in Dallas, TX., US, and at the 8th international workshop on Agent-based Approach in Economic and Social Complex Systems in the Shibaura Institute of Science and Technology in Tokyo, Japan. The author expresses his gratitude to all the participants for their active involvement in the workshop.

Appendices

Technical Note on Model Comparison

This section summarizes the matrix notations for deriving the test distribution. The formal test is constructed under the assumption that the misspecified model can be evaluated using a non-optimal weight matrix. In our study, the SMM allows the weight matrix to include the correlation of the moment conditions for computing the objective function; see the supplementary paper by HMT. In that paper, the moment estimates and the unique elements of a random weight matrix are asymptotically normally distributed under standard assumptions[7]:

$$\sqrt{T}\left[\{m_T - \widehat{m}(\theta)\}', \left(\xi_T - \widehat{\xi}\right)\right]' \underset{d}{\rightarrow} N\left(0, \widehat{\Sigma}_0\right), \tag{12.16}$$

where ξ is the unique elements of W. They can determine the degree of sampling variability of the moment estimates.[8]

As mentioned earlier, the weight matrix is set to $W = \widehat{\Omega}_{BB}^{-1}$. We then calculate the selection matrix C_W from its simple multiplication of vec $(W) = C_w\widehat{\xi}$. Note that the matrix C_w has the dimensions $n_m^2 \times d$ where d denotes the number of unique elements of W. The block bootstrap method can provide a consistent estimate of the variance-covariance matrix $\widehat{\Sigma}_0$; the matrix dimension is $(n_m + d) \times (n_m + d)$.

Now, we see that the matrices $D,\ F,\ M$ are non-singular in the neighborhood of θ:

$$\begin{aligned} D^I &= \left(W\ E_I \otimes \left(\widehat{m}_T - m^I\left(\theta^I\right)\right)' C_W\right) \\ F^I &= \frac{\partial m^I\left(\theta^I\right)'}{\partial \theta^I} W \frac{\partial m^I\left(\theta^I\right)}{\partial \theta^{I'}} - M^I \\ M^I &= \left(E_I \otimes \left(\widehat{m}_T - m^I\left(\theta^I\right)\right)' W\right) \frac{\partial}{\partial \theta^{I'}} \operatorname{vec}\left(\frac{\partial m^I\left(\theta^I\right)}{\partial \theta^{I'}}\right), \end{aligned} \tag{12.17}$$

where E_I is the identity matrix of which the dimension is $n_\theta^I \times n_\theta^I$. Note that the dimensions of the matrices $\frac{\partial m^I(\theta^I)}{\partial \theta^I}$ and $\frac{\partial}{\partial \theta^{I'}} \operatorname{vec}\left(\frac{\partial m^I(\theta^I)}{\partial \theta^{I'}}\right)$ are $(n_m + d) \times n_\theta^I$ and $(n_m + d) \cdot n_\theta^I \times n_\theta^I$. The dimensions of F^I and M^I are n_θ^I by n_θ^I.

The theorem S.4 of HMT-sup states that the QLR test distribution converges in distribution to $z'\ \widehat{\Sigma}_0^{\frac{1}{2}}\left(U^B - U^A\right)\widehat{\Sigma}_0^{\frac{1}{2}} z$, where $z \sim N\left(0,\ E_{n_m+d}\right)$. The $n_\theta^I + d$ by $n_\theta^I + d$ matrix U^I is defined as $U^I = U_1^I - U_2^I - U_3^I - U_4^I$. The matrix notation $(W\ 0)$ suggests that the $n_\theta^I + d$ zero matrix is stacked into the $n_\theta^I \times n_\theta^I$ weight matrix. The dimension of $(W\ 0)$, then, is $n_\theta^I \times \left(n_\theta^I + d\right)$.

[7]The term "random" indicates a full weight matrix without imposing any restriction on the off-diagonal elements. The matrix is data-dependent as the elements are estimated from empirical data.

[8]For example, the uncertainty about the first moment is measured by the second moment, while the uncertainty about the second moment is represented by the fourth moment (kurtosis). Note that the uncertainty about those unique elements are estimated using the double block bootstrap method.

$$U_1^I = D^{I'} \frac{\partial m^I(\theta^I)}{\partial \theta^{I'}} \left(F^{I'}\right)^{-1} \frac{\partial m^I(\theta^I)'}{\partial \theta^I} W \frac{\partial m^I(\theta^I)}{\partial \theta^{I'}} \left(F^I\right)^{-1} \frac{\partial m^I(\theta^I)'}{\partial \theta^I} D^I$$

$$U_2^I = (W\ 0) \frac{\partial m^I(\theta^I)}{\partial \theta^{I'}} \left(F^I\right)^{-1} \frac{\partial m^I(\theta^I)'}{\partial \theta^I} D^I + D^{I'} \frac{\partial m^I(\theta^I)}{\partial \theta^{I'}} \left(F^{I'}\right)^{-1} \frac{\partial m^I(\theta^I)'}{\partial \theta^I} (W\ 0)$$

$$U_3^I = D^{I'} \frac{\partial m^I(\theta^I)}{\partial \theta^{I'}} \left(F^{I'}\right)^{-1} \left(M^{I'} + M^I\right) \left(F^I\right)^{-1} \frac{\partial m^I(\theta^I)'}{\partial \theta^I} D^I$$

$$U_4^I = \left(0\ E_I \otimes \left(\widehat{m}_T - m^I(\theta^I)' C_W\right)\right)' \frac{\partial m^I(\theta^I)}{\partial \theta^{I'}} \left(F^{I'}\right)^{-1} \frac{\partial m^I(\theta^I)'}{\partial \theta^I} + D^{I'} \frac{\partial m^I(\theta^I)}{\partial \theta^{I'}} \left(F^{I'}\right)^{-1} \frac{\partial m^I(\theta^I)'}{\partial \theta^I} \left(0\ E_I \otimes \left(\widehat{m}_T - m^I\left(\theta^I\right)\right)' C_W\right)$$

A sequential testing procedure is used to compare the overlapping models; see Vuong (1989). First, we test the hypothesis that the fit of the models to the empirical moments is equivalent. If this hypothesis is rejected, the second step is to evaluate the uncertainty about the rejection, based on the asymptotic distribution of the QLR statistic (see theorem S.5 in HMT-sup). In our application, in the first step we could not reject the equal fit of the models; we do not need to consider the second step.

Double Moving Block Bootstrap Method

This section discusses the moving bootstrap method for estimating the covariance matrix; also see Lahiri (2003). The double block bootstrap method is used to estimate variation of the moment conditions and the unique elements of the weight matrix.

Now, we assume that the random variables $X_1, \cdots, X_N$ are weakly dependent and stationary. We use χ_n and l to denote the sample and an integer for the sub-sample; i.e. $\chi_n = \{X_1, \cdots, X_N\}$, $l \equiv l_n \in [1, n]$. The following routine generates 1,000 resampled data points from the sub-blocked samples of $B_i = (X_i, \cdots, X_{i+l-1})$:

- Draw the data replacing a fixed block length, and generate the bootstrap sample, of which the size is T. Let B^* denote the resampled data; i.e. $B^* = \{B_1^*, \cdots, B_k^*\}$, where the elements in B_i^* consist of $\left(X^*_{(i-1)l+1}, \cdots, X^*_{il}\right)$ with $i = 1, \cdots, k$.
- Shuffle B^* again using random interval point and generate a double bootstrapped sample of size T. Let B^{**} denote the double resampled data; i.e. $B^{**} = \{B_1^{**}, \cdots, B_k^{**}\}$, where the elements in B_i^{**} consist of $\left(X^{**}_{(i-1)l+1}, \cdots, X^{**}_{il}\right)$ with $i = 1, \cdots, k$.
- Compute the variance-covariance matrix of B^{**}; i.e. $\widehat{\Sigma}_0$. The matrix will be inserted into the simulated test distribution for the model comparison (see Eq. (12.16) in Appendix 1).

References

Amilon H (2008) Estimation of an adaptive stock market model with heterogeneous agents. J Empir Finan 15:342–362

Brock W, Hommes C (1997) Rational routes to randomness. Econometrica 65:1059–1095

Brock W, Hommes C (1998) Heterogeneous beliefs and routes to chaos in a simple asset pricing model. J Econ Dyn Control 22:1235–1274

Bühlmann P (2002) Bootstraps for time series. Stat Sci 17(1):52–72

Chiarella C, He X (2002) Heterogeneous beliefs, risk and learning in a simple asset pricing model. Comput Econ 19:95–132

De Grauwe P, Grimaldi M (2006) Exchange rate puzzles: a tale of switching attractors. Eur Econ Rev 50:95–132

Duffie D, Singleton K (1993) Simulated moments estimation of Markov models of asset prices. Econometrica 61(4):929–952

Fagiolo G, Birchenhall C, Windrum P (2007) Special issue on "empirical validation in agent-based models". Comput Econ 30(3):195–226

Franke R (2010) On the specification of noise in two agent-based asset pricing models. J Econ Dyn Control 34(6):1140–1152

Franke R, Westerhoff F (2011) Estimation of a structural volatility model of asset pricing. Comput Econ 38:53–83

Franke R, Westerhoff F (2012a) Structural volatility in asset pricing dynamics: estimation and model contest. J Econ Dyn Control 36(8):1193–1211

Franke R, Westerhoff F (2012b) Converse trading strategies, intrinsic noise and the stylized facts of financial markets. Quant Finan 12(3):425–436

Gaunersdorfer A (2000) Endogenous fluctuations in a simple asset pricing model with heterogeneous agents. J Econ Dyn Control 24:799–831

Gaunersdorfer A, Hommes C (2007) A nonlinear structural model for volatility clustering. In: Teyssiere G, Kirman A (eds) Long memory in economics. Springer, Berlin, pp 265–288

Gilli M, Winker P (2003) A global optimization heuristic for estimating agent based models. Comput Stat Data Anal 42(3):299–312

Goldbaum D, Mizrach B (2008) Estimating the intensity of choice in a dynamic mutual fund allocation decision. J Econ Dyn Control 32(11):3866–3876

Hnatkovska V, Marmer V, Tang, Y (2011) Supplement to "Comparison of misspecified calibrated models". Working paper, Vancouver: University of British Columbia

Hnatkovska V, Marmer V, Tang Y (2012) Comparison of misspecified calibrated models: the minimum distance approach. J Econ 169(1):131–138

Horowitz JL, Lobato IN, Nankervis JC, Savin NE (2006) Bootstrapping the Box-Pierce Q test: a robust test of uncorrelatedness. J Econ 133(2):841–862

Jang T-S (2015) Identification of social interaction effects in financial data. Comput Econ 45:207–238

Lahiri SN (2003) Resampling methods for dependent data. Springer, Berlin

Lee B-S, Ingram BF (1991) Simulation estimation of time-series models. J Econ 47:197–205

Lee S, Lai P (2009) Double block bootstrap confidence intervals for dependent data. Biometrika 96(2):427–443

Longtin A (2003) Effect of noise on nonlinear dynamics. In: Beuter A, Glass L, Mackey MC, Titcombe M (eds) Nonlinear dynamics in physiology and medicine. Springer-Verlag, New York, pp 149–189

Manski C, McFadden D (1981) Structural analysis of discrete data and econometric applications. The MIT Press, Cambridge

Pagan A (1996) The econometrics of financial markets. J Empir Finan 3:15–102

Vuong Q (1989) Likelihood ratio tests for model selection and non-nested hypotheses. Econometrica 57(2):307–333

Winker P, Jeleskovic V (2006) The unconditional distribution of exchange rate returns: statistics, robustness, time aggregation, Working paper 008-06. University of Essex, Colchester
Winker P, Jeleskovic V (2007) Dependence of – and long memory in – exchange rate returns: statistics, robustness, time aggregation, Working paper 011-07. University of Essex, Colchester
Winker P, Gilli M, Jeleskovic V (2007) An objective function for simulation based inference on exchange rate data. J Econ Interac Coord 2:125–145

Chapter 13
An Agent-Based Implementation of Service System Interactions Based on the ISPAR Model

Chathura Rajapakse and Takao Terano

Abstract We present a method to develop agent-based models based on the service system abstraction and the ISPAR model, to study market systems in the light of Service-Dominant logic. Service-Dominant logic is a mindset that acts as a lens, through which we can see the world in a different way. More precisely, it intends to bring new insights into the marketing domain by perceiving the market as a system of resource integrating actors, who exchange resources in the form of services. The service system abstraction and the ISPAR model of service system interactions provide a reasonable starting point for this endeavor. We explain how the service system abstraction and the ISPAR model could be implemented computationally through an agent-based model of a hypothetical market system. We further argue that the proposed method could be successfully applied to study various real market phenomena.

Keywords Agent-based modeling • Service-dominant logic • Service systems • Service science • ISPAR model • NKCS model

1 Introduction

The mindset of Service-Dominant Logic, also known as S-D logic, is a lens, which enables to look at market interactions and value creation in a different way (Vargo and Lusch 2011). More precisely, it intends to bring new insights into the marketing domain by perceiving the market as a system of resource integrating actors, who exchange resources in the form of services (Vargo and Lusch 2011). According to Ostrom et al. (2010), S-D logic has a staggering potential to continue to be a catalyst for important research in the field of services. Concurrently, service system is a term coined in the field of Service Science, Management and Engineering (SSME) to abstract the market into identifiable entities to study the nature of service and the ways and means to understand and improve service (Maglio et al. 2009; Maglio and

C. Rajapakse (✉) • T. Terano
Department of Computational Intelligence and Systems Science, Tokyo Institute of Technology, 4259, Nagatsuta-cho, Midori-ku, Yokohama, Japan
e-mail: chathura@dis.titech.ac.jp; terano@dis.titech.ac.jp

Y. Nakai et al. (eds.), *Agent-Based Approaches in Economic and Social Complex Systems VIII*, Agent-Based Social Systems 13, DOI 10.1007/978-4-431-55236-9_13

Spohrer 2008). The service system abstraction largely buys in concepts from S-D logic and helps defining the structure and behavior of resource integrating actors in a market system. ISPAR model is a process model, which explains the behavior of different service systems such as people, businesses, government agencies, etc., in an interactive market environment (Maglio et al. 2009).

Markets are social systems with lots of dynamics due to complex adaptive nature of the interactions among individual actors. Therefore, the study of complex macro-level market patterns requires a focus on the dynamic, micro-level interactions among market entities. This makes the Agent-based Modeling (ABM) (Terano 2008; Epstein 2006; Casti 1997) a suitable approach in the study of market systems since a market could be modeled and simulated using ABM as a complex adaptive system of individual agents such as customers, firms and government agencies. Given that the S-D logic provides a new lens to look at market systems, we suggest research combining S-D logic and ABM would be highly beneficial to the progress of the marketing theory. In this endeavor, the service system abstraction and the ISPAR model are very important conceptualizations as they extract the essence of S-D logic to provide a starting point for agent-based modeling of market systems. In other words, the service system abstraction resembles agents and the ISPAR model guides the implementation of their behavior.

In this paper, we present an agent-based model of a hypothetical market comprising providers and customers of one particular service. We propose a method to computationally represent service systems and implement their interactions based on the guidance of the ISPAR model. We then present some preliminary results of our simulations on the evolution of service provider agents with respect to customer arrivals over time. Finally, we discuss a potential application of this method in the domain of consumer behavior. The rest of the paper is organized as follows. In Chap. 2 we discuss the relevant literature and in Chap. 3 we explain our method to computationally represent service systems. In Chap. 4, we introduce our agent-based model and some preliminary results. Chapter 5 contains a discussion on the results and a potential real-world application of the proposed method. Chapter 6 concludes the present work.

2 Literature Review

2.1 Service Science

As the share of service sector in the economies of most industrialized and non-industrialized nations has continued to grow over the past three decades (Central Intelligence Agency – USA 2012), Service Science, which is also called Service Science, Management and Engineering (SSME) has become an emerging research discipline (Spohrer et al. 2007; Spohrer and Maglio 2008). Service science aims at understanding service systems and their interactions to create the basis for systematic service innovation. Service-Dominant logic (S-D logic) (Lusch et al.

2006) has been acknowledged as the provider of right perspective, vocabulary, and assumptions, on which a theory of service systems, their configurations and interactions could be built (Maglio and Spohrer 2008). In other words, S-D logic provides a lens through which the world could be seen in a different way; as multiplicities of various types of service systems exchanging services for the mutual well being (Vargo and Lusch 2011).

Service system is proposed as the basic abstraction of service science, which is formally defined as a configuration of people, technologies, and other resources that interact with other service systems to create mutual value (Maglio et al. 2009). The service system abstraction eliminates the traditional producer vs. Consumer distinction, in which the producer plays the role of value creator where as the customer plays the role of value destroyer (Maglio et al. 2009). Instead, it adopts the S-D logics notion of exchange of services, in which value is being co-created through the combined efforts of firms, employees, customers, stakeholders, government agencies and other entities related to a given exchange, but determined always by the beneficiary (customer) (Vargo et al. 2008). A service system possesses a value proposition, through which it interacts with other service systems (Maglio et al. 2009). A value proposition is a combination of value creating attributes, along which the resources of the service system are organized (Rajapakse and Terano 2013a). According to this service system abstraction, anything ranging from individuals, firms and agencies to worlds and planets could be a service system, which agglomerates resources and interacts with other service systems through different value propositions.

The ISPAR Model An interaction between two service systems has been presented as a model of ten possible outcomes in the ISPAR (Interact-Serve- Propose-Agree-Realize) model (Maglio et al. 2009). In the ISPAR model, an interaction can be either a service interaction or a non-service interaction. Service interactions are value co-creation interactions where each service system engages in three main activities: (1) proposing a value co-creation interaction to another service system (proposal), (2) agreeing to a proposal (agreement), (3) realizing the proposal (realization). A non-service interaction may involve a welcoming behavior such as exchanging pleasantries on the street or an unwelcoming behavior such as committing a crime. Non-service interactions basically acts as determinants of future value co-creation interactions. Figure 13.1 is an illustration of the ISPAR model.

2.2 *Agent-Based Modeling*

Agent-based modeling takes the generative approach in social science, in which a generativist looking forward to explain the emergence of macroscopic societal regularities, such as norms or price equilibrium, would like to know how the decentralized local interactions of heterogeneous autonomous agents could generate

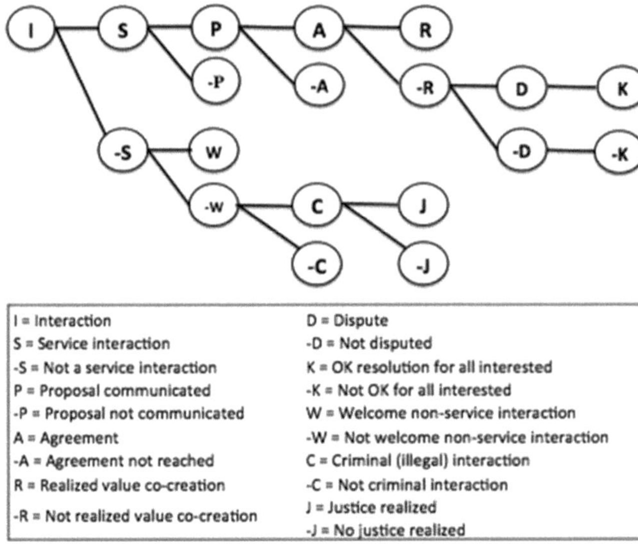

Fig. 13.1 The ISPAR model of service system interactions

the given regularity (Epstein 2006). Generally, the interdependency, emergence and non-linearity inherent in the underlying processes make it difficult for humans, unassisted by computer simulations, to effectively reason about the consequences of actions in a complex system (Carley 1999). An agent-based model enables to generate a would-be world (Casti 1997), in the form of a computer simulation, in which a group of heterogeneous, autonomous, bounded rational agents interact locally in an explicit space (Epstein 2006). The creation of such silicon surrogates of real-world complex systems allows researchers to perform controlled repeatable experiments on the real McCoy (Casti 1997).

3 Representing Service Systems as Agents

Our method to represent service systems computationally (as agents) uses Kauffman's NKCS architecture (Padget et al. 2009) as the basis. The NKCS model has been originally developed to mimic the co-evolution of multiple species in biological ecosystems through actions and reactions of individual species (Padget et al. 2009). This can be likened to the co-evolution process of interacting service systems, both individually as well as systemically, through value co-creation on service interactions (Rajapakse and Terano 2013a). More details of the NKCS model and the possibility of its application to the domain of service systems could be found in Rajapakse and Terano (2013a and Padget et al. (2009).

According to Maglio et al. (2009), a service involves at least two service systems, one applying competence and another integrating the applied competences with other resources to determine the benefit (value co-creation). A given service system is an instance of a particular service system entity such as customers, service providers, etc. For example in a tourism market, instances of Tourists entity interact with instances of Hotels entity for lodging service. Therefore, we begin with defining the structure of service systems.

According to the definition, each service system has a value proposition (Maglio et al. 2009) and a value proposition could be identified as a combination of value creating attributes (Ng et al. 2012). More precisely, service systems mobilize their resources into these attributes and develop their competences along them. For example, 'providing Internet access' could be one attribute of a hotel's value proposition in the tourism market. Thus, we represent the structure of value proposition of each entity as a combination of N such attributes. A given attribute is set to be at a particular state out of D possible states, where D could be an integer from the set $\{0, 1, 2 \ldots d - 1\}$. For example, providing Internet access could be done by different ways such as setting up Wi-Fi zones inside hotel premises, giving access on request at a charge, giving in-room Wi-Fi access to all residents, etc. and each of these ways corresponds to a particular state of the attribute. States of all N attributes of a given service system in combination make the overall state of that service system. In other words, instances of a given service system entity could be at any of D^N possible states at a given time. For example, if we define the value proposition of hotels as $N = 5$ and $D = 2$, hotel A's state could be 10101 where as hotel B's state could be 01010. This reflects the differences of resources and competences of the two instances of the same entity. In other words, if two hotels are identical in every aspect, they should bear the same state string.

According to Maglio et al. (2009), a service interaction between two service systems results in co-creation of value. We define a utility landscape for each service system entity considering their service interactions with other classes using the dependency structure of the NKCS architecture. First we consider each value-creating attribute of a given value proposition as depending on K number of other attributes of the same value proposition. By doing so, we could control the complexity of the value proposition. For example, the state of Internet accessibility at a hotel would depend on the structure and materials used to build its rooms. Furthermore, we consider each value-creating attribute of a given value proposition as depending on C number of attributes of each of the value propositions of other entities, which are likely to get involved in a service interaction. For example, the impact of 'providing Internet accessibility' at a hotel to the co-created value would depend on (1). Whether the customer possesses a laptop and (2). Whether (s)he knows how to connect it to the network. Due to this dependency structure, the co-created value from a given value-creating attribute not only depends on its state but also on the states of other attributes, upon which that attribute depends. Therefore, in a service interaction that involves two parties, there could be D^{1+K+C} possible state value combinations for each value creating attribute of one party to determine its utility (value) contribution to the total utility (value) co-created by the other party. Thus, each of such state value combination associated with a given attribute is assigned a utility value drawn from a random number distribution. The possible state value combinations associated with all attributes of a given value proposition and their respective utility values resemble a utility landscape.

4 The Agent-Based Model

This section contains a description of our agent-based model that uses the IPSAR model as the basis to implement service system interactions. As mentioned in the previous section, ISPAR model incorporates ten possible outcomes that may occur in a typical service system interaction. However, for the current version of our model we use only a branch of the ISPAR model; the branch with outcomes that are more likely to occur generally. Figure 13.2 illustrates the selected branch of the ISPAR model for the current implementation.

According to Maglio et al. (2009), the non-service interactions are expected to impact future service interactions. However, such impacts are contextual and thus would be used in a specific application setting later on. Similarly, not being able to communicate a proposal is also a special scenario, which we would like to omit in this discussion. Here we are rather interested in frequently occurring well-defined proposals for value co-creation such as buying a snack at a fast-food restaurant or booking a hotel room during a travel. However, depending on the context, it is possible to alter this implementation as it complies with the omitted branches of the ISPAR model. We use the ODD (Overview, Design concepts and Details) protocol proposed by Grimm et al. (Polhill et al. 2008) to elaborate the details of our model. However, due to the space constraints, we are compelled to omit some extensive details.

4.1 Overview

Purpose This model is developed to formulate a method to understand market dynamics through the lens of S-D logic. More precisely, we intend to apply this method to study the consumer behavior and the evolution of providers in service markets.

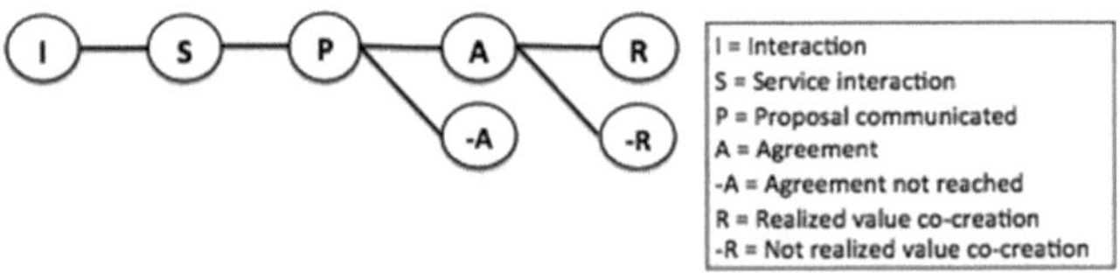

Fig. 13.2 The branch of the ISPAR model implemented in the model

State Variables and Scales The model contains only two service system classes: service provider class and the customer class. Entities are defined according to the description in Chap. 3. Each service system class can have a user specified number of instances (agents) as customer agents and service provider agents. All agents, irrespective of their class, have a current state, which determines the current state of their value proposition. According to the definition in Chap. 3, current state of a service provider reflects its current service level based on the resources and competences it possesses. In the simulations, service providers' current states were initially chosen randomly and kept constant throughout the simulation run. On the other hand, customers' current state reflects their current profile in terms of their characteristics and resources. In order to attain a diverse population of customers, customers' current states were also selected randomly.

Another important common state variable is the 'expectation'. Both customers and service providers have an expected utility (value), which determines the adequate or acceptable utility from a service interaction. We setup a zone of tolerance for expectations based on Zeithaml and Leonard (1993) with the upper margin set to 100 % and the upper margin set randomly. However, customers' zones of tolerance are assumed to be squeezing after successful value co-creation experiences, to reflect the increase of expectations, which usually happens. The percentage increase of the lower (ad- equate) margin here is determined by a parameter. Apart from these, customer agents keep a memory of their past experience with providers. A need for the service is determined for each agent at each time step based on a probabilistic value determined by another parameter.

Process Overview and Scheduling The model basically considers one major process; the process of fulfilling a need of a customer. This process is implemented according to the branch of the ISPAR model presented in Fig. 13.2. Once a customer gets a need, he looks for a suitable provider in his memory. If there is no provider in the memory (first timer), he picks a provider randomly. Otherwise, he checks the potential value obtainable by interacting with each provider in the memory and selects the provider that best meets his expectation. If no provider in the memory can meet his expectation, the agent then looks for any previously unvisited providers and picks one randomly if available. If not available, the agent seeks for better potential values at the one-mutant neighboring locations on its state space following the greedy strategy (Padget et al. 2009). In any case if a suitable provider could not be found, the agent gives up that need. This is further illustrated in Fig. 13.3.

Once a suitable provider is found, the agent initiates a service interaction (S) by contacting the selected provider through a service proposal (P). In the current implementation, we consider that a proposal is well defined and communicated. With a service proposal, the respective provider agent gets to know the current state (profile) of the customer agent and determines the potential utility (value) from the service interaction by referring to his landscape. If the potential value is greater than the expectation of the service provider agent, it agrees (A) to serve that customer or reject otherwise (-A). Getting the consent of the service provider agent

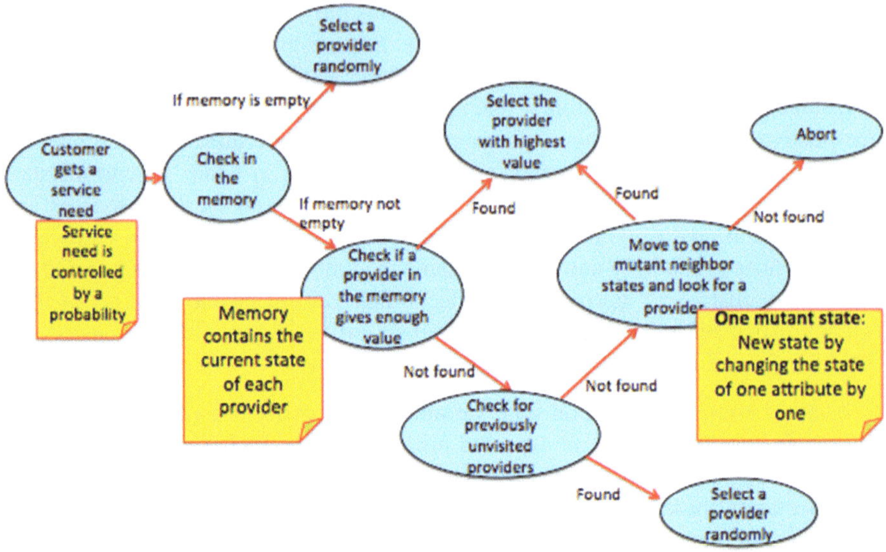

Fig. 13.3 The process selecting a service provider by a customer

brings the service interaction to the value co-creation phase. The customer agent will determine its utility (value) of the service interaction by referring to its landscape. If the perceived utility is greater than the expectation of the customer agent, value co-creation becomes successful (R) but not otherwise (-R). In both cases, the customer agent updates its memory about the provider for future use. This is further illustrated in Fig. 13.4.

4.2 *Design Concepts*

Emergence According to Maglio et al. (2009), abstraction enables measurement. In this simulation, we measure the customer arrivals of each service provider at each time step to study the emerging evolution patterns of the providers.

Adaptation In this model, only customer agents display an adaptive behavior. When they are unable to find a service provider who can meet their expectation, they search for a better state in their one-mutant neighboring states of the state space. Moving to the one-mutant neighboring states can be likened to the process of changing one's own profile in terms of a given aspect; for example acquiring more knowledge or buying some equipment.

Fitness/Objectives In this implementation, only the customer agents have an objective. They try to meet their increasing expectations through value co- creation interactions with the available providers.

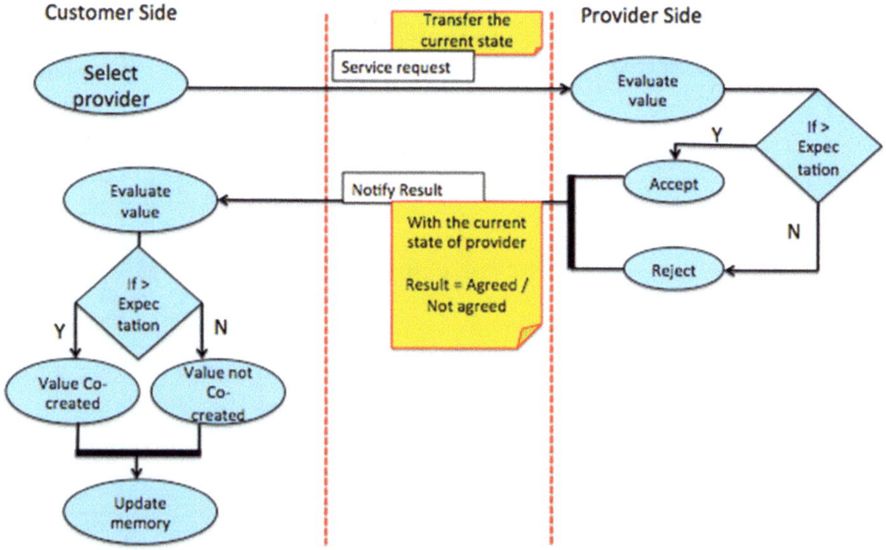

Fig. 13.4 The process of service interaction between a customer and the selected provider

Prediction If a customer agent interacted with a service provider before, his memory contains the current state (service level) of the provider, which helps to predict the potential for value co-creation in future interactions.

Stochasticity If customer agents consume the service for the first time or if the service providers in memory prove no potential for value co-creation, customer agents randomly select a new provider (if any).

5 Results

Here we present some preliminary results of the model. For all our simulation runs, we set N = 8, K = 2, C = 2 and D = 2. We selected those values because of the limit of computational resources and to ensure faster execution of the simulation. Furthermore, all simulations were conducted for a market with 1,000 customers and 5 service providers. In our first experiment, we set the need probability to 0.25 to ensure a less frequent service such as booking a hotel room for a travel, and the corresponding result of a simulation run is shown in Fig. 13.5. In our next experiment, we set the need probability to 0.9 to ensure a high frequent service such as buying food from a fast-food restaurant, and the corresponding result of a simulation run is shown is Fig. 13.6.

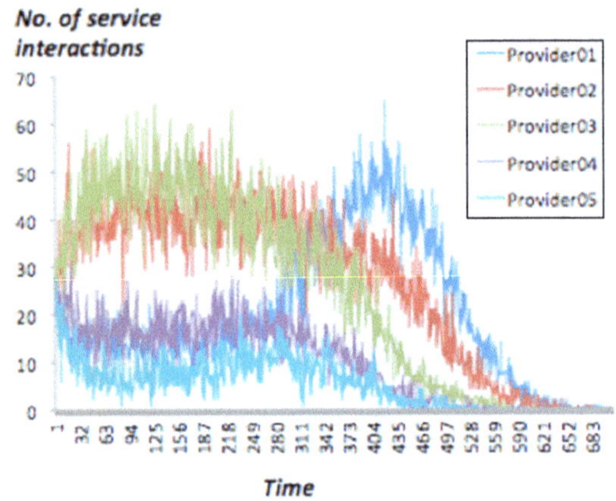

Fig. 13.5 The evolution pattern of five service providers with customer need probability set to 0.25

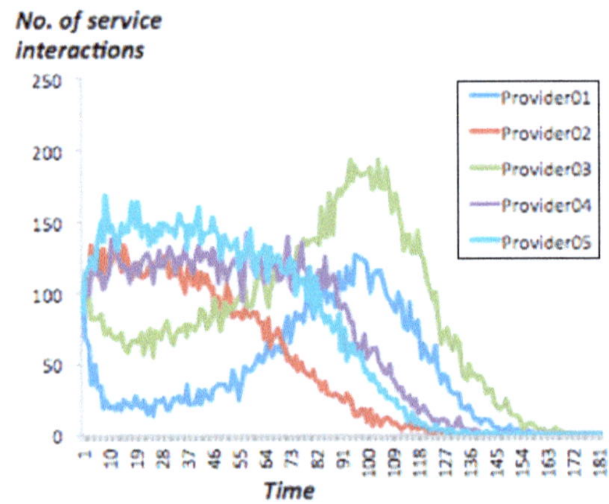

Fig. 13.6 The evolution pattern of five service providers with customer need probability set to 0.9

6 Discussion

Since the current states of the service provider agents were selected randomly, trying to interpret the resulting curves with respect to individual service providers does not make any sense. In fact, we are rather interested in the shapes of the resulting curves in general. The curves on the two graphs, regardless of the frequency of getting the service need, show the known phases of the product life cycle (Rink and Swan 1979). For example, we can clearly see growth, stagnation and decline phases in most of the curves where as some shows a recovery phase after decline as well. S-D logic discards the differentiation of goods and services of the traditional Goods-Dominant logic (Vargo and Lusch 2011); (Lusch et al. 2006) and defines all goods as means of offering a service. Thus, based on this results, we could reasonably argue that the service interactions in markets between providers and customers lead the respective services to a life cycle pattern, which is quite similar to the product life cycle. We would like to call this Service Life Cycle (SLC) (Rajapakse and Terano 2013b).

Notably in both graphs, all service providers complete their SLC quite early and almost together. However, this kind of simultaneous and early convergence is very unlikely to happen in a real market environment as different service providers perform differently letting some to sustain for longer periods while some decline early. In our opinion, this limitation could be avoided by modifying the behavioral rules of customer agents. In the current implementation, customer agents select a service provider either randomly or based on the experience of the previous service interaction. However, in a real environment of customer choice, these behavioral rules would not be accurate. Hence, this is a major limitation that is necessary to be addressed in the applications of this model.

The computational model presented in this paper could be applied to study various real world market phenomena that involve service interactions and value co-creation. In our on going research, we apply this model to the context of consumer behavior. Why customers switch providers despite their attempts to improve the service level has been a research question with a substantial history (Bowden 2009). However, looking at the recent rises and collapses of market giants in different industries, that research question is highly significant even today. Understanding customer retention has been recently shifted to the study of the means of attaining customer loyalty, in which customer engagement plays a vital role (Bowden 2009). In our research, we attempt to build an agent-based model to study customer engagement in the light of S-D logic. For this we use the computational model presented in this paper with significant improvements.

According to the customer engagement process model presented in Bowden (2009), customer loyalty emerges from an affective commitment of individual customers towards a particular brand. We define affective commitment as stemming from 'trust' and 'recommendation strength'. Based on Bowden (2009), we define trust as a function of delight, which is the difference between the expected value and the co-created value. Thus, trust component of affective commitment relates to the branch of service interactions of the ISPAR model. On the other hand, recommendation strength component relates to the branch of non-service interactions. For example, a peer recommendation of a particular brand may help an individual to purchase the same brand in the future. Or else, an influential advertisement by a provider may position a brand in customers' minds influencing them to switch to that brand in the future. The affective commitment of customer agents thus gets updated individually and dynamically with their service and non-service interactions affecting their engagement with each brand. Our future work thus involves improving and implementing this model as a descriptive and predictive model.

7 Conclusion

The service system abstraction and the ISPAR model of service system interactions provide a very good starting point to study market systems in the light of S-D logic. Here we introduce a method to develop agent-based models based on the service system abstraction and the ISPAR model. We present the modeling details and some preliminary results with respect to a hypothetical market system comprising customers and service providers of one particular service. We propose that this method could be successfully applied to study various real market phenomena in the light of S-D logic. To support our proposal, we briefly introduce our ongoing work in the domain of consumer behavior to study customer engagement with brands.

References

Bowden JL (2009) The process of customer engagement: a conceptual framework. J Mark Theory Pract 17(1):63–74

Carley KM (1999) On generating hypothesis using computer simulations, DTIC Online: Information for the Defense Community

Casti JL (1997) Would-be worlds: how simulation is changing the frontiers of science. Wiley, New York

Central Intelligence Agency – USA (2012) The World Factbook. https://www.cia.gov/library/publications/the-world-factbook/fields/2012.html

Epstein JM (2006) Agent-based computational models and generative social science. In: Epstein JM (ed) Generative social science: studies in agent-based computational modeling. Princeton University Press, Princeton

Lusch RF, Vargo SL, Malter AJ (2006) Taking a leadership role in global marketing management. Organ Dyn 35(3):264–278

Maglio PP, Spohrer J (2008) Fundamentals of service science. J Acad Mark Sci 36(1):18–20

Maglio PP et al (2009) The service system is the basic abstraction of service science. IseB 7(4):395–406

Ng I, Parry G, Smith L, Maull R, Briscoe G (2012) Transitioning from a goods- dominant to a service-dominant logic: visualising the value proposition of Rolls- Royce. J Serv Manage 23(3):416–439

Ostrom AL, Bitner MJ, Brown SW, Burkhard KA, Goul M, Daniels WS, Demirkan H, Rabinovich E (2010) Moving forward and making a difference: research priorities for the science of service. J Serv Res 13(1):4–36

Padget J et al (2009) Sendero: an extended, agent-based implementation of Kauffman's NKCS Model. J Artif Soc Soc Simul 12(4):824–844

Polhill JG, Parker D, Brown D, Grimm V (2008) Using the ODD protocol for describing three agent-based social simulation models of land-use change. J Artif Soc Soc Simul 11(2):3

Rajapakse C, Terano T (2013a) Modeling value co-creation process in complex service systems using Kauffman's NKCS architecture. In: 7th international KES conference on agents and multi-agent systems – technologies and applications, Hue, Vietnam

Rajapakse C, Terano T (2013b) An agent-based model to study the evolution of service systems through the service life cycle. Int J Energy Inf Commun 4(5):45–60

Rink DR, Swan JE (1979) Product life cycle research: a literature review. J Bus Res 7(3):219–242

Spohrer J, Maglio PP (2008) The emergence of service science: toward systemic service innovations to accelerate co-creation of value. Prod Oper Manag 17(3):238–246

Spohrer J et al (2007) Steps toward a science of service systems. Computer 40(1):71–77

Terano T (2008) Beyond the KISS principle of agent-based social simulation. J Socio Inform 1(1):175–187

Vargo SL, Lusch RF (2011) It'sallB2B . . . and beyond: toward a systems perspective of market. Ind Mark Manage 40(2):181–187

Vargo SL, Maglio PP, Akaka MA (2008) On value and value co-creation: a service systems and service logic perspective. Eur Manag J 26(3):145–152

Zeithaml VA, Leonard LB (1993) The nature and determinants of customer expectations of service. J Acad Mark Sci 21(1):1–12

Chapter 14
Snowball Sampling Analysis of Viral Marketing Campaigns Targeting Market Mavens

Takashi Yoshida and Setsuya Kurahashi

Abstract We showed the fact that market mavens are included more among communicative consumers than average and act as information hubs between communities by analyzing a research about consumers' word-of-mouth activities using snowball sampling technique. We also designed research questions to seize the feature of community structure inside social networks. On the basis of these outcomes, we developed a network model that reflects community structure and a multi-agent simulation model. The agreement between research and simulation results endorsed the factors premised in the model such as four consumer types, type dispositions on network, and effect of local diffusion. Moreover, we used this simulation model to propose a method for improving the effect of a referral program. An advantage of this method is that marketers need not to have special information about individual customers.

Keywords Snowball sampling • Market maven • Social network • Community structure • Multi-agent simulation • Referral program

1 Introduction

Consumers talk and share their views about a product with others. Today marketers consider the way to stimulate consumers to share and spread marketing-relevant information, called "word-of-mouth marketing" or "viral marketing" (van der Lans et al., 2010). Individual consumer's behavior with respect to viral marketing has been researched (Toubia et al., 2011). In addition, diffusion strategies in theoretical social network models have been argued (Hinz et al., 2011). However, marketing-relevant information diffuses in a complicated path within social networks. To understand the effects of viral marketing, marketers need to know not only about

T. Yoshida (✉) • S. Kurahashi
Graduate School of Business Sciences, University of Tsukuba, 3-29-1 Otsuka, Bunkyo-ku, Tokyo 112-0012, Japan
e-mail: yoshida.takashi@live.jp

Y. Nakai et al. (eds.), *Agent-Based Approaches in Economic and Social Complex Systems VIII*, Agent-Based Social Systems 13, DOI 10.1007/978-4-431-55236-9_14

individual consumer's behavior but also about interactions between consumers and the real structure of social networks where marketing-relevant information flows (Bampo et al., 2008). We carried out detailed researches to clarify interactions between consumers. A preliminary analysis has already reported (Yoshida et al., 2008). In this research, we developed a multi-agent simulation framework that consists of the network model and consumer type dispositions on the network considering the influence of a group of consumers, called market mavens, who spread their capricious knowledge widely. As an application of our simulation framework, we analyzed the method for improving the effects of referral program. An advantage of this method is that marketers need not to have special information such as degree of customers.

2 Research Methodology

The research subjects were *Edy*, an electronic payment service, and *mixi*, a web-based social networking service. We expected *Edy* to be preferred by people who have deep knowledge and *mixi* by ones who have modish personality. To compare this contrast, we chose these two items as the research subjects. We applied snowball sampling (Ikeda and Huckfeldt, 2001). In this technique, a researcher asks the main respondents to recruit further subjects among their acquaintances, so the extracted sample grows like a rolling snowball. This technique is an ideal way to acquire samples of influential individuals.

A research using this technique consists of three steps. In screening research, we sent a set of questionnaires to a broad sample of potential respondents and asked whether they would introduce the people who talked with them on their decision to apply a product. From among all respondents, we chose respondents (main respondents) who agreed to introduce other respondents (snowball respondents). In snowball research, we asked the main and snowball respondents to answer questions about any communication they had previously been exposed to regarding a product. The answers of main and snowball respondents are compared for verification. In complementary research, the respondents are randomly extracted among the respondents of the screening research.

The research started in October 2007 and ended in January 2008. We used an internet research assistance service. In the screening research, we sent e-mail containing the URL of the questionnaire page to about 30,000 affiliates whose ages were 20–49. We received 19,172 responses and 5,978 of them were valid. In the snowball research, we chose 985 and 1,038 main respondents for *Edy* and *mixi*. We sent them e-mail containing the URL of the questionnaire page and invitation to snowball respondents. 721 and 719 snowball respondents sent us responses. As the combination of both respondents, 577 and 513 were valid. In the complementary research, we sent e-mail to randomly extracted affiliates whose ages were 20–49. We acquired 1,001 and 1,000 replies, with 725 and 741 being valid.

3 Consumer Interaction Analysis

3.1 Four Consumer Types

In the screening research, respondents were asked to answer the questions on a four-point scale about one's attitude to marketing information. The answers of the questions were subject to factor analysis. Two factors were identified: opinion leader factor and market maven factor. The opinion leader score (OL-score) reflects how likely is that a consumer will tell others one's views about a product. The market maven score (MM-score) reflects how likely it is that a consumer will gather and distribute information about a variety of products (Feick and Price, 1987). We set the borders between high and low scores at the arithmetic means of these values. By these borders, consumers are classified into four types.

Consumers who have high OL-score and high MM-score are called "leading consumers" (LC). LCs gather information widely and provide it to wide range of people. Consumers who have high OL-score and low MM-score are called "opinion leaders" (OL). OLs state their subjective opinions about special products to others within a narrow range of acquaintances. Consumers who have low OL-score and high MM-score are called "market mavens" (MM). MMs have capricious knowledge about products, but spread their knowledge much more swiftly and widely. Consumers who have low OL-score and low MM-score are called "followers" (FL). FLs are cautious about adopting innovative products. Consumer types of research respondents are shown in Table 14.1. By snowball sampling, we acquired the sample

Table 14.1 Consumer types of research respondents

	LC	OL	MM	FL	Total	$\chi^2(3)$	p
Screening research	543 (9.1 %)	2,020 (33.8 %)	1,923 (32.2 %)	1,492 (25.0 %)	5,978 (100.0 %)		
Edy complementary	78 (10.8 %)	222 (30.6 %)	224 (30.9 %)	201 (27.7 %)	725 (100.0 %)		
Edy main	122 (21.1 %)	166 (28.8 %)	219 (38.0 %)	70 (12.1 %)	577 (100.0 %)	65.2	<0.001* <0.001*
Edy snowball	98 (17.0 %)	151 (26.2 %)	220 (38.1 %)	108 (18.7 %)	577 (100.0 %)	27.3/11.4[a]	<0.001*/ 0.0096**,[a]
mixi complementary	81 (10.9 %)	260 (35.1 %)	233 (31.4 %)	167 (22.5 %)	741 (100.0 %)		
mixi main	101 (19.7 %)	173 (33.7 %)	180 (35.1 %)	59 (11.5 %)	513 (100.0 %)	37.9	<0.001* <0.001*
mixi snowball	85 (16.6 %)	149 (29.0 %)	194 (37.8 %)	85 (16.6 %)	513 (100.0 %)	19.7/8.39[a]	<0.001*/ 0.039***,[a]

Sum of each row equals 100 %

$^{*}p < 0.001$; $^{**}p < 0.01$; $^{***}p < 0.05$

[a]The left side number is the chi-square value and the p-value between random and snowball respondents. The right side number is the chi-square value and the p-value between main and snowball respondents

of influential individuals concerning the use of *Edy* or *mixi*. The ratio of MMs of snowball respondents was significantly higher than that of screening research respondents in the case of *Edy*, as well as in the case of *mixi*. These results mean that MMs played influential role in the diffusion process of not only *mixi*, which was preferred by MMs, but also *Edy*, which was preferred by OLs.

3.2 Six Phases and Phase Transitions

Each consumer has an interest level about a product. We assumed there are following phases that consumers pass through: no-interest, recognition, attention and possession. A consumer in the no-interest stage does not know about the product. During the recognition phase, the consumer has a vague idea about it. In the attention phase, the consumer has a concrete opinion about the product and craves or dislikes it. In the possession phase, the consumer has acquired and is using the product. We subdivided consumers in the attention or possession phase into those holding either positive or negative attitude because they have a concrete idea about a product. In sum, we consider six consumer phases: no-interest (N), recognition (R), positive attention (A+), negative attention (A−), positive possession (P+), and negative possession (P−). The consumer phase transition can follow the following paths: N to R, R to A+, R to A−, A+ to P+, A+ to A−, A− to A+, P+ to P−, P− to P+. These phase classification and possible phase transitions are shown in Fig. 14.1. Our research included questions about respondents' current phases and emergence times of phase transition. Figure 14.2 shows the estimation about each respondent's phase at a specific point of time.

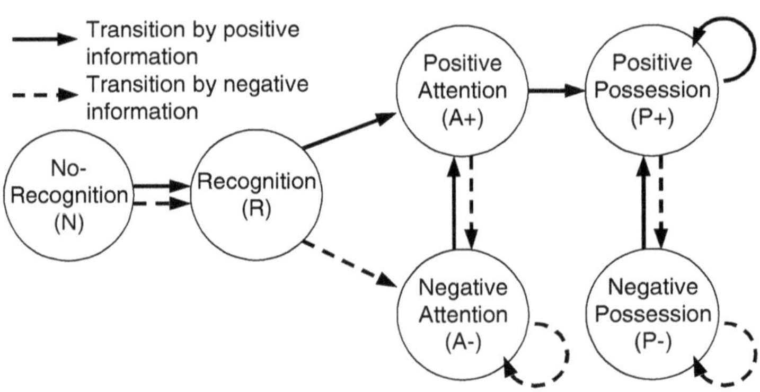

Fig. 14.1 Six consumer phases and eight phase transitions

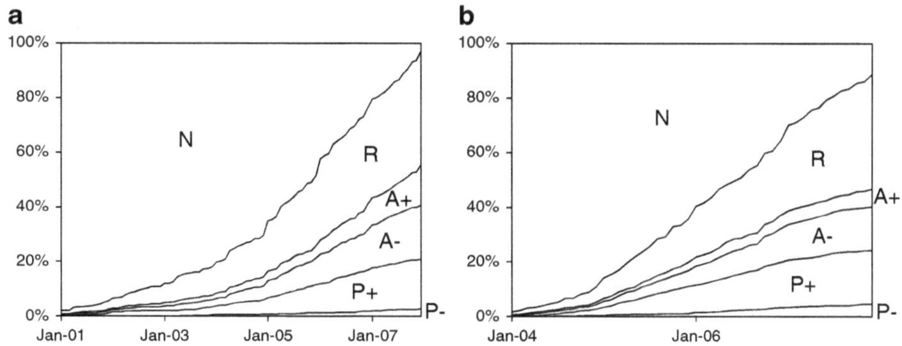

Fig. 14.2 Estimated phase history. (**a**) *Edy*. (**b**) *mixi*

3.3 Recommendation Frequency and Phase Transition Probability

We assumed consumer phase transition occurs in two ways. The first way is when a consumer receives a word-of-mouth recommendation from other consumers through a social network. The recommendation can be positive or negative. The second way is when a consumer receives information from an external source such as mass media. Information reception occurs according to exogenously determined probabilities. The frequency that a respondent talks and hears word-of-mouth recommendation is questioned in the research. We also questioned that phase transition was occurred by whether recommendation or mass media information. Based on the answers to these questions and phase transition history, parameters shown in Table 14.2 were obtained.

Word-of-mouth recommendations between different acquaintances occur at different probabilities. The frequency is considered to follow a power low. The power index estimated with a research question was -0.12 in 1 month. We assumed that recommendation frequency from a consumer to an one's acquaintance follows $p_n = a(n + 5.0)^{-1.2}$, where p_n is recommendation frequency to nth person in decreasing order of frequency and a is the coefficient of each consumer.

4 Social Network

Human relations between consumers can be described as a graph theoretical network by regarding consumers as vertices and the human connections between consumers as edges. Some simplified network models that exhibit the features of large-scale networks in the real world have been reported (Newman, 2003). Our focus is on an internal structure of real world networks. Some members form a group and are more closely connected with each other than with other parts.

Table 14.2 Estimated parameters: (**a**) Number of people to recommend per month, (**b**) Probability of recognizing a recommendation, (**c**) Phase transition per hearing a recommendation, (**d**) Phase transition by other reasons except recommendations per month, (**e**) Local diffusion coefficient on phase transition rate by other reasons

(a)

		LC	OL	MM	FL
Edy					
R	Pos.	0.121	0.104	0.086	0.039
R	Neg.	0.157	0.136	0.112	0.050
A+	Pos.	0.705	0.082	0.287	0.237
A+	Neg.	0.485	0.057	0.198	0.163
A−	Pos.	0.101	0.103	0.303	0.032
A−	Neg.	0.087	0.089	0.262	0.027
P+	Pos.	1.464	0.547	0.682	0.273
P+	Neg.	0.488	0.182	0.227	0.091
P−	Pos.	1.579	0.045	0.253	0.001
P−	Neg.	3.421	0.098	0.547	0.001
mixi					
R	Pos.	0.297	0.111	0.125	0.113
R	Neg.	0.239	0.089	0.101	0.091
A+	Pos.	1.023	0.227	0.258	0.262
A+	Neg.	0.777	0.173	0.196	0.199
A−	Pos.	0.425	0.086	0.273	0.099
A−	Neg.	0.960	0.195	0.616	0.223
P+	Pos.	2.129	0.523	0.734	0.519
P+	Neg.	1.081	0.265	0.373	0.264
P−	Pos.	1.038	0.623	0.498	0.166
P−	Neg.	1.462	0.877	0.702	0.234

(b)

	Probability of recognition
Edy	0.656
mixi	0.951

(c)

			Edy	*mixi*
N	Pos.	N to R	0.034	0.133
N	Neg.	N to R	0.034	0.133
R	Pos.	R to A+	0.030	0.169
R	Neg.	R to A−	0.036	0.049
A+	Pos.	A+ to P+	0.037	0.480
A+	Neg.	A+ to A−	0.010	0.023
A−	Pos.	A− to A+	0.028	0.020
P+	Neg.	P+ to P−	0.003	0.001
P−	Pos.	P− to P+	0.001	0.001

(d)

	LC	OL	MM	FL
Edy				
N to R	0.025	0.022	0.019	0.017
R to A+	0.030	0.025	0.024	0.010
R to A−	0.019	0.015	0.015	0.012
A+ to P+	0.040	0.070	0.064	0.063
A+ to A−	0.002	0.011	0.007	0.009
A− to A+	0.012	0.007	0.013	0.008
P+ to P−	0.001	0.005	0.009	0.002
P− to P+	0.001	0.001	0.001	0.001
mixi				
N to R	0.020	0.022	0.016	0.016
R to A+	0.022	0.016	0.017	0.012
R to A−	0.014	0.018	0.009	0.008
A+ to P+	0.030	0.023	0.045	0.042
A+ to A−	0.009	0.013	0.019	0.050
A− to A+	0.020	0.003	0.001	0.001
P+ to P−	0.011	0.009	0.010	0.011
P− to P+	0.001	0.001	0.001	0.001

(e)

	0–5 %	5–10 %	10–20%	20–100%
Edy				
N to R	0.971	0.971	1.126	1.028
R to A+	0.600	0.761	1.673	2.606
R to A−	0.928	0.928	1.194	1.512
A+ to P+	0.750	0.858	1.302	1.187
A+ to A−	1.088	1.088	1.011	0.496
A− to A+	0.791	0.791	0.934	4.869
P+ to P−	1.167	1.167	1.277	0.245
P− to P+	1.000	1.000	1.000	1.000
mixi				
N to R	0.995	0.995	1.122	0.875
R to A+	0.600	0.616	1.050	2.771
R to A−	0.926	0.926	1.024	1.317
A+ to P+	0.750	0.780	0.613	2.068
A+ to A−	1.838	1.838	0.378	0.675
A− to A+	0.726	0.726	1.654	0.996
P+ to P−	3.049	3.049	0.566	0.634
P− to P+	1.000	1.000	1.000	1.000

This structure is called community structure (Fortunato, 2010). In our assumption, communities are overlapping reflecting that each consumer participates in several groups of people, based on family, friends, workplace, social activities, and so on. Furthermore, consumers are thought to exchange information densely inside communities. We define a community as "a complete or nearly complete subgraph within a social network." Palla et al. (2005) used the term *k-clique* to indicate a complete graph with k vertices. To simplify, in the following analysis, a community consists of k members is assumed to be *k-clique*.

To estimate the number of acquaintances a respondent has, we applied the number of people whose phone number or e-mail address are registered in the one's cell phone directory (Ishiguro and Tsuji, 2006). Research questions designed to acquire degree distribution and the distribution of the number of community members were as follows:

Q1. How many people are registered in your cell phone directory?
Q2. Choose a typical acquaintance from your cell phone directory. Among the people in your cell phone directory, how many ones know both you and the chosen acquaintance?

The answer to Q1 can be seen as degree. However, the answer to Q2 cannot be seen directly as the number of community members. Supposing there were one community of three members and one community of six members in a society, three respondents would answer "1 acquaintance knows both I and the chosen one." and six respondents would answer "4 acquaintances know both I and the chosen one." Therefore, to acquire the number of community members, at the first step we add 2 to the answer to Q2, and at the second step we divide the count by the number of community members itself. We received 19,172 responses. Responses that answered with multiples of 5, such as "25", "50", and "100", were judged to be invalid because these answers were possibly based on dubious estimates done without checking cell phone. 5,978 responses were valid under this condition.

Table 14.3 summarizes network attributions of each consumer type and the results of Steel-Dwass-Critchlow-Fligner multiple comparison tests. The number of joining communities, which means how many different groups of people a respondent takes part in, was calculated by dividing degree by the number of community members minus 1. The reason for subtracting 1 is to exclude the respondent oneself. As shown in the table, MM's number of joining community was significantly larger than that of OL. This result means that a MM, in comparison with an OL, takes part in more communities and acts as a bridge between communities that spreads information from one community to others.

Table 14.3 Multiple comparison tests of network attributions between all pairs of consumer types

	LC	OL	MM	FL	*t*	*p*
N	530	1,941	1,846	1,370		
Degree						
1st Q.	38.3	33	36	23		
Median	76	62	69	51		
Mean	116.0	98.3	105.3	71.9		
3rd Q.	151.8	119	131	91		
LC-OL	*	–			3.92	<0.001
LC-MM	n.s.		n.s.		1.91	0.268
LC-FL	*			–	8.55	<0.001
OL-MM		–	**		3.26	0.006
OL-FL		*		–	7.44	<0.001
MM-FL			*	–	10.14	<0.001
Number of community members						
1st Q.	4	4	3	3		
Median	6	6	6	5		
Mean	13.92	10.23	10.19	8.25		
3rd Q.	12	12	11	10		
LC-OL	n.s.	n.s.			1.04	0.729
LC-MM	n.s.		n.s.		2.28	0.103
LC-FL	*			–	6.36	<0.001
OL-MM		n.s.	n.s.		1.97	0.199
OL-FL		*		–	8.05	<0.001
MM-FL			*	–	6.14	<0.001
Number of joining communities						
1st Q.	3.85	3.92	4.33	3.20		
Median	8.20	7.17	8.57	6.91		
Mean	13.76	11.86	13.81	10.58		
3rd Q.	15.24	12.95	15.49	12.66		
LC-OL	n.s.	n.s.			1.94	0.21
LC-MM	n.s.		n.s.		0.86	0.824
LC-FL	*			–	3.77	<0.001
OL-MM		–	*		4.52	<0.001
OL-FL		***		–	2.92	0.018
MM-FL			*	–	6.78	<0.001

– The smaller side of a pair of significant population means; *n.s.* not significant
$^{*}p < 0.001$; $^{**}p < 0.01$; $^{***}p < 0.05$

5 Scenario Analysis by Simulation

5.1 Outline of Simulation

To analyze the effect of word-of-mouth recommendation in the diffusion process of *Edy* and *mixi*, we implemented multi-agent simulations based on the results of consumer interaction analysis and social network analysis. In the simulation, a consumer is considered to be an agent. The agent is classified into four consumer types and disposed as a node of our network model. The agent talks word-of-mouth recommendation and raises phase transition by recommendation or mass media information in specific probabilities estimated by our research. The real time scale of one step is one month. The duration of simulation is from the 0th step to the 73rd step in the case of *Edy*, which is equivalent to between November 2001 when the service launched and December 2007, and to the 46th step in the case of *mixi*, which is equivalent to between February 2004 and December 2007. The number of agents was 10,000 because we thought the number was large enough to neutralize the extreme influence of the agents whose degrees were more than 500. The simulation results were arithmetic mean of 100 replicates. Table 14.4 shows the factors of the base model and reference models that were used for sensitivity analysis.

Table 14.4 Factors of base model and reference models

	Base model	Reference models
Number of agents	10,000	
Replicates	100 times, see arithmetic mean	
Number of steps	(*Edy*) 74 (*mixi*) 47	
Phase transfer parameters	Table 14.2	
Referral program	(*Edy*) Not (*mixi*) Do	(a) (*mixi*) Not
Effect of local diffusion	Separate [0,5 %) from [0,10 %)	(b1) Not separate [0,5 %)
		(b2) Not consider LD
Consumer type classification	4 types (LC 908, OL 3,379, MM 3,217, FL 2,496)	(c) Not distinguish types
Type disposition on network	Consider degree and community (Table 14.5)	(d) Not consider type disposition on network
Network model	Community structure model	(e1) Configuration model
		(e2) BA model
		(e3) WS model
WoM concentration	$\gamma = -1.2$	(f) $\gamma = -3.0$

5.2 Network Model

The following network generation procedure called "Configuration model" can reproduce any degree distribution (Newman et al., 2001):

1. Allocate arbitrary degree k_x of the node x.
2. Chose two nodes by stochastic means according to degree allocation number and draw an edge between these nodes.
3. Subtract 1 from edge allocation number of chosen nodes and repeat Step 2.

This model, however, cannot reproduce community structure. In addition, although cluster coefficients of real social networks are 0.2–0.4, that of this model is around 0. Therefore we developed another network model:

1. Allocate arbitrary degree k_x of the node x. Obtain the total number of edges by $\sum_x k_x/2$.
2. Set arbitrary probability distribution function of the number of community members $p(m)$ where $m \geq 2$.
3. Determine the number of communities $C(m)$ where m is the number of community members, provided that the distribution of $C(m)$ subjects to $p(m)$ and the total number of edges equals the result of Step 1.
4. Determine m_{max} that satisfies $C(m) > 0$. Chose m_{max} nodes by stochastic means according to allocated degree and draw an edge between every pairs of these nodes.
5. Subtract 1 from $C(m_{max})$. Subtract $m - 1$ from the allocated degree of chosen nodes. Repeat Step 4 until $C(2)$ becomes 0.

This model can reproduce research results of degree distribution and the distribution of the number of community members. Cluster coefficient is also reproducible. The way of allocation of degree k based on the research results was, in the interval of $1 \leq k \leq 55$ the distribution was uniform with 47.47 % nodes, in the interval of $56 \leq k \leq 150$ the distribution followed power law ($\gamma = -1.39$) with 35.67 % nodes, and in the interval of $k \geq 151$ the distribution followed power law ($\gamma = -2.50$) with 16.86 % nodes. Distribution of the number of community members $p(m)$ was, in the case $m = 2, 3, 4, 5$, and 6, 15.77, 10.22, 13.28, 16.24, and 7.12 %, respectively. In the interval of $m \geq 7$ the distribution follows power law ($\gamma = -3.76$). When the number of nodes was 10,000, the total number of communities included in the model became 17,398. Table 14.5 compares research results, (A) configuration model of 10,000 nodes, and (B) our community structure model of 10,000 nodes. Figure 14.3 illustrates this network generation procedure.

Table 14.5 Comparison of research results and network models

		Research results	A	B
Degree (all)	1st Q.	28.0	29.0	29.0
	Median	58.0	59.0	59.0
	Mean	92.5	91.5	91.5
	3rd Q.	117.0	116.0	116.0
Degree (LC)	1st Q.	38.3	38.0	38.0
	Median	76.0	72.4	72.4
	Mean	116.0	112.1	112.1
	3rd Q.	151.8	148.9	148.9
Degree (OL)	1st Q.	33.0	31.1	31.1
	Median	62.0	59.7	59.7
	Mean	98.3	92.4	92.5
	3rd Q.	119.0	114.5	114.5
Degree (MM)	1st Q.	36.0	34.2	34.2
	Median	69.0	67.2	67.2
	Mean	105.3	101.1	101.1
	3rd Q.	131.0	128.1	128.1
Degree (FL)	1st Q.	23.0	20.3	20.3
	Median	51.0	46.9	46.9
	Mean	71.9	70.4	70.4
	3rd Q.	91.0	88.0	88.0
Number of community members (all)	1st Q.	3.0		3.0
	Median	5.0		5.0
	Mean	6.5		6.2
	3rd Q.	7.0		8.0
Cluster coefficient			0.044	0.306

A: Configuration model; B: Community structure model

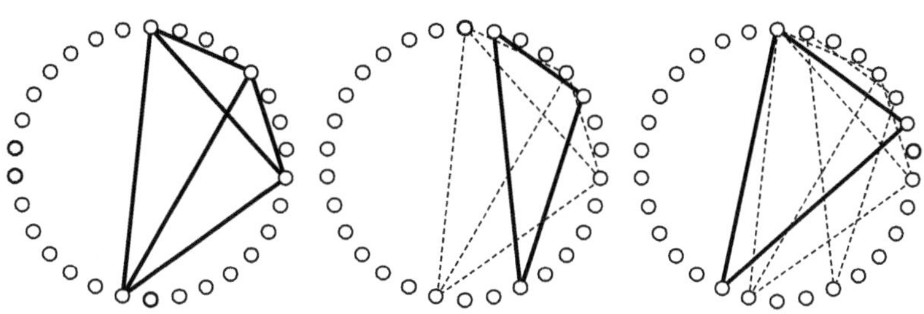

Fig. 14.3 This figure illustrates the network generation procedure. As an example, from the *left figure*, 4, 3, and 3 nodes are selected as community members. Draw an edge between every pairs of these nodes and pile the edges

5.3 *Results of Base Model*

Figure 14.4 overlays the simulated diffusion rate of base model of *Edy* and *mixi* on those of research results. Diffusion rate transition of *Edy* was close to research results. In contrast, diffusion rate of *mixi* at the last step was close to research results but the timing of adoption was different. The research respondents are considered to have answered that they were "senior participant" of *mixi*. Figure 14.4 also shows the number of participants announced by the *mixi* administrator. The transition of this number is close to the simulation results. Table 14.6 shows the details of simulation results. (a) Diffusion rates at the last step, (b) rate of phase transitions that recommendations aroused, and (c) type composition ratio who gave influence when started using are fact data that are not used to develop the simulation framework. The research and simulation results well agree. Reference models shown in Table 14.4 were tested for sensitivity analysis. The results of base model was the most close to the simulation results. These agreements verify the correctness of the simulation framework.

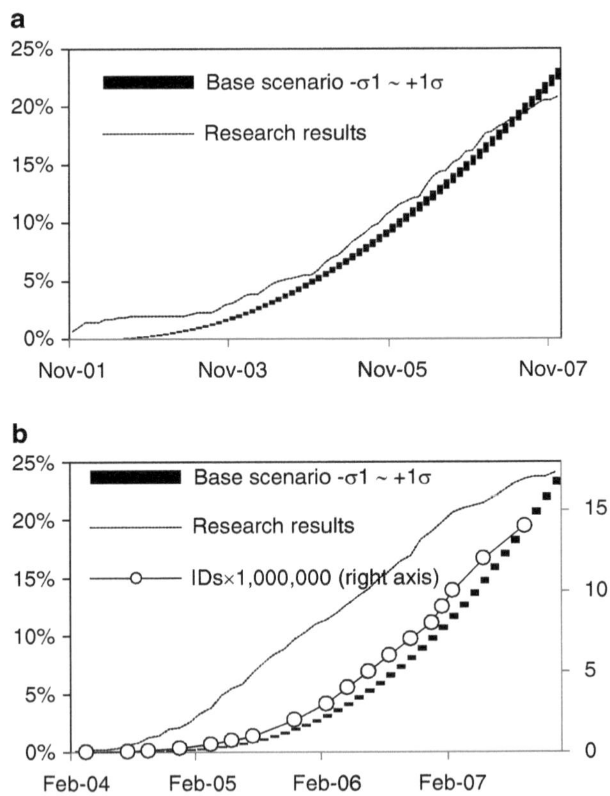

Fig. 14.4 Diffusion rate transitions of *Edy* and *mixi* under base model simulation results and research data. Bars mean -1σ and $+1\sigma$ of 100 replicates. (**a**) *Edy*. (**b**) *mixi*

Table 14.6 Simulation results of base model: (**a**) Diffusion rates at the last step, (**b**) Rate of phase transitions that recommendations aroused, (**c**) Type composition ratio who gave influence when started using

(a)

	LC (%)	OL (%)	MM (%)	FL (%)	All (%)
Edy base model	28.0	25.8	25.3	13.4	22.7
(s.d.)	(1.73)	(0.80)	(0.74)	(0.70)	(0.49)
Edy research results	29.2	24.4	23.6	10.8	20.8
mixi base model	34.0	23.8	27.1	15.6	23.8
(s.d.)	(2.06)	(1.01)	(0.95)	(0.93)	(0.81)
mixi research results	29.4	27.7	27.3	13.4	24.2

(b)

	Recognition (%)	Attention (%)	Possession (%)
Edy base model	10.9	12.8	7.6
(s.d.)	(0.35)	(0.46)	(0.53)
Edy research results	8.0	10.7	8.4
mixi base model	40.9	54.7	78.0
(s.d.)	(0.55)	(0.74)	(0.86)
mixi research results	40.8	50.0	81.7

(c)

	LC (%)	OL (%)	MM (%)	FL (%)
Edy base model	23.5	29.2	39.2	8.1
(s.d.)	(3.23)	(3.94)	(3.84)	(2.25)
Edy main respondents	21.1	28.8	38.0	12.1
Edy snowball respondents	17.0	26.2	38.1	18.7
mixi base model	29.5	24.7	32.9	12.9
(s.d.)	(1.22)	(1.04)	(1.08)	(0.91)
mixi main respondents	19.7	33.7	35.1	11.5
mixi snowball respondents	16.6	29.0	37.8	16.6

5.4 *Improving the Effect of Referral Program*

As an option of a simulation, we considered "referral program", a type of viral marketing campaign. In this program, a marketer asks a consumer to introduce another consumer. If the introduced one buys a product, marketer pays rewards. In the simulation, an agent that joins in the program searches another agent that has not bought a product and talks positive recommendation. However, announcing the program needs costs. We analyzed the method for alleviating the costs and improving the effects of the program by scenario analysis of the simulation framework.

Table 14.7 Effects of referral program strategies. Scenario 1: 10 % of agents in Possession stage join in referral program campaign. Scenario 2: marketers register the information of agents and let them join in the campaign from the next step. Scenario 3: if an agent does not introduce another agent for 12 months, marketers exclude it to sieve influential agents

	Number of invited agents	Number of registered agents (last step)			
		LC	OL	MM	FL
Edy Scenario 1	30.83				
(s.d.)	(4.81)				
Edy Scenario 2	30.26	7.27	8.87	9.57	1.67
(s.d.)	(5.48)	(2.65)	(2.84)	(2.92)	(1.31)
(Type composition ratio)		(26.5 %)	(32.4 %)	(35.0 %)	(6.1 %)
Edy Scenario 3	30.91	3.41	3.16	3.71	0.82
(s.d.)	(5.74)	(1.80)	(1.70)	(1.91)	(0.88)
(Type composition ratio)		(30.4 %)	(26.2 %)	(32.5 %)	(10.8 %)
mixi Scenario 1	335.1				
(s.d.)	(22.3)				
mixi Scenario 2	364.5	64.32	51.71	68.13	18.68
(s.d.)	(27.1)	(7.87)	(7.27)	(7.35)	(4.65)
(Type composition ratio)		(31.7 %)	(25.5 %)	(33.6 %)	(9.2 %)
mixi Scenario 3	368.1	44.48	29.28	37.34	10.98
(s.d.)	(24.1)	(5.32)	(4.82)	(6.12)	(3.15)
(Type composition ratio)		(36.5 %)	(24.0 %)	(30.5 %)	(9.0 %)

Scenario 1 Marketers announce the campaign by advertisement and 10 % of agents in Possession stage join it. Joining agents choose an adjacent agent and talk positive recommendation.

Scenario 2 Marketers judge that an introducing agent is an influential type such as LC and MM if the introduced agent buys the product. Marketers register the information of the agent and let them join in the campaign from the next step. On the other hand, marketers continue the announcement by advertisement. The total joining ratio is kept 10 %.

Scenario 3 Some registered agents might not be truly influential type who succeeded the introduction accidentally. Although marketers let a registered agent join in the campaign, if it does not succeed to introduce another agent for 12 months, marketers exclude it to sieve truly influential agents.

Table 14.7 shows the results of these three scenarios. In scenario 1, 30.83 and 335.1 new customers were introduced in the cases of *Edy* and *mixi*. In scenario 2, the number of invited customers was almost the same or increased to 30.26 and 364.5. In scenario 3, the number of invited customers increased to 30.91 and 368.1, as well as the number of registered agents was streamlined from 27.38 to 11.10 and from 202.8 to 122.1. Table 14.7 also shows the types of registered agents at the last step of scenario 2 and 3. The ratio of LC and MM was, in comparison with that the average of total 10,000 agents were 42.9, 61.5 and 65.3 % in scenario 2 and 62.9

and 67.0 % in scenario 3, in the cases of *Edy* and *mixi*, respectively. Therefore truly influential consumers were sieved. An advantage of this method is that marketers need not to have special information about individual customers.

6 Conclusions

We implemented multi-agent simulations and analyzed the effect of viral marketing based on a research results about consumers' word-of-mouth (WoM) activities using the snowball sampling technique. Our simulation framework consists of two outcomes: consumers' activity of WoM recommendations and social network structure. The subjects of consumer research were *Edy* (an electronic payment service) and *mixi* (a social networking service).

The research results show that a type of consumers, called market maven, is included more among influential consumers than average. Moreover, we calculated five parameters needed in the simulation: (a) number of people to recommend per month, (b) probability of recognizing a recommendation, (c) phase transition per hearing a recommendation, (d) phase transition by other reasons except recommendations per month, and (e) local diffusion coefficient on phase transition rate by other reasons. In social network analysis, we focused on community structure that some members form a group and communicate more frequently with each other than with other parts. We created a research question to reveal the structure inside social networks. By analyzing the answers to this question, market mavens were shown to act as an information hub between communities.

Based on these outcomes, we developed a network model reflected community structure and a multi-agent simulation framework. Simulation results endorsed our framework that consists of the network model and consumer type dispositions on the network considering their degrees and the numbers of joining communities. Moreover, as an application of our simulation framework, we analyzed the method for improving the effect of referral program. According to our simulation results, by accumulating the information of introducers, and moreover by removing the information of introducers who does not introduce extra ones within particular period, marketers can sieve influential consumers. An advantage of this method is that marketers need not to have special information about individual customers.

References

Bampo M, Ewing MT, Mather DR, Stewart D, Wallace M (2008) The effects of the social structure of digital networks on viral marketing performance. Inf Syst Res 19(3):273–290. doi:10.1287/isre.1070.0152

Feick LF, Price LL (1987) The market maven: a diffuser of information marketplace. J Mark 51(1):83–97

Fortunato S (2010) Community detection in graphs. Phys Rep 486(3):75–174

Hinz O, Skiera B, Barrot C, Becker JU (2011) Seeding strategies for viral marketing: an empirical comparison. J Mark 75(November):55–71

Ikeda K, Huckfeldt R (2001) Political communication and disagreement among citizens in Japan and the United States. Political Behav 23(1):23–51

Ishiguro I, Tsuji R (2006) Address chou no riyouritsu to touroku ninzu no network size no sihyou tositeno datousei. Riron to houhou (Sociol Theory Methods) 40(2):295–312

Newman MEJ (2003) The structure and function of complex networks. SIAM Rev 45(2):167–256

Newman MEJ, Strogatz SH, Watts DJ (2001) Random graphs with arbitrary degree distributions and their applications. Phys Rev E 64(2):026,118

Palla G, Derényi I, Farkas I, Vicsek T (2005) Uncovering the overlapping community structure of complex networks in nature and society. Nature 435(7043):814–818. doi:10.1038/nature03607

Toubia O, Stephen AT, Freud A (2011) Viral marketing: a large-scale field experiment. Econ Manag Financ Mark 6(3):43–65

van der Lans R, van Bruggen G, Eliashberg J, Wierenga B (2010) A viral branching model for predicting the spread of electronic word of mouth. Mark Sci 29(2):348–365. doi:10.1287/mksc.1090.0520

Yoshida T, Tomizawa N, Gotoh T, Iguchi H, Sugioka K, Ikeda K (2008) Consumer phase shift simulation based on social psychology and complex networks. In: IEEE congress on services-part I, Honolulu, pp 289–296

MIX
Papier aus verantwortungsvollen Quellen
Paper from responsible sources
FSC® C105338

If you have any concerns about our products,
you can contact us on
ProductSafety@springernature.com

In case Publisher is established outside the EU,
the EU authorized representative is:
Springer Nature Customer Service Center GmbH
Europaplatz 3, 69115 Heidelberg, Germany

Printed by Libri Plureos GmbH
in Hamburg, Germany